Also by Frieda Hughes

GEORGE

A Magpie Memoir

Frieda Hughes

AVID READER PRESS

New York   London   Toronto
Sydney   New Delhi

To George and his children.

AVID READER PRESS
An Imprint of Simon & Schuster, Inc.
1230 Avenue of the Americas
New York, NY 10020

First Avid Reader Press hardcover edition June 2023

AVID READER PRESS and colophon are
trademarks of Simon & Schuster, Inc.

For information about special discounts for bulk purchases,
please contact Simon & Schuster Special Sales at
1-866-506-1949 or business@simonandschuster.com.

The Simon & Schuster Speakers Bureau can bring authors to
your live event. For more information or to book an event contact
the Simon & Schuster Speakers Bureau at 1-866-248-3049
or visit our website at www.simonspeakers.com.

Interior design by Patty Rennie

Manufactured in the United States of America

1   3   5   7   9   10   8   6   4   2

Library of Congress Cataloging-in-Publication Data is available on file.

ISBN 978-1-6680-1650-3
ISBN 978-1-6680-1652-7 (ebook)

A Note on the Text

This book is based on diary entries made between May 2007 and January 2009, which I returned to when I decided I wanted to write about my life with George. It seemed to me that the diary entries best captured the speed and manner of George's sometimes dramatic daily development—and so I have kept them in place, but have added useful information that I only came across later on, where it felt appropriate.

George.
3?/8/19

Prologue

I magine wanting something since you were old enough to be conscious of wanting it. Imagine a longing for something; a place, a state of being, or a situation, that worked away inside your head all those early years, directing you consciously or unconsciously towards achieving that place, or way of being, or situation that you longed for, because, as my late father always said, if you truly want something you should visualise it and make a space for it in your life.

He also added that we should be very careful what we wish for, because sometimes when we get it, it's not quite what we imagined. If, for instance, you wished for a cash injection of a substantial amount, and you wished with all your heart for this lucky windfall, and then someone you loved dearly died and you inherited a sizeable amount of money in their will, that would be a tragic way to achieve the realisation of your longing. Or if you wished for some time off work and then found yourself afflicted with Covid, monkeypox or a broken leg, that would be counterproductive, as you would be too ill to enjoy your time off. Even as a child, these thoughts occurred to me; I'd read too many myths and fairy stories not to have absorbed the life lessons around which they were based.

No, the things I wanted had to be achieved without causing pain to others, or to myself—except, perhaps, from exhaustion: my own happy exhaustion as a result of my sincere mental and physical efforts.

The things I longed for, other than health, happiness and wealth, probably in that order, were plants, pets, and a home of my own that I would never have to move from. The plants and pets were the embellishment and confirmation of the permanent home and, therefore, the sense of stability and belonging that I craved.

Plants were a direct connection to nature; oh, to have somewhere to grow and propagate them, to smell their earthy roots as I repotted them or planted them out, to possess flowerbeds and herbaceous borders where I could arrange them by colour and leaf-shape, interspersing perennials with evergreens and so never having nothing in the soil when winter came. I didn't understand how anyone could live with bare flowerbeds through the seasons of rain and snow.

I can still remember how exciting I found the smell of lily corms in my late teens and early twenties, fecund and engaging in their sawdust when they came out of their plastic bags from beneath the big, brightly coloured lightweight cardboard squares of label, photograph and description. The anticipation of their future growth and flowering would dig into my chest like a happy mole. Succulents too, with their fluid-filling and prehistoric appearances . . . and delphiniums and foxgloves, pieris and mahonia, campanulas looking as if they were leaking on to the ground like purple-blue milk as their blooms spread, and nasturtiums in orange, pouring over walls and the edges of windowsills. Cherry blossom, lilac and magnolia . . .

In my mind I had images of flowerbeds and combinations of blooms, and I wanted to sculpt gardens out of plants and grow trees tall, so I could clear-stem them to support blowsy crimson or purple clematis. I longed to arch leylandii into interesting shapes and prune everything, that could be so pruned, into a sphere; I had a strange affinity to spheres.

Looking back at the small child I was at the age of, I think, six, I see an impish little girl with hair like a scarecrow; I always brushed just the top of my fine, scraggy hair, as the knots underneath made it impossible for the useless cushioned brush with short bristles. I tended the French marigolds that my father's older sister, my Aunt Olwyn, once planted during one of her extended stays, in a little round flowerbed cut out of the patch of weedy grass and clover that my father optimistically called "the lawn." The "lawn" constantly encroached over the cut-earth edges, instilling in me a lifelong dislike of any flowerbed–lawn border that doesn't have a defined edge such as pavers, or raised stones, or some means by which to keep them entirely, easily separate.

What astonishes me now was my childish lack of self-consciousness when I picked the marigolds and took them to the town hall to enter them in the flower competition there one year, among all the adults with their prized and fertilised marigold blooms, their specially bred combination marigolds, their nurtured, competition-ready sodding great golden and crimson flowerheads. What sheer brashness! What delightfully deluded optimism I possessed, to think that I was in with anything so much as half a chance. I was so sure that my little marigolds were the best, because in my eyes they were so incredibly beautiful, so unbelievably perfect— made up, as they were, of the crimson and orange halo of the tightly packed petals that framed their cushiony heads, which were themselves made up of many more tightly packed and crimped smaller petals.

Of course, my connection to plants and my desire to grow them was not just born of my wonderment that nature could sprout so many breathtaking creations; it was also an expression of my desperate longing to put down roots.

I felt as if the ground on which I stood was constantly changing and shifting, and that if I looked away for just a minute, then looked back, the landscape would have altered, and I'd have a whole other universe to acclimatise to because, following the suicide of my mother, Sylvia Plath, on 11 February 1963, my father, Ted Hughes, found it difficult to settle. His peripatetic lifestyle meant that I never had my few clothes all in one place, or my books (I did not have toys), or make friends (I did not have any real friends). Wherever he went my younger brother, Nick, and I followed, like two trailing limbs. Possessions would have been an encumbrance, but that was OK because as very young children we didn't have any, and that was something else: I longed for possessions.

It wasn't that I wanted to *have* things simply for the sake of it, but I longed to use the responsibility for them, and the size and number of them, as weights with which to anchor myself, so that my father's unpredictable urge to continually uproot us could not shift me from my chosen seabed.

By the time I went to my last school, a boarding school in Hampshire—Bedales—at the age of thirteen, I had, by my count, been to twelve schools, including two of the schools twice—yo-yoing between them—a school in Southern Ireland, and being home-schooled once. Sometimes Nick did not join me and I would attend for little more than a couple of weeks. Bedales was thirteen.

My father would follow his girlfriend, or an idea, or an apparent urge to move somewhere he could escape the associations of his past or forge a new and brighter future; there was never time to buy a uniform and I wouldn't be anywhere long enough to warrant the expenditure, so I was forever an oddity, not belonging. The other children would always have their friendship groups established at the point where I was propelled into their midst like a clumsy cuckoo in outgrown street clothes in the middle of a week, in the middle of a term, in the middle of a year. I learned two opposites: to make casual friends quickly, and to live without good friends at all. But any kind of friend didn't last long in any case, because I was never around to form a proper bond; as a result, even now, I have a strong desire to escape or run whenever a friendship begins to mature, because my inner fear is that the friendship will somehow be snatched away when I least expect it, and I must prepare to be bereaved all over again. It is an echo from those years of travelling through England and Ireland, dangling from one of my father's hands, while Nick hung on to the other.

Nick appeared to simply endure the light-switch speed at which our daily environment could change—he was often mute and sullen and wouldn't engage—while I registered every aspect, every passing adult face, every room in every bed and breakfast, every father's friend's spare room, as if it were some kind of electrical pulse. Sometimes shocking.

Animals and birds were my other passion: they were unheard, just as I felt unheard; they needed someone to speak for them and anticipate their needs, just as I did. I had a belief that they could hear me thinking and that they identified with me as I identified with them. I felt I could trust them the way I did not feel I could trust human beings. Many human beings did not appear to have my best interests at heart, and the only person I really trusted was my father. Whereas I felt that I knew where I was with a ferret, cat, rabbit or a dog.

My belief as a small child was also that if I had a pet it should mean that I'd have found a home in which to be stationary; surely Dad would then stop moving around? In reality, having an animal didn't mean Dad would stay put at all, so I couldn't have pets in the proper sense that another little girl might be able to keep a rabbit or a pony or a dog. We had a goat once, that got pregnant and produced a bad-tempered Billy-the-kid when Dad took us away and left it with a local farmer, so it had to be rehomed. There was a tabby cat called "Tabby" that accompanied many years of my childhood, but went feral because Dad kept taking us away and leaving it to the mercy of the neighbour. It would come home when we did. There was a stunningly beautiful white cat that was given to us as a stray; it had to be rehomed because Dad thought it was bad luck (on the basis that black cats were lucky so white cats were the opposite), and when it bit a hole in my upper arm I was deprived of any powers of persuasion to change his mind. There was a Labrador puppy given to us by my Aunt Olwyn, who thought it would stay the size it was when she bought it. I can still hear my father wailing, "Didn't you look at the size of his paws? They're huge! And they tell you that he's going to be a BIG DOG!" Peter only lasted a matter of weeks until Nick pulled his tail so hard it almost detached and the dog squealed in agony, and then bit Nick's lip badly enough to give Dad the excuse to give Peter away to the sound of my breaking heart. Guinea pigs in Yorkshire ate each other when my father took us away again and left the guinea-pig care to his father, who forgot to feed them. And, when I was thirteen, there was a badger called Bess that Dad rescued from a tiny cage in a pet shop, rehousing her in a shed in the yard where I found ways through marzipan and sliced cow-lungs to befriend her. Hugging a badger is like hugging a warm, squishy ball of muscle—a wombat in Australia feels a bit the same. The calm joy I felt at sitting on the straw-covered floor in Bess's shed, having her snuffle round me and lie in my lap of her own volition, made Bess the creature that I wanted to spend most time with.

But Bess had other ideas; the shed was made of cob, and although a cob wall is several feet thick, it is only mud and straw. It didn't take her too many weeks to dig her way to freedom. I was happy for her; I reasoned that she must have felt ready to go and be able to feed herself. The tadpoles that I kept in an enormous blue-and-white glazed bowl beneath my old iron bed were equally unsuccessful, because they eventually grew legs and I had to let them go; I couldn't bear the idea of someone vacuuming my bedroom and accidentally hoovering up half-developed frogs.

*

To have a "forever home"—one where I could plant trees and not have to move and leave them behind, where I could own a dog, and not have to rehome it because I had to leave, where I could buy furniture and keep it because I wasn't going to live anywhere else—was what I longed for all my life. To be in a place where I could walk down the street in a nearby town and know at least three people to talk to before I got home. Stability, and a sense of permanence. I never had that as a child; the nearest thing was the physical being of my father. If my father was in the room, then he represented warmth and safety just in his very being, because he cared for and loved me and my little brother and made sure that we knew this. But during my early childhood he was not stationary, and I longed to be stationary, just so I would have time to put down those damn roots.

This ferocious desire meant that every time I bought a new home I wanted to make it THE LAST home, even though I knew—absolutely knew without a shadow of doubt—that it was only one of the many dwellings on my journey. My father was the first to point this out, giving voice to my uncomfortable secret inner admission.

However, I had to treat each new home as if it was "the last" or I wouldn't pour my love and effort into it, which were the things that brought a profit and made it possible to buy another property, and fix it up, and another, and another, and so climb the property ladder, buying homes that other people didn't love, so that I could transform them into something desirable.

But I drew the line at the garden. I simply couldn't plant up the gardens, because I knew I'd never be able to take them with me. My last house in south-east London, which I bought as three derelict apartments and turned back into a magnificent Victorian family home while living in it with my then husband, sometimes with no kitchen or no bathroom, had a large garden that I left as lawn. When I designed and built a sunken terrace, I populated it with scores of terracotta pots of plants, which I brought with me when I found THE house, THIS house in Mid Wales, where I have been living since 2004. By the time I moved, there were so many pots they required an entire truck of their own.

When that truck arrived in Mid Wales, I knew, for the first time in my life, that I would never have to move again. I had finally found a house that I could grow into, develop, reorganise, paint and write in, garden for, and fill with PETS. I only wished my father had been alive to see it.

Having imagined your heart's desire, imagine getting it. Achieving, by dint of effort and the passage of years, the very thing that you so longed for. Imagine the sheer intoxicating elation that it had, at last, come to pass. I was in a state of joy and disbelief that I had managed to buy this part-Georgian/part-Victorian hall in the once resplendent grounds of which a small hamlet had been built, leaving barely an acre of field as garden.

The hamlet consisted of three short dead-end roads—each one populated by between six and fifteen red-brick houses—a postbox, a pub and a railway-station house that had been converted into a home. Once, the trains stopped here and would take you all the way into London, 200 miles away. The old coach house and stables that once belonged to the hall had been converted into ten little apartments, and beyond the hamlet were farms, smallholdings, other hamlets and the River Severn.

The hall itself had an imposing frontage, but inside it was in dire need of plumbing and wiring, the replastering of ceilings and walls, and the replacement of several windows. In the meantime, it was habitable. It was semi-detached with a neighbouring smaller building, which was once the kitchens, dairy, pantry, scullery and servants' quarters for the big house, and was now owned by a rather lovely woman in her seventies called Jean.

The fact that the house sat on only an acre was good for me; it was enough to construct an interesting garden, but not so big that I would need to borrow sheep to keep the grass down.

I moved here with my husband on 30 June 2004. We had met eight years earlier, when I was living in Australia, just before moving back to England the following year when my father had cancer. He died a year later, but I never returned to Australia to live. I wanted to stop moving. I wanted roots and I felt very strongly that they should be English roots, because England was where, even when living in Australia, I derived an income from my painting and writing.

In hindsight, I may have said things that persuaded my husband to think I might go back with him one day, although I fervently hoped that England would be enough for him to want to stay permanently, and that he'd find the kind of success as an artist that I knew he craved. Or perhaps he simply heard what he wanted to hear. In any case, the surface of the past closes over and never lets you visit the same place; when you return to somewhere in the past, it has moved and shifted and evolved and life in it now would never be like the life you once had. So, I wanted to stay in Britain: I wanted to make friends and keep them, own dogs and have them die of old age in my ownership, develop the garden of my wildest dreams, and embellish my home with possessions that would keep me rooted.

From the beginning my husband always maintained that he wanted to go back to Australia when he was "older." I had imagined that "older" meant ninety, or ninety-five, not sixty-five or seventy. Because, as he was already fourteen years my senior, I had the uneasy feeling that he was hankering to return even when we moved here. I pushed that fear of future upheaval to the back of my mind, hoping that the renovation of this house in Wales would somehow glue us together and take his mind off the longing. But just as I longed for my home, he longed for his.

I turned a blind eye even as our foundations crumbled, and ultimately, none of the things I hoped would save us were enough. In this book, although we were married, I refer to him as The Ex.

After our move into our new, very large, semi-detached "fixer-upper," the proceeds of the sale of the London house gave us a certain financial boost, and, for a while, I felt almost as if I were on holiday, something that I'd rarely felt even when I *was* on holiday.

The move also gave me the physical and mental space to write and paint, which I'd longed for all my life, and a couple of years in, I started to write a weekly poetry column for *The Times*, which added to my financial security. I could hardly believe my good fortune and counted my blessings daily.

Every morning I'd drive to the tiny nearby town to buy a newspaper, find myself with a view of the valley beyond, and wonder at the sheer beauty of my surroundings. Then I'd return to the fixer-upper and be aghast and elated at the sheer size of the challenge, and feel deeply happy that this was my home now.

Shortly after we moved in, one of the locals was standing outside my house with me, looking at the patch of land I was digging holes in to form circular flowerbeds, almost all the garden being at the front. He and his wife owned a gift shop in the nearby town, which is how we'd met.

"How often are you going to be here?" he enquired, eyeing several mountainous heaps of rocks with which I was going to build raised flowerbeds, with the aid of a sack truck, a cement mixer that I'd had to assemble myself out of the box, a lot of enthusiastic optimism, and considerable disregard for my increasingly debilitating lower back pain.

I gazed up at him (he was very tall), slightly puzzled. "I've moved here. Permanently," I replied.

"No, I mean, how many days a week will you spend here?" he asked. I was confused. He explained that most people who moved to Wales from London went back during the week.

"I'm going to be here all the time," I assured him firmly. He smiled.

"You'll last about two years, then," he replied.

That was eighteen years ago.

By my third year in Wales, the Reader's Digest *New Encyclopedia of Garden Plants and Flowers* had become my bible. It was an unexpected gift from Aunt Olwyn. Olwyn wasn't prone to giving me presents, unless she had some ulterior motive: shoes that were too big for me (too uncomfortable for her), a scarf of golf-ball-sized rabbit-fur-covered pieces attached together (unwearable unwanted gift to Olwyn), a crochet mustard-coloured bikini that shrank in the sea and barely covered my modesty (and therefore had no hope at all of covering the much larger Olwyn's modesty). One year when she came to stay for Christmas and I collected her from the station, she presented me with my Christmas present on the platform: an empty balsa-wood box that had contained two pounds of glacé fruit (I *love* glacé fruit). A lifelong chain smoker until dementia rendered it impossible, she'd eaten the entire contents on her journey to Wales from London in an effort to assuage her cravings for a cigarette.

But the encyclopedia of plants was a joy to me; I pored over it whenever I stopped to eat a meal (three times a day), and I'd gleefully list the useful shrubs or flowers for my next garden-centre visit (three times a week at least)—I was totally addicted, and I knew it. This was also an addiction that I could, for a short while, afford to indulge.

Creating the garden gave me a tangible purpose, a sense of fulfilment, and, although I knew it couldn't last forever, I was going to follow this obsession as far as it would go, not least because it was harmless, made me intensely happy, and was incredibly productive—albeit perhaps only in my own eyes. I experienced a deep satisfaction from watching plants take root, grow and multiply. And being outside, surrounded by nature, made the clamour of humanity subside. All other interests fell away and I became single-minded, rooted in dirt.

Certain forms of happiness are found by creating or identifying a need, finding out what is necessary to feed that need, then supplying it: I dug more and more circular flowerbeds, then bought plants to fill the new spaces. Oh, the sheer luxury of it! To fulfil a longing for ericaceous bushes and be able to buy not one, but ten at a discount. Camellias, hellebores and tsugas crowded the flowerbeds as fast as I could dig them. The word "euonymus" filled me with affection for the little evergreen bush of soft, two-tone leaves of gold and green or cream and green.

I'd pick up a potted pieris and feel a sense of wonder at the delicate pink leaves at the end of otherwise green twigs; the smell of tulip bulbs was like catnip to me, and the mental image of a sweeping curve of miniature azaleas would set me off digging the trench for them.

At the Derwen Garden Centre, near Guilsfield, I was bewitched by their alphabetical rows of flowering trees and berried bushes, their hip-high tables of hellebores and euphorbias, and their pools of swamp-loving greenery. I finally gave up buying by the carload and saved up instead for a truckload at a time.

My desire to garden had been fermenting since that first childhood flowerbed of marigolds, and now I could channel all of my energy (or passion?) into this plot of land. The only things that limited me were the hours of darkness, unavoidable commitments, a certain amount of painting and writing, and the physical pain from my bad back. The garden was my daily destination and sometimes threatened to take over even from my own work completely, because I kept thinking: when it is finished, I'll have more time to paint and write, but I'll be doing it in this extraordinary environment full of colour and life. Creating the garden had a visible end, whereas painting and writing were my lifelong companions; so, getting it finished to the point where there was no more room for landscaping or planting would, I thought, free me. Then, of course, I'd need someone to help me weed . . .

But I was unexpectedly interrupted three years into all of this, by the arrival of a tiny, feathered scrap who was going to instantly demand top billing on my priority list: enter George.

May

Saturday 19 May 2007

Working in the garden daily, I noticed a pair of magpies building a huge nest in the neighbour's copper-leafed prunus tree, which rose out of the hedge between our two gardens about 50 yards from the front of my house.

Twig by twisty twig, they knitted this wooden bag for their babies; it hung in the highest of the branches like a dark lantern, a testament to their skill at construction, a very large, twiggy nest, shaped like a tall, inverted pear, with a twiggy lid that was attached by a spine at the back, but sat above the rim to allow parental access from the sides while protecting from the worst of the rain. I'd never seen anything quite like it.

The tree's heavy presence and purple-dark leaves were now made more threatening by the habitation of these magpies and their staccato laughter; their noise sounded as if hard wooden blocks were being thrown at a wall, so they clattered to the ground. Toiling beneath them as I dug narrow trenches for flowerbed edging pavers, and planting hellebores and miniature azaleas, I had the idea that they were the jokers and we humans were their fools.

They screeched and made strange chugging noises; king and queen of the garden, they challenged the wood pigeons and doves and teased the jackdaws and crows without shame. They skipped and flounced and appeared hideously happy as they performed their quick little dance steps, wearing their black-and-white shiny suits with that tinge of oil-slick blue-green like a stain on their inky feathers. Where crows possessed gravitas, jackdaws possessed curiosity, and magpies possessed a tangible sense of humour.

Magpies are vermin, I was told by farmers and friends alike, and anyone who cared to voice an opinion, as if they *knew* all about magpies. Their seemingly universal verdict sounded trite and rehearsed rather than being a warranted judgement that any one of them had come up with on their own. So, I disagreed with them, but nevertheless, when the twelve wild duck eggs started to vanish from the nest on the island in the middle of the large fishpond I'd constructed, I began to regard the magpie nest with some suspicion.

Every morning I'd find another egg missing, and broken bits of shell littering the pond edge. It seemed the egg-eater was coming for an egg a day. Three eggs into the carnage, the duck stopped sitting and deserted the nest; the eggs continued to disappear until there were none left. It was magpies, someone told me, although in truth it could have been any number of creatures: crows, ravens, ferrets, mink, foxes, rats. Even lovable hedgehogs crave a raw egg and there are several of them in my garden. Jackdaws eat eggs too; sometimes I'd look out of the kitchen window and there would be eight or a dozen of them perched on the table and benches that stood on the bit of grass I called "the front lawn." (I've since turned it into a rockery and series of winding flowerbeds full of low-growing evergreen bushes.)

The jackdaws and crows hung around the front yard like mourners waiting for the funeral in their sooty blacks, but I liked them; they had dignity and poise, unlike the magpies who were imps. If I put bread out for the birds, the big black crows would fly over, their slow, powerful wingbeats bringing them down like burnt-out space junk until they littered the crumbling tarmac of the circular forecourt, where they got on with the business of devouring bread. The jackdaws would step aside for their larger cousins. But the magpies would sidle in, cackling and fizzing, hyper-energetic and focused on food.

The bread had to be brown; I was amused to find that the birds ignored white bread altogether, which festered outside, becoming soggy heaps in the first rain and eventually washing away as a sort of greying, diluting slime. Even the rats and mice weren't interested.

The night before, there had been fierce winds. Inside the house the windows had felt to be shaking free of their box frames, their weights rattling inside their hidden sash-coffins. The large house, beaten by the storm, gave me a sense of being in a ship on a wild sea. Our bedroom on the third floor at the back was like the bridge; looking out over the neighbours and forging a path through the stormy skies. The slimmer trees had leaned and bowed, the bigger ones had lost branches, and now here, when I looked up, was the broken, torn-apart tatter of the magpie twig-nest.

Good, I thought firmly, no more magpie nest meant no more magpie eggs, so fewer magpies to eat duck eggs. Even as the thoughts crossed my mind, I felt a stab of guilt; I'd damned them without evidence, and I've spent so much of my life rescuing wounded birds and animals (a compulsion begun in childhood, which eventually grew to include friends, boyfriends, and derelict houses), trying to patch them up and keep them alive until they mended, that being glad of the destruction of the nest, and the eggs that could have been inside it, was alien to me.

There was no sign of the magpie pair. They had simply vanished.

In the raised rockery beds that I'd built adjacent to the tree, a small feathered scrap caught my eye. I parted the foliage around it and found an injured baby magpie; it was almost the size of my palm—too young to walk or fly, and with only the most rudimentary feathers. Its stumpy wings were like a bundle of fan-sticks still awaiting fluff. So, the magpie eggs had already hatched. Immediately, I wanted to save it.

Although I've picked up various injured birds over the years, I've only ever seen baby birds when they've fallen out of the nest, already dead. This little thing was just about alive and in desperate need of care.

The baby magpie's open beak was full of fly eggs, which didn't bode well for the bird. I gently flushed the eggs out under a dribble from the outdoor tap; the bird was bleeding in patches all over its body, and I guessed the neighbour's cat must have had a go at it—it looked torn in places, like a bloodied rag. I took it indoors and gave it a lukewarm bath to flush out the fly eggs from the wounds on the rest of its body; I had to use a tiny watercolour paintbrush to get the fly eggs out of its nostrils. I didn't know what else to do, but I remembered clearly how quickly fly eggs can turn into maggots, and the idea of any egg hatching, eating flesh as a maggot before becoming a chrysalis from which would emerge a fly, made gigantic by the minuteness of its tiny, flesh surroundings, revolted me. I made sure I fished out every single one.

When I was a small child my father, who was a fanatical fisherman, forgot that he'd left a tin of maggots on the dashboard of his old black Morris Traveller. In the summer heat they turned into flies in record time, exploding the top of the old tobacco tin he'd put them in as the bulk of their bodies swelled up like miniature Hulks, clouding the interior of the car with tiny black shiny pissed-off engine-driven lunatics. When he opened the car door my father was engulfed in a cloud of quickly dispersing fizzing black dots, and I was engulfed in peals of laughter, tempered only by a sense of revulsion at the seething mass.

The magpie chick didn't fight or struggle; on the contrary, it put up with my ministrations with the air of a creature that no longer cares. I dried it off, and got it to eat a small worm, which I dangled into its open upturned beak and dropped to the back of its throat, so it swallowed. Then I wrapped it up warmly in a T-shirt and put it in a small cardboard box. I left it to recover and hoped it might, although given its condition I had my doubts. If it lived, I'd call it George.

The sun was blazing down; it was a hot day and I didn't want to miss the weather for planting, so I got back outside as soon as I thought George was settled and there was nothing more that I could do for him; his little head was sunken on his tiny chest and he appeared to be sleeping.

I was planting miniature azaleas beneath a couple of tall silver birches at the bottom of the garden, far away from the spot where I'd found the magpie chick, when I heard a single desperate cry. It wasn't plaintive at all, but demanding and outraged. I searched the bushes and leaves at my feet and found a second baby magpie. It was cold and dead. Puzzled, since it couldn't have been the source of the noise, I buried it beneath one of the cupressus trees I'd planted, and searched again, for the source of the bird call.

Thinking that it might have been my imagination—or a sound from something on the other side of the hedge, out on the road— I got on with shovelling earth, wondering how many weeks it would be necessary to find worms for the baby bird before it could feed itself. I made my way back down to the bottom of the garden where I started filling a jar with the worms I dug up. It didn't occur to me to look up worm suppliers on the internet, because my internet connection in those days was so slow that I could barely send an email, let alone access useful information. So, I'd ask someone who knew, or I'd wait to find out, and until then, I'd dig worms.

I was turning over spadeful after spadeful of the dried leaves and woodchips that covered the ground 6 inches deep, when suddenly another, quite deafening shriek tore right through my eardrum; I had been about to dig the spade into the earth by my feet, but now stopped. Bewildered, I searched through the leaves and debris on the ground, my fingers digging deep, safe in the confines of my black Marigold rubber gloves, which, in the heat of the day, had filled with sweat from my hands so my fingernails were paddling in pools forming at the fingertips of the gloves, but I could still see nothing. Then, just in time, right there by the toe of my boot, next to the blade of my spade and camouflaged by the leaves on the ground, was a third magpie chick. It squatted belligerently, peering up at me with magpie fury. I realised that I might have cut it in two had it not made a noise.

With cheery visions of rearing magpie twins, I took it back to the house and wrapped it up in the T-shirt nest with its sibling. It didn't struggle. It reminded me of one of those plump, rounded toys that are weighted at the bottom; you can knock them over and they always swing up again, but they don't possess the means to walk.

For a while I had happy thoughts of naming them Samson and Delilah and waving them off to freedom in tandem when old enough, but when I came back later to check on my two guests I found the first chick was dead. If only I could have found it before the cat and the fly eggs . . . if only I had a magic wand.

I fervently hoped that rinsing the fly eggs off the first bird had not contributed to its death, although when I remembered those fly eggs I really believed that I had no choice but to remove anything that might become a maggot. This thought didn't stop me berating myself, however: should I not have bathed it? Should I not have cleaned all the fly eggs off it? Could I have got to it before the cat did? Was it too warm? Or not warm enough?

The second chick was leaning away from its sibling as if disgusted. The little corpse must have been getting chilly to cuddle up to. I extracted the dead chick and buried it next to its other sibling beneath the twisty cupressus, seething with frustration at not knowing what would have made the difference between its life and death.

I should have kept it warmer; I should have toasted it in the bottom oven of the Rayburn. I should have tucked it into my shirt so that it felt as if it was being mothered. Perhaps then it would have had more of a chance. But of course, shock is the real killer. Shock, and cats.

In my early twenties, I took in unwanted cats—I loved those cats and ended up with thirteen of them before I managed to rehome them all. But they killed things, and after living in Australia in my thirties and seeing cats kill so many of the indigenous marsupials, I went right off cats altogether.

Now I was determined to try and save the third bird. I chose not to think about how people would judge me bringing up a bird held in such high disregard.

Magpie food became a preoccupation all afternoon; I worked my way through planting azaleas and denuding the garden of worm life, small slugs, and a couple of woodlice. Every so often I'd take a break to feed George. (Who could just as easily have been Georgina: the name moved from the dead bird to the survivor; I like to recycle.) He'd raise his head on a neck that looked a foot long in comparison to his tiny, squat body, and open his mouth with an ear-splitting screech when he wanted food.

In the process of answering George's dietary calls, I discovered an interesting thing about worms: they genuinely didn't want to die; they didn't think that a bird's gullet was a nice, moist hole to slip into, so they fought like hell to escape George's eager beak, twisting and writhing as I tried to dangle them into his throat. It was as if they were all eyes and aware of impending doom.

It wasn't long before I developed the knack of pushing the end of the worm down George's throat with the tip of my finger, and quickly shoving the rest of it into his jaw, before the other end of the worm got a curling grip on the side of his beak and hauled itself out. I noticed the back of the magpie's tongue had a sort of two-pronged ledge that pointed down into its throat, as if to deter anything living that might want to scramble out again.

If worms had only a single thought in their little nematode bodies, it was that they wanted to LIVE.

The really big worms (and I found a couple of whoppers about 5 inches long) were so strong that it was almost impossible to get their whole length into the bird before they forced his beak open to effect their escape. And they could move fast. I caught one fleeing from a high-sided bowl and slithering rapidly across the kitchen worktop. Perhaps it would have been better to chop them up, but whenever I accidentally cut them in half with a spade, it made me cringe terribly, as if I expected to feel the cut myself. And they wriggled in apparent agony—not that being digested alive in a bird's belly is any more pleasant. In any case, George seemed to have no trouble accommodating any size of worm, so chopping up worms was, I reasoned, thankfully unnecessary.

George's temporary accommodation became the bundled T-shirt at the bottom of the dogs' small wire-mesh carry-cage, placed on the floor by the Rayburn in the kitchen.

The kitchen was the only room in the huge house that actually had any space; all the other rooms were filled with stacked furniture, boxes of possessions that hadn't been unpacked because there was nowhere to put the contents, bags of cushions and curtains and clothes, and then all the glass and crystal chandeliers I'd constructed from bits bought in a chandelier breaker's. (This was a warehouse that contained nothing but the broken-up parts of chandeliers of all descriptions: long, dangling spiky crystals; pear-drop crystals; chains of crystals; boxes of new bead crystals; the wire pins used to curl through the holes in crystals to fix them to their base; green, red, yellow and orange glass ball pendants; glass arms; chandelier skeletons to adorn . . . these items and many, many more were heaped in boxes on rows of trestle tables, through which I would rummage for hours at a time during the two years I'd been house-hunting.)

Green plastic units inherited from the previous owners—some glazed, and mostly propped up on top of each other as opposed to being fitted—filled the kitchen. The aged dark green Rayburn slogged along in an effort to be warm but went cold every time I put something in it to cook, and the oven was a crock. The bare dark oak floorboards dated back to the Victorian rear part of the house, although the kitchen was in the Georgian front part. Everything was in a permanent state of "being unfinished," which, for someone like me who likes to make order out of chaos, was a form of torture.

I could never get it properly clean or tidy because of all the rubble, boxes and bags; I felt demoralised by years of "camping out" in our own home, which is what we'd done for five years in the London house until it, too, was done. (It took another two years to sell.) But this house was going to take very much longer, and in the meantime, the seemingly never-ending state of the house made it so much easier for me to remain in the garden, where I was not constantly reminded of what a depressing shit-heap the inside of my home was. In the garden I could make a visible difference daily because the work necessary was something I was capable of, and didn't require the costly employment of others; the electrician and plumber were slowly working their way through rewiring and plumbing indoors. When they finished, the house would already have cost much more than I would ever realise if I sold it again. In overcapitalising, I was confirming my intention of staying rooted to the little plot the house stood on. In constructing the garden, I was making it very difficult to sell in any case; after all, who would want to take on the work required for the upkeep?

Never before had I cared for a bird so young, so I was fascinated when George demonstrated that he was nest-trained and shoved his bottom over the side of the T-shirt I'd folded to put him on, in order to expel crap from his living area. Unfortunately, there was no height to allow for the clearance of bird crap, so it dribbled off the edges. His parents didn't teach him to do this; it was wired into his brain, just as the colour of his feathers and the size of his beak were determined by his DNA.

The parents of some birds will wait for the faecal sac produced by their babies, grab it in their beaks and fly off to drop it like a miniature missile somewhere else. Sometimes they will eat it, supposedly because the matter still contains useful nutrients. George did not expel his poop in a faecal sac, so I could be certain that magpie projectile-pooing was now going to be a regular feature of my kitchen landscape.

If that was the case, George was going to need a more efficient nest to allow him better access to an edge over which he could dangle his posterior. In a forgotten corner of a kitchen cupboard I discovered a shocking-pink plastic salad bowl with a lime-green interior; for the price of £1 it had seemed like bright and happy value, although I'd never used it for anything. I filled the bowl with screwed-up newspaper, then arranged the T-shirt into a sort of nest shape on top.

Now George was raised off the newspaper-covered floor of the dog cage and could properly crap over the side of his nest. Although he could wobble and rock, he was unable to walk, so he remained squatting, gazing at the dogs outside the bars until he was hungry. Then he opened his mouth again, so that the top of his head looked about to flip off, and let out another of his blood-curdling shrieks: "FEED ME!" The only time he moved was to shuffle his backside to the edge of his nest.

I worked outside until around ten that evening, when it was too dark to see, and fed the bird a couple more worms that I'd saved. Then, as soon as the very last glimmer of light outside vanished, it was as if someone had switched him off; George's neck retracted, his eyes shut, his body fluffed into an untidy ball of plastic-looking feather-sticks, and he was instantly asleep. He could have been a toy in which the battery had suddenly run out of juice.

Now I had a chance to examine him more closely; his rudimentary flying feathers were still contained in what looked like black plastic tubes that were breaking away at the ends, allowing the feathers inside to fluff out and give the bird a more appealing appearance. His underbelly was bald, and his papery pink skin allowed a clear view of the intestine that curled from his neck to his rear end. He wasn't remotely beautiful, but he was certainly interesting.

I hoped he'd be alive in the morning.

Sunday 20 May

When I opened the kitchen door, George was chirping in a high-pitched rather pretty way; it was a sort of trilling sound and the dogs were delighted, padding around the cage beside the Rayburn and panting encouragingly at him. Widget, the runty Maltese terrier midget sister of Snickers, who was a slightly larger white mophead of a dog, watched the bird with devout interest as if she was watching a cooking programme on television; glance away and you won't know how much tarragon to add to your frying chicken thighs in wine and crème fraiche, or whether you should use a bain-marie to cook the soufflé. Mouse, the old Maltese-cross, was largely uninterested and walked around him without acknowledgement. She was a princess and this thing in her living area was an untidy, smelly knot of strange bird-squeals.

Snickers, however, clearly wanted to adopt him. Wishfully, she paced the outside of the cage, while Widget stood watching her with an air of bafflement. She tried to lick George through the bars. I wondered if it was because he tasted interesting, or because she wanted to clean him as if he were her own, or if she would bite his head off were he more accessible.

George ate the rest of the worms that I'd glad-wrapped in a bowl with a tiny air hole last night to keep them fresh. The very, very big ones were obstinate again. Feeling dreadful as I dunked them in water (which also seemed to shock them into stillness) to make them more slippery to swallow, I then dangled their two ends into the back of George's throat. One of the worms hooked the loop of its body over George's beak as he tried to swallow both ends, so the more he swallowed the tighter the loop on his beak became: cartoonish. I unhooked the loop, stretching it over the tip of George's eager beak so that he could swallow the worm.

He was gaining weight so rapidly, literally in front of my eyes, that the plastic bowl of his nest now rocked and tilted when he moved around in it. I weighted it with a couple of large stones in the bottom, so that when George stuck his backside over the edge, he didn't topple the bowl over.

He also appeared to be more comfortable with the dogs and with me. I picked him up from time to time; he liked having his feet secured on my fingers as he nuzzled into my chest for support, because he couldn't balance in my hand, he was too unsteady by far. OK, so he was cute, I thought, but he's still a magpie with exploding dandruff.

As the hours passed, more and more of the plastic-looking black tubes containing new feathers, like super-thin straws with spiky ends, emerged from the small outgrowths—papillas—in his skin. They each began to fray at the ends, crumbling away to expose the soft feathers underneath, leaving heaps of grey dandruff at the bottom of his cage.

George was growing fluffier by the minute. Disconcertingly, I found that I wanted to be with him all the time, watching his almost visible development, feeding him until he couldn't squeeze in another worm; I was transfixed, and felt that if I left the room for a moment I'd miss a whole other stage.

When George slept in between feedings he tried to tuck his head into his wing, but his feathers weren't plentiful enough, his neck was too short, and his head was rather large and clumsy, so it didn't work; he just appeared to be trying unsuccessfully to fold himself in half.

He was also, I must be honest, a little eating–shitting machine. "Don't write the grotty stuff," said a friend who was visiting during George's adolescence when I mentioned my desire to record his existence. But why not? Birds crap, and baby birds crap enormous amounts because they eat vast quantities to fuel their prodigious growth rate, in some cases doubling in size every three days. My friend, I think, was quietly repelled by the proximity to a real live wild bird and its effluent, whereas all I saw was the most miraculous little creature doing what every creature does.

Vast quantities of projectile magpie poo were propelled sometimes out of the cage bars altogether, and on to the kitchen floor. On one occasion Snickers had a near miss when she was keeping vigil, facing his cage in a sphinx-like pose, head up, front paws forward, eyes, nose and ears alert when George shuffled to the edge of the makeshift nest in his colourful bowl, raised his tail feathers and aimed right at her; a shaft of flying magpie poo narrowly missed her right ear and hit the side of the kitchen unit behind.

My own wonderment at George was that he had blown in from the wild and, driven perhaps by a primal instinct to survive no matter what, had decided to let me take over his feeding and care. Adapt and survive, they say, and George was adapting—it was up to me to help him survive.

I tried not to worry about what would happen if George made it into adulthood; whether he would fly off, or whether I would have to accommodate him forever. I could only take one day at a time, especially as I didn't want him to leave. When anyone asked what I was going to do with the bird, I told them that "the bird will decide," which was true: it all depended on George, and I was going to have to accept his decision, even if I disagreed with it.

Monday 21 May

My days had come to follow a sort of pattern: bed late, then up before I'd had enough sleep. That way I felt as if I was somehow "making" extra time to get more done, while often feeling guilty that I was spending hours in the garden rather than on my next poetry book or painting.

Guilt is self-inflicted, and sometimes it is useful in driving us on to get things done—most of the time, however, it is pointless and painful. Guilt for me is what makes me get up in the morning to write and paint—or I will finish the day having added nothing to it: no little painting, no written word, no small effort that will go towards building a finished book, or an exhibition.

The unfortunate truth about my work is that it is all self-generated. No one is directing me; I am wholly responsible for succeeding or falling flat on my face. Ideas pop into my head and I have to decide if they are exciting enough to imbue me with the energy for their completion, in the hope that others will enjoy the results as much as I enjoyed the creating.

Working on poems for *The Book of Mirrors*, I was developing characters around "Stonepicker," which was the title poem of an earlier collection, about a woman who harbours grievances against others in the belief that they are to blame for all that's wrong in her life—she will never take responsibility for anything. I was creating a family for her: Stunckle, Stonepicker's uncle, the man who believes everything is his right, and that he is elevated above all others; and Stunckle's cousin, based on a self-appointed critic and arbiter of opinion who is so deeply insecure that he must bring others down in order to feel equal, which is one of my favourite wickedly brutal poems. *The Book of Mirrors* itself was my vision of a book that we open to see ourselves (or those we have met) as we (or they) really are—or could be.

All the experiences I've ever had with people who I'd like to avoid in future helped me to add flesh to my Stonepicker family.

Other life continued; renovations progressed slowly. In the early days we had an au pair, a Hungarian girl who wanted to improve her English, to help out around the house; she had no objection to a lack of children—I gave her the least awful bedroom while The Ex and I slept in a room with bare boards, pinned-up sheets as curtains, and the entire contents of my future linen cupboard in a heap of black bin bags piled in the corner.

But one night she came to find me to tell me her ceiling was making strange noises.

The ceiling creaked and groaned and spectacularly collapsed in front of me just as I opened her bedroom door, making a sandwich of the double bed. Clouds of dust billowed up from the debris, and, from the exposed rafters that were left behind, dead flies and crumbs of rubble continued to drop, like little afterthoughts, into the air cushion of plaster particles that swirled and eddied in an excited frenzy. I quickly shut the door on it; there was nothing that could be done, and the poor woman had to move to the only other available bedroom, which was full of light fittings. She lasted six months in Wales, and then either the renovations or the isolation from any interesting nightlife (or both) took its toll and she returned to London.

Friends came and went in a desultory fashion. I felt rather cut off; I'd enjoyed a hectic social life in London, although it would have crippled my efforts to work had I allowed it to. Here, I knew no one. But now I had other company; George was the new guest and I was besotted by what appeared to be his rapidly developing little bird-personality. This particular morning he was already the first thing on my mind, above even the dogs. I felt slightly guilty about that, but the dogs had food out all the time, so they could help themselves, and their water bowl was always full, whereas George couldn't fend for himself in any way at all; he was helpless and needed me, and now my purpose was to keep him alive. The joy of such a purpose is that it gives you a reason to ignore everything else. There is nothing so effective in taking one's mind off the practical concerns of our lives as a living creature that needs immediate care without which it will die, if we are so inclined to try and save it. And I was.

I was now living in my gardening clothes. The silk shirts I loved to wear when out and about in London hung limply in the wardrobe boxes, and I lived in men's work trousers from a local shop, and tatty old T-shirts. I looked like a bag lady, permanently in green wellingtons or muddy trainers, and occasionally lipstick; blazing sun, howling wind and occasional sleet are very drying for the lips. I wore no other make-up. I felt very far removed from my old city life, when I wouldn't go out of the door without a face full of warpaint.

Having always felt that small talk stultified my brain, and being rubbish at it, I was now spared an enormous number of conversations altogether, as my social life dwindled and calls to visit London almost vanished. Exciting London parties went on without me as I grew roots and flowered in the Welsh Marches.

My own conversation was limited to the names of plants that filled my head from morning until night; names that I can't remember now, but which consumed me with desire back then. On this particular Monday I drove to the Derwen Garden Centre; there was a sale on. Even as I drove I could feel my heart rate increase with excitement at the idea of being able to buy multiple plants at bargain prices. I was uncomfortably aware that my addiction might seem odd to others. I was once addicted to cigarettes. Before I gave up on 8 March 1993, I smoked eighty cigarettes a day. Buying them had given me joy (in answering the need) and a sense of security (having enough for the next few hours), although getting down to one packet used to fill me with anxiety, because a single packet wouldn't last me more than four hours at best, and that knowledge filled me with panic. Smoking had brought me a feeling of being "in the company of a friend," albeit a friend who gave me a hacking cough, permanent phlegm and the breathlessness of a person three times my age.

Nicotine causes a constriction of the blood vessels; so, blessed with a normally very low blood pressure in any case, I now froze. I was cold everywhere and my feet and hands suffered terribly during winter gardening. I wondered if shrinking the blood vessels in my brain would contribute to dementia later and I increased my efforts to bin cigarettes forever. But I found it nigh on impossible.

When I did finally give up smoking, my skin appeared to plump up and soften, and I realised how cigarettes had dried me out. After years of trying and failing to kick the habit, I'd finally given up by repeatedly telling myself, "I'm not giving up, because I'VE NEVER SMOKED!" If giving something up was too difficult because it deprived me of a habit I enjoyed, then telling myself over and over "I've never smoked" meant that I wasn't depriving myself of anything, and the withdrawal symptoms were aberrations that would pass. Which, after six months of weight gain (I put my head in the fridge and didn't come up for air for three months), night terrors, muscle spasms and a phlegm-clearing cough, they did.

But now I had a new friend—George—and he wasn't bad for my health in any way I could see, and his care could be neatly accommodated alongside my gardening obsession.

My father once told me what he described as a Chinese proverb, "Hair by hair you can pluck a tiger bald," which was in the back of my mind as I faced the canvas painting hairs on to tigers, rabbits, cats, wolves, bears and chinchillas over the years. Every small effort contributed to a much larger picture—this belief, even before my father's proverb, governed my life from childhood. I could see how starting something now, not next week, and sticking at it, would achieve goals as a result of my sheer doggedness if nothing else. In the back of my mind were all the projects, all the paintings and all the stories that I'd never finished, and "finishing everything" was going to be my new motto. I only hoped that the garden would be worthwhile; I had a suspicion that it was going to look a bit mad when completed. But better that than remaining a dream, like all the other gardens in my imagination over the years.

With a view to "finishing," I did a bit more work on trying to dig up the ground elder in the flowerbed down the side of the house, but it was a thankless task; the smallest piece of root left would grow another healthy plant. I knew how indestructible it was, and the frustrating—and seemingly endless—effort of removing the ground elder demoralised me, because I knew it wasn't worth planting anything in the soil afterwards. It was only a question of time before it returned again, having grown a whole new root system out of sight, before presenting itself afresh in all its vile greenery. The idea of clearing it over and over again at various points in the future simply added itself to a litany of other tedious but necessary tasks that I would have to keep repeating if I wanted to keep from being subsumed. I turned my thoughts to George instead, and found myself smiling.

There are always priorities in life, and often it is up to us to designate more importance to one responsibility or obligation above another. But when a living creature that cannot speak for itself enters the equation, it must come as a top priority by default. George's sudden, unexpected presence in my life gave me the excuse to ignore everything that didn't require immediate attention.

I noted today that George was quieter and less demanding. I'd run out of worms halfway through the day. (Have you any idea how exhausting it is to dig constantly for worms? It was just as hard a job for me as it would be for a parent bird.)

It seemed that I'd exhausted the worm-supply for the time being, or the worm-word had got out and they were sinking deeper into the ground for safety. (Only much later did it occur to me that I could have bought maggots and worms from a shop only 7 miles away that sells everything from chainsaws, horse nuts, goldfish and furniture to gardening supplies . . .)

So, now I was making little pellets out of minced beef when George screeched for food. Each time I would wet a pellet of the meat in a bowl of water so it slipped down more easily, and was less likely to stick to his beak. Usually after the first mouthful, he edged his bottom over the side of the nest and crapped; he was like a bird version of those plastic dolls that you give a toy bottle of real water to, that then pee on to your lap because you forgot it needs a nappy, because it is a DOLL.

As I child I had one once, but not for longer than it took me to dismember it; it was horribly life-sized, with batting eyelids when I tilted it one way or another. No one who really knew me would have given such a disgusting fake-human thing to me—I would much rather have had a train set.

Having disconnected the travesty of its rubbery limbs, I buried the evidence in the garden at the family home, Court Green in Devon, the house that was bought by my mother and father when they were very much still together in 1961, and where my brother, Nick, was born.

That doll revolted me; it was testament to the expectation that I would grow up to have a baby and be a mother; the weight of this expectation on me, just because I was a girl, was something I was conscious of even at the age of seven or eight, and I felt it was an imposition on what I regarded as my freedom of choice.

Many years later, when I was in my mid-teens, someone was digging a flowerbed at the family home when I heard a cry of horror. I ran to see what the matter was and found them holding up one of the doll's arms, complete with hand; I suspect their first reaction had been to think it might be real, as it was life-sized. Plastic baby dolls apparently don't compost.

Tuesday 22 May

George was more demanding today; I fed him little and often on worms and minced beef. He appeared to like being held, although if I picked him up I had to hook his feet over my fingers as he wasn't very coordinated himself. He was beginning to develop quite a firm grip, although his toes felt soft against my skin; he wasn't scratchy at all.

Everything I did, be it cooking a meal, or gardening, or working at the computer, or painting, I did with one eye on George.

I was having a look at a job that was being done by a local workman to patch the plaster on the walls and replace the windows in the living room on the middle floor when suddenly I heard Mouse barking from downstairs in a desperate warning fashion. She had a deep voice, that dog, for something that was so small, old, white and fluffy.

I raced towards her bark, Snickers and Widget skittering and slipping down the worn, dark oak Victorian stairs ahead of me.

Mouse was still in her basket in the kitchen, and I glanced around frantically to see what was causing her to panic.

The first thing I did was check the dog cage for George. But although the doors of the cage were firmly fastened, George wasn't there. For one awful moment I thought Mouse might have eaten him, then I remembered that Mouse had hardly any teeth; she'd still be chewing and there would be telltale feathers. She looked at me indignantly, raised to her full sitting height of barely 12 inches.

Then a plaintive squawk arose from the dogs' food bowls in the corner of the kitchen floor by the sink, and there was George, clumsily perched on the edge of one of them, his tail propping him up in a rather lopsided fashion because one of his rudimentary wings drooped slightly, perhaps as a result of his fall from the family nest. It seemed that George had taken to self-service. I couldn't understand how he'd escaped, as he appeared to be much too large to get between the cage bars.

Gently scooping him up, I placed him back on his T-shirt nest in the cage, but two minutes later all three dogs were barking; they had now tuned in to George and George's actions directed them. So, my eyes were first on George. I watched, impressed, as he waddled to the edge of his makeshift nest on his heels, and fell over the side. Then, unsteady, he raised himself up, stumbled towards the bars like a drunk, turned sideways and slid one wing out of the cage. He squeezed his chest through, which must have hurt because he let out a cry of complaint, then the other wing followed. He was free. George, I discovered, was developing brains; this sideways crab-waddle seemed to me to be an extraordinary deduction for the little bird.

Magpies (*Pica pica*) have a brain-to-body mass ratio that is apparently only exceeded by humans. They can learn to imitate human speech, use tools, recognise people and remember who or what is dangerous and who or what is safe to be around. George's deduction that, if he turned sideways, he could escape, meant that he'd thought about his size and shape in tandem with the narrow space available between bars. Most other birds—sparrows, pigeons, pheasants, chickens—would simply ram their heads through the opening and wonder why their bodies refused to follow. A buzzard or red-tailed kite might not think about the sideways waddle, but I can't imagine that they would be so undignified as to try to cram themselves through a seemingly impossible gap.

Now George toppled forward in a heap on the floor outside the cage and tried to stand up. But he was too uncoordinated for this, so I picked him up and he snuggled into the crook of my arm. I gazed at his cage, racking my brain for a solution to his Houdini-like abilities, trying to judge the width of the bars against the size of his little breast; it would only be a couple of days until he was far too big to get through, so the solution only had to be temporary.

Then I had it! Cling film. I cling-filmed the sides of the cage including the main access door at the front. There was a door in the top of the cage that I could use instead.

But before I put him back, I thought George could do with some space to try out his new legs, so I set him on the kitchen floor for a bit. He was like a half-wound clockwork toy, reeling and stumbling this way and that, his wings out for support, tottering as if he were on vertiginous heels. The dogs followed his every move: Snickers licked George's beak (presumably attracted by all that beef-mince flavour) and I let her, watching closely to make sure that she didn't suddenly lunge forward and snap the little bird's head off. She wouldn't let Widget near George; she snarled at her smaller sister and Widget scampered away, only to come back for another look at the new plaything.

When he stretched, George's legs were so long in comparison to his body they looked like stilts. He stumbled to a halt on his spiky little toes, shuffled his shoulder feathers so they ruffled, then raised himself unsteadily on his pins as if seeing how far they would go. Higher and higher he went, until he looked like a tiny black-and-white ball of wool on two very thin knitting needles. He peered down at the floor as if surprised to see it so far away.

When I put him back in his cage, he immediately tried to get out again; his new freedom had been snatched from him and he wasn't having it; he bounced off the cling film over and over again until exhausted, and only then did he give up. He appeared to sulk like a child, squatting sullenly on the floor of his cage. I reached in from above and put him back in his bowl of a nest, turning the kitchen lights out so he'd sleep. I noted how he was quickly becoming a sort of magpie version of a belligerent teenager with attitude; I had visions of waking up in the morning to a magpie hoodie.

Because of George, rolls of paper kitchen towels would have to be a major purchase; they were the handy wipes for all the baby-bird excrement that escaped the confines of the cage. No bird-mother could have been more attentive than I was, and George's screeches for attention dragged me from whatever I was doing; if he were to live, then he must be fed.

Wednesday 23 May

Further evidence was stacking up that life must, whether I liked it or not, return to a more work-focused ethic. It meant that I had to feed George only on bits of mince; there wasn't time to find worms because I was working in the office on the following week's poetry column for *The Times* all day, and it required dedication to go out and dig up the reluctant magpie snacks in enough quantity to satisfy George's increasingly demanding appetite. How could he possibly eat so much?

And yet I found that I could not keep away from him; he was a little feathered magnet. Now and then I took him out to stroke him, having persuaded myself that I needed to make another cup of tea—and another—and another, so that I could justify deserting my computer.

George was totally trusting when I held him; he'd let me pick him up, put him down and move him around. The speed at which he was developing meant that a few hours made all the difference to his appearance and behaviour: it was amazing to see how his instinct for survival had easily allowed him to swap one black-and-white winged mother for a large, fleshy, beige-pink, fabric-covered one that was many times his own size, just as long as food was delivered on demand.

The dogs were now also fixated by George. When he was in his cage on the floor, they sat and waited outside it, napping when they weren't watching him, but always keeping close.

On this particular afternoon I felt terribly tired—exhausted in fact, so much so that my efforts to work on my column were becoming counterproductive; I found myself sitting, dozing, and listing like a beached boat in my swivel office chair in front of the computer, unable to concentrate. I thought it might be a result of too much late-night work in the office, so I took a nap on the kitchen sofa. There is a protocol to this:

First, I fetch a blanket. The three dogs see what I am doing and line up in front of the sofa with expectant expressions on their little white faces, each punctuated by the three perfect black coals of eyes and nose. I stack a couple of cushions at each end to support my feet and my shoulders so that I'm in a nice, comfortable "V" shape, which is the only lying-down position that my arthritic disc-compromised back ever truly enjoys. At the time of writing this I have lost an inch and a half in height, which, when the doc measured me for some statistical requirement or other, shocked me as if I'd been punched.

Once I lie down with the blanket over me, doggy hierarchy is always imposed; Snickers is first up and tucks herself beneath my chin, as close to my face as she can manage without suffocating me. Widget is next, but, being shorter-legged than her sister, she uses a tiny footstool that I bought her for the purpose, to scramble on to the sofa in order to reach my lap, where she lies down next to Snickers. Then Mouse, as old as she is, scrabbles up the side of the heap; she tentatively uses the footstool, but only sometimes, because the dogs are all conscious that the stool is primarily for Widget. Only Widget will curl up on it and Snickers will never use it to access the sofa even if I attempt to persuade her. But she is able to jump up unaided in any case.

This afternoon, once the dogs were settled, I put George on my chest too, up against Snickers and on a T-shirt in case he felt the need to relieve himself. If I was taking time away from work in order to nap, spending time with all my animals simultaneously was a way of multitasking. Occasionally I'd open one eye and check on George; he was fast asleep as were the dogs. From time to time Snickers would lean over and lick George's face, which really meant licking his beak. George tolerated it, visibly bracing himself against the pressure of her relatively large tongue against his tiny head. It was the closest thing to heaven (if a little weird) to lie there with three contented pooches and a napping magpie. I felt warm, loved and in good company. What they felt was presumably that they were a) near their food source, b) near a decent heat source, and c) they wouldn't miss anything that might go on, since we were all there together in a big heap.

Thursday 24 May

Not missing out was important to George. Today I noticed that he never took his eyes off me; he didn't miss a single action or movement that I made. I left him out for longer and longer periods of time, and he would just sit, observing me and the dogs, growing quietly, and shedding more and more dandruff from the sheaths of his feathers.

Stretching is a big thing with young birds; they test their legs and wings to the extreme, as if checking everything works for their maiden flight, since a second chance is often not an option if they crash and break their necks, or are found by a cat while semi-conscious.

George regularly tested his legs, rising up as if he were on pistons, then stretching his wings behind him and downwards; it was if he were breaking out of his physical restraints. If he could balance so he didn't fall over, he'd look quite dignified, like a little man getting ready for a night out in his dinner jacket and white shirt, but usually he'd stumble and fall.

Most of the time he levered himself around, squatting on his heels, waddling like someone kneeling; he still couldn't walk yet. What appeared to be his knees pointed backwards, but those were his heels, since his knees were really the bones up at the top of what appeared to be his thigh. I wondered if he had a birth defect when I noticed his ear openings were different heights and sizes.

Recently, in *Bird Brain: An Exploration of Avian Intelligence* by Dr. Nathan Emery, I found a mention that owls have one ear opening higher than the other in order to receive mismatched sound waves and so pinpoint prey. Although the ear holes of corvids aren't mentioned, it describes George.

Six days after finding him the sheaths of George's wing and tail feathers were almost all powdered off; he just had a couple of little bits left that Widget tried to nibble away. Dandruff was a daily feature of the kitchen floor; it gathered in heaps in the corners of the old, dark oak Victorian floorboards, and eddied and whirlpooled in the draught of opening and closing doors, prompting me to drag out the vacuum cleaner over and over again.

George seemed to enjoy affection, although maybe for him it was simply the need for food and warmth. But if he was out of the cage, he wanted to be close to me; my lap was his favourite place. This slowed me down terribly, as once he sat on my lap I was reluctant to move. But I had a sense that it wouldn't be long before the chances to stroke this tiny magpie would evaporate as he developed independence.

Thinking I might never raise another magpie, I tried to keep a photographic record of me with this fascinating little bird, but it was hard to get a picture of us together, because I had to rely on the good nature of The Ex, who wasn't the least bit interested. George, it seemed, was the competition.

Friday 25 May

For the first few days of his stay with me, I continued to see George as a magical creature. I was like any owner with a new pet: watching, worrying, fascinated as this little being did simple things, from his leg-stretching to his wing-arching. When he arched his wings, he'd bring them over his head like an angel, and he tried to clean his chest feathers, but his neck, while it stretched upwards, somehow wouldn't let him reach his front.

Although he still screeched to be fed, he'd begun to peck occasionally at the meaty dog food that I kept topped up in dishes on the floor for the dogs, which was good, because it heralded the time when he could feed himself. Sometimes he managed to get a bit of dog meat in his beak and threw it back down his throat. I found it interesting that he developed increasingly adult habits so quickly and without any parent bird to copy. (Which was fortunate, as I was never going to demonstrate my dog-meat-eating skills for his benefit.)

Mostly, he liked company, and was very happy to sit on the table beside me, or on my lap. He was also happy just sitting in my hand as I moved around doing chores: cooking, tidying up, whatever I could do one-handed. Sometimes I held him in one hand while I painted with the other, and he'd watch my face, or my paintbrush as it moved, and seemed captivated. So was I. Of course, I realised that everything took twice as long to do with a magpie hanging off me, but I also wanted to make the most of every minute. His warmly feathered presence was like having an emissary of the natural world grounding me daily.

Today, George only fell off the kitchen table on to the floor twice. Gravity was his latest lesson. He did this a lot, as if trying to fly, but his little chin would hit the ground and he'd be in a heap. I don't know if his fall was an intentional effort to see if he could fly or if it was just because he didn't know what to do about the edge of the table. When I picked him up and put him on the crook of my arm, he climbed on to my shoulder and snuggled into my neck. I could feel his warm feathered body pressing against my skin.

Saturday 26 May

The Ex and I were invited out to have dinner with friends. It was the first time that I'd had to leave George at home for a whole evening. Going out to buy plants, or pots, or food for the house, I could rush back for the next feeding, but a whole dinner party would take hours. I found myself beset with anxiety for the bird: what if he suddenly got terribly hungry and I wasn't there to feed him? What if he found out how to get part way—but not all the way—through the cling film that now swaddled the sides of his cage, and injured himself? What if he escaped and Snickers, in her excitement, ate him?

No sooner had we dressed for dinner, and left the house, than I wanted to turn around and come back home. Desperately, I thought up excuses: we had a flat tyre and the spare was missing or also flat; perhaps I'd developed an unexpected stomach bug and found myself throwing up in a lay-by. But if I did not accept invitations, I was never going to expand my almost non-existent circle of acquaintances.

All through the evening my mind was back at the house, imagining how George was. I smiled, I ate, I drank, I know I spoke to people but have no idea what I said. I hope I was a good guest; I felt warm and friendly towards the other guests, but also alien—they seemed so removed from reality for me. Inside my head I was hearing George making "feed me" noises. I made my honest excuses—I had to feed a baby magpie—and we left just slightly early, no doubt leaving behind us the impression of eccentricity.

When we got back, George was all curled up, perched on the edge of his nest, facing outwards rather than inwards; this was a new development. Snickers and Widget lay side by side in watchful attendance beside his cage, paws out in front of them, heads held high, necks taut, noses forward. I wondered if they'd moved at all since we left. George was doggy telly and they found him riveting.

As soon as he laid eyes on me, George gave a loud, demanding squawk, so I fed him another mouthful of minced beef and balanced him on my shoulder, where he stayed as I made a cup of tea. The practicalities of the makeshift kitchen meant that the teabags were a long way from the kettle, which was a long way from the cold tap, and the fridge was a satellite at the edge of the large room; the kitchen measured about 21 feet by 23 feet. As I moved about, I could feel George's little toes gripping softly.

That night he curled up in his cage when I put him back, perching on the edge of the bowl instead of resting in the middle as he used to. Every day he was a little more aware, and since the sheaths of his feathers had pretty much gone now, he looked like a real magpie, only in chubby miniature. He was shabby, with bald patches on his head exposing his lopsided different-sized ear openings; his tatty appearance tugged at my heartstrings.

Sunday 27 May

As much as possible, I lived with George on my shoulder, his little claws digging in as he perched. For some reason he liked to face backwards when I walked. He'd crap on the arm of the work shirt I wore for the purpose, because he couldn't lever his bum far enough over the edge of my shoulder. I cleaned it up. He was quite happy as I moved around the house, as long as I didn't hurry; it unsettled his balance. The dogs played together on the floor and occasionally, when they came over to peer up at George, he let out a "feed me" screech as if he thought they could do just that. He talked to the dogs in a squeaky, chittery way, but they had no idea what he was saying. I'd never heard a bird make those sounds before. The chittering in adults is a really harsh sound, but this was gentle and almost musical. Sometimes it was as if he was asking a question.

He also made strange cackling, gurgling noises when he tried to communicate, which gave me the opportunity to shove minced beef down his throat every time he opened his beak; his screech was deafeningly loud in my ear . . . the piercing shard of his little cry would stab me right down to my cerebellum.

George's appetite appeared to have increased suddenly, as if his metabolism had accelerated. In the previous week he'd already eaten countless worms, numerous slugs and almost an entire 1lb packet of minced beef.

Within days of taking up residence, George was trying to fly in earnest. This wasn't just a falling-off-the-table effort, but a real attack on the process of becoming airborne. A week earlier, when he fell out of the bowl-nest, he couldn't even stand up, but now he was demanding attention, regarding my shoulder as his very own perch, and was striding up and down the kitchen floor flapping his tatty wings, followed by Snickers who had definitely adopted him, and Widget, who wouldn't let her sister have all the fun.

I wondered if I should pick George up and throw him into the air—after all, how else could I teach him to fly? But mother birds can't teach their offspring to fly either; the babies have to get airborne on their own, and flying for birds is not always something that works first time.

First, there is the idea of owning wings: stretching, flapping, folding, the moment they have their first rudimentary feathers. The more developed their feathers, the more they are able to get an idea of the lift that flapping gives them. Then there is the distance between the nest and the ground below, which they will risk usually only when they are fully feathered, although the fluff may still be clinging on in places and their tails may be short and undeveloped.

Many common garden birds can't fly right away and must spend a couple of days on the ground while their flight feathers grow that little bit more. Then their flight is necessarily unpredictable and badly executed. They might fly directly into an object instead of landing on it. They must practise, practise, practise.

Once they have flown the nest, they don't return. The fledglings end up scurrying around the ground with their parents feeding them at intervals. Overnighting is the problem here; they have to find shelter and safety. But it is only a matter of a few short days before they are properly airborne.

One year I had three baby robins, three baby wrens and three baby blackbirds all arrive around my bird feeder during the same week. It was like having a kindergarten for feathereds. A window painter who was working for me at the time brought me two of the wrens, one after the other, thinking they needed help because it was possible to catch them, but they were perfectly healthy and very active; they just couldn't get off the ground properly quite yet, although it would only be a day or two until they could.

The parents were always somewhere nearby, feeding them under my car, or on the bench near the bird feeder. There were plant pots and overgrown campanulas behind which they could scuttle and hide when they heard me coming. Most of the time they ignored me and just got on with the business of living, and I had the joy of watching them twitter and feed daily until the fledglings finally left altogether and the parents' job was done.

Tuesday 29 May

Leaving the dogs and the magpie at home and making sure the magpie had food within reach should it be hungry, The Ex and I drove to London for the day for the first time in what seemed like an age. I didn't want to go; I wanted to stay with George. However, he was old enough to feed himself if I left him with a bowl of dog food, and he wasn't trying to escape his cage, so I was persuaded that the bird would be fine.

We got up early, packed a change of clothes and arrived at my Aunt Olwyn's in Kentish Town about four hours later. Olwyn was in good spirits when we got there; I'd printed some photos of the evolving garden to show her, and she wanted to keep two or three of them, which was quite a compliment from someone so critical. Then, feeling rather excited at the idea of actually being able to dress up for the first time in many weeks, I changed into a smart, silky black trouser suit that hadn't seen the light of day since I moved to Wales, and went off to meet my friend, a novelist and poetry anthologist, at the Wolseley. How surreal to go from mixing cement in trainers, combat trousers and skinny T-shirts, covered in drying mud, and wiping a magpie's bum, to wearing an elegant outfit and 4-inch heels for tea at the Wolseley, followed by a party!

Looking around at the wind-tunnel faces, elegant manicures, expensive clothing and languid demeanour, I felt suddenly conscious of my dirt-ingrained fingernails (no amount of scrubbing could get them spotless) and my puppyish enthusiasm for everything from the other diners to the food. I was as curious as George was about every aspect of his new environment.

I managed to refrain from the boiling topic of magpie-rearing; it was difficult enough to resist talking about the garden, since that was the other main focus of my life at this point. Once or twice, when seeing friends, I'd mentioned that I mixed my own concrete and could see their eyes glaze over.

After changing at Olwyn's into jeans and trainers, we drove back to Mid Wales in the middle of the night—all because of George, the miles stretching out before us until we reached the Welsh border and I felt a sudden wave of affection for my home. The dogs were delighted when we got back, and George, woken by the kitchen lights, was attentive and interested. He was still alive; that was the main thing.

Wednesday 30 May

The following morning, I got something of a surprise. Every day, without fail, the dogs lined up at the kitchen door so that, when I opened it, I was met by a row of three happy little faces, panting and eager for food and attention and a run in the garden. This time there was a row of the three dogs—and George at the end, wings out to support him, panting and happy and expectant just like the dogs. The four of them danced around my feet, giddy with excitement. I was astonished; the dogs had not eaten George. He didn't even look slightly chewed around the edges, and as for George, he appeared to be imitating the dogs in every way, right down to the gallopy-prancing.

But I couldn't work out how he'd escaped from his cling-filmed cage. On closer examination of the cage, the sides of which were still intact, I could see that George was, in fact, now too large to escape through the side bars, and I could remove the cling film if I wanted.

However, the bars in the top door of the cage, which I now used as access to get him out to play, alternated between narrow and wide. It seemed George had just discovered this too, and somehow squeezed through one of the wider gaps. But it would still have taken a magpie contortionist; how the hell did he get up? Even if he'd been able to fly, he'd have had to flap up (and wouldn't be able to get through by doing that, as his wings would be in the way), then hang upside down from the bars by his feet, before hauling himself out. I just couldn't see how his escape was possible; there were no conceivable means by which he could have got up and out between the wider-gapped bars without a ladder.

In hindsight, I wish I'd put George back in the cage and let him demonstrate his method, because once he'd found a way of doing something that worked, he'd do it again and again.

But I didn't. Instead, I wrapped the top door in cling film too.

Often, I'd put George on the kitchen table, which was varnished, so it was very easy to clean. He'd hop about, examining me and pecking at objects: roses in a small vase, the salt and pepper, the gardening book, the newspapers; everything interested him and went into his beak to be picked at, dragged a bit, or dropped over the edge of the table on to the floor. He'd peer down after it as if questioning the fact that it existed at all, as it had now gone somewhere else.

When he tired of my shoulder, I kept a folded-up old T-shirt on the table at my elbow where George would sit, fluffing out his feathers, to watch me. His probable departure at some stage in the future was a thought that I pushed further and further to the back of my mind, but keeping him would be problematic; he had been a wild bird in the beginning, so shouldn't he be a wild bird again? Though the knowledge that he could fly off and simply be shot was unbearable. The Ex was determined, however, that the bird should leave.

Time and again I told him that the bird would decide. I knew very well that I wanted the bird to stay with me; I longed to have George be a part of my daily life until one day in an unforeseeable future he dropped off his little perch from natural causes. I was astonished at the affection that I felt for this little black-and-white bundle after only twelve days.

While the dogs were a daily delight, having a wild bird adopt me was an inexplicable joy. At night, when I put out the kitchen light, with the dogs curled up in their baskets by the Rayburn, and George curled up in his bowl of T-shirt and newspaper in his cage on the floor next to them, I felt a real sense of peace. That little scene made me feel that everything was OK, and I could sleep, happy in the knowledge that my charges were a) still alive and b) apparently content.

After I'd had George for a couple of weeks, I found a bit of wood in the cellar, which I wedged between the bars of his cage so he had a proper perch. George liked his perch; he managed to hop up on to it from time to time. I might not have been a natural magpie-mother, but I was trying.

June

Saturday 2 June

Today was a notable day—the first time George flew. He flew from my shoulder to the kitchen island in the morning and from my shoulder to the side of my studio in the evening, while I stood painting at the easel. I was working on a series of emotionally-based abstracts called *Mental Mechanics* which reflected my thought processes. By this time, George had grown really comfortable with his ability to hang on when I moved around; I was his surrogate mother who doubled as a tree.

He didn't falter or stumble on his take-offs and landings, but he was inelegant. There was no skill or grace yet; it was as if he was just happy to have "made it" from one perch to another.

He amused himself between his early flights by pecking at the rings on my fingers. His actions seemed more specific than merely pecking at an object; he studied the rings carefully and tried to peel off the reflection of the lights, or the windows—those fascinating moving things that must have looked like tiny fireflies darting this way and that on the small gold bands. I noticed how he pecked at the reflection on the glass face of my watch sometimes; as the gleam shifted, George would try to get his beak around it as if he thought he could pick it off.

He had begun his forensic examination of all the elements of his new world, starting with everything attached to me. He was insatiably curious. How much did this weigh? Could that be lifted? Would the other thing break if dropped? Peck, peck. I wondered about stories of gold and magpies—having cared for George I know they really are thieves, because they squirrel away odd-ments; if they see something shiny or reflective they want it because it interests them, and they are curious—unlike other birds that don't appear to have much of a thought process. You'll never get a pheasant playing with a shiny bit of anything, or flying off with the sponge from the kitchen sink, simply because it is a curious object and might become useful later.

It takes a thought process of some kind to act upon an acquisitive idea, because the bird must consider what could or should be taken, and what the risks are. A shiny bell on the neck of a cat wouldn't be a good idea; the earring in my ear was maybe a much better one, or so George appeared to think, when he yanked at it.

Watching George trying to handle food and objects, I could only imagine that for a magpie so quick and clever, it must have been frustrating not to have fingers.

George was now eating tinned dog meat all the time. The relief of being freed from worm-digging was marvellous (although with the benefit of hindsight I think George could have lived on dog meat from the beginning). I think I was digging worms for me more than him; it made me feel as if I was making a proper effort and that he was getting to eat something he might have been given by his parents. Although it's entirely possible they would have fed him only rotting bits of roadkill.

I put some dog meat in an upturned coffee-jar lid in his cage because he was so often hungry when I wasn't available to feed him, and because he didn't always seem to want to eat the minced beef. When I left the mince in his cage and he pecked at it, it stuck to his beak no matter how he tried to shake it off. The tinned dog meat, unlike the mince, didn't stick to him when he tore at it, so he could swallow the bits once he'd shredded it. In those days I didn't know about day-old frozen chicks—the clean version of roadkill for raptors and corvids. (And even if I had, I might not have been able to stomach it at the time; I was introduced to chopping up defrosted day-old chicks at a much later date.)

Now that he was able to fly short distances, George began to use me as a jumping-board. He'd sit on my shoulder and occasionally flap to the ground where the ever-watchful Snickers and Widget would lick his face and his beak. Then he'd squawk and stand there, wings akimbo for balance, and legs spread, as if he were actually enjoying the bath, and I think he must have been or he wouldn't have let them do it. His face received the brunt of the attention to the point where he'd become slightly soggy and I'd have to call a halt to the slobbering.

He was happy, then, to have me pick him up. Sometimes he made little purring noises, which were extraordinary coming from a tiny bird. I'd have liked him to do it more often; it was so much easier on the ear than his shriek.

Monday 4 June

I was now having dreams of a magpie on my shoulder as I painted or wrote every day: Frieda Hughes, painter-and-poet-with-magpie. A magpie has this advantage over man's best friend: it can nuzzle your cheek and nibble your ear as you work at a computer, as long as you don't mind the bird shit running down your back. A dog just paws your knee, looks pleadingly at you, then goes off to pee on a rug when it realises the magpie is getting more attention.

My fantasy of painter-and-poet-with-magpie was further encouraged when I painted for an entire afternoon with George sitting on my shoulder. Occasionally he'd hop on to some other surface or nearby chair-back, then to the floor to be licked by dogs. I'd pick him up and put him back on my shoulder, where he'd pull at my ear, my shirt buttons, my earrings. He crapped down the arm of my thick, woolly work shirt at least five times; I kept mopping it up. Just as I was thinking loving things about George, and putting a dash of chrome yellow across a bit of leaf green on a canvas, George crapped again and I felt compelled to wipe the worst of it off. But it was a work shirt so I didn't care, except that in the back of my mind stood the imaginary critics who might see me dripping magpie shit and disapprove.

Maybe, I thought, I'd stop brushing my hair (better as nesting for birds), or having a bath (so my fragrant cleanliness didn't put him off), or changing my clothes (why bother, when there's just going to be more bird shit later?) or picking up the phone to talk to friends (after all, who'd want to listen to a mad magpie-woman who talks about mixing concrete? Although I did once meet another woman with her own cement mixer at a friend's party, and we had a completely hysterical evening together).

Being totally focused on one thing frees us up from everything else. It also isolates us. Attaining a balance is better—I made a note that I must work on that.

Sometimes George would trot around the back of my head from one shoulder to another, then crouch down and puff himself out like a mini-feather duster, and give his feathers a little shake—it's astonishing how much feather-sheath dust there is in a baby-bird's feathers when they do that; clouds of detritus would fall to the ground like thin, grey papery shavings.

Thankfully, the bird mess decreased almost daily as George got older. I fervently wished he would always be there, on my shoulder, reassuringly warm and solid.

He worked better as a constant companion than almost anything else. When living in Australia in the 1990s, I had a guinea pig for a while, and used to carry it around in my handbag and take it to parties. It was winter, and cool, and the guinea pig wasn't very big, so I tucked him into the roll neck of my sweaters, and if anyone thought I had a goitre, they were polite enough not to mention it, and I had a real, live neck-warmer that occasionally squeaked.

One day George only crapped down my back once, spending his time occasionally picking imaginary bugs from behind my ear. In fact, he was noticing stray hairs that had escaped my ponytail, and his sharp eyesight had picked up on the fine wisps. Then, suddenly, he flew to the top of the painting I was working on and tried to grasp it so he could perch. But because it lay flat against the sloping white background board of my wall easel, his head hit the hard surface. His little black feet were desperately clutching the edge of my picture, but his beak was pointing upwards, his chin flattened against the white board, his wings splayed like a moth's and his eyes wide with surprised indignation; he'd somehow thought the white sheets of ply that I use as a gigantic easel were open space; he had not registered that they were solid.

Once I'd stopped laughing, I detached him from my canvas, wiped the oil paint off his little toes and put him back on my shoulder, where this time he stayed.

By now he was hopping around the kitchen daily and the dogs loved it; he'd run after them, wings out, feet pattering and beak open, directing his velocity at their bouncing white curly tails, and then they would turn and chase him right back. I'd watch, like a parent, waiting for the first wail or squeal to warn me that something had gone wrong, that a dog had bitten the bird, or the bird had bitten the dog, but it never came.

Slowly, other aspects of my life seemed to be coming together: by now I'd put up a curtain pole and curtains in one of the spare rooms, which had been painted so I could furnish and make nice the room I hoped we would be filling with a stream of visitors. The rest of the house, however, was still a building site, and, after three years, it was grinding me down to live that way.

When we first moved in, The Ex was ebullient, striding from room to room and, to my horror, picking at the corners of the scruffy, magnolia-painted wallpaper and pulling strips of it off right up to the ceilings, exposing patchy ancient paint or plaster beneath, to my cries of "Noooo, we have to live with the house like this for a long time!" He argued that we were going to be doing the whole place up, so it didn't matter. But it did to me; I knew how long it could take and that I would have to look at those walls of torn wallpaper every day for years, and they would be as depressing as hell. And they were.

The entrance hallway had 8-foot-high fake panelling made of plywood and pine and painted pale green. It wasn't unpleasant to look at, but The Ex regarded it as a travesty and pulled it off the wall, exposing the old Victorian plaster, patchy paint and holes. There was no disguising it now.

We could only renovate the house as fast as I could bring in money, and because of this, it was often frustrating. The Ex made up for it by working on the house himself, albeit reluctantly, because he felt he should be painting. I understood his feelings very well, and suffered similarly, but his paintings hadn't been selling at our exhibitions (they were too big for most people's walls), at a time when another income would have transformed our lives.

There was good news, however, when an art buyer for an investment bank chose to purchase one of my largest paintings AND one of The Ex's; we did open a bottle of champagne for that, and the confidence boost was sorely needed.

And my Uncle Gerald in Australia—my father's elder brother—had been in touch; he was on his way to getting his memoir, *Ted and I*, published. Over a period of several months I had tried to persuade him to write down what he remembered before it was too late, not least because he was exhausting himself answering the questions of numerous Ted Hughes researchers—and now he had! I was in awe of his efforts; he was ninety-one when he started it, and ninety-four when the book was published. (He died one month short of his ninety-sixth birthday.)

Over the years I'd tried to persuade my Aunt Olwyn (who, as my father's older sister, was once also his literary agent) to write a memoir too, but she flatly refused, and was simply furious that

Gerald had written something. She made certain that he knew how she felt. In one of our regular phone calls he told me how, in one letter she sent him, her fury was not satisfied by the insults contained in the letter alone; she had to write more on the back of the envelope, much to Gerald's embarrassment when the postman handed it to him. Her fury was such, he said, that she had scored through the paper with the pen she was using, and then stabbed a hole in it with the final full stop.

Saturday 9 June

In the absence of photographs of me with my magpie, because The Ex still displayed a remarkable reluctance to oblige, I recorded George's progress on a mini-DVD recorder. Everything seemed to interest him; when he pecked at the floorboards I couldn't understand why he'd want to, until I watched more closely and realised he was actually targeting the gaps between, as if they were three-dimensional.

But George didn't give up that easily; over and over again he tried to get hold of the dark space between the floorboards as if he thought he was picking up a ribbon, and he was visibly puzzled when he couldn't get a grip on it. I wondered how he saw things; what did a floor crack look like in order for him to think it was something he could get his beak around?

Humans have binocular vision to better judge distance and perspective. The majority of birds have their eyes on the sides of their heads, giving a wide expanse of monocular sight to the left and right, and only a narrow front band of binocular vision where the sight of one eye overlaps with the sight of the other—notable exceptions being owls and, to a lesser degree, hawks. Owls' eyes face directly ahead and are actually tubes held in place by bony structures called sclerotic rings. As a result, they cannot move their eyes at all, a limitation that is compensated for by the extraordinary extent to which they can turn their heads.

Because it is the binocular vision that aids our judgement of distances between things, I could only imagine that George's largely monocular sight perceived the gap in the floorboards like a piece of dark string resting on the floor. But like everything else, it didn't take long for George to work it out.

He tried to peck through a pack of AA batteries, he pulled and tugged at bits of paper that were wedged between the pages of a closed book, and tried to pick up the scratches in the paintwork on the backs of the white kitchen chairs. He had a hack at the tall, wooden salt and pepper grinders that towered over him when he stood on the kitchen table. It seemed that he was testing the resistance of objects—were they real or imaginary?

Curiously, as the days passed, George's "feed-me" screech became a purr like a cat's when the dogs were close to him. It was like a sound of contentment, warm and gentle. And one morning I thought there was a man in the kitchen when I heard words being spoken—but they were words that I didn't recognise. When I opened the door I found it was George practising what sounded like fragments of a strange human language. I swear he was trying to talk, emulating the sounds that humans made around him. It IS rumoured that magpies can be taught to speak, and after all, George was surrounded by words because I talked to him and the dogs all the time. Rubbish, mostly; they were never going to learn anything of a deeply philosophical nature from me, since my philosophical thoughts were not something I'd try and share with a dog.

I remembered a mynah bird—found in South and South East Asia and related to starlings—at a friend's house when I was about thirteen. It spoke actual words, although the meanings of those words were lost on the bird. The cage was such a small dome-shaped thing, however, that he couldn't even open his wings, and it pained me not to be able to set him free. I felt as if I could sit in his head and feel his frustration at possessing wings that he couldn't spread or stretch, and his despair at the sense of atrophy of his flight muscles. I wanted to rescue him. I never forgot my sense of claustrophobia on behalf of that bird.

George's increasing ability to fly encouraged me to try and get him to come to me when I called, but I wasn't having much luck. Food, predictably, was the only persuasion that worked, although he was dithery about it and could be easily distracted—just like a child. Those who train birds properly weigh their birds to make certain they are hungry enough to fly to the fist or the perch, but all I wanted was for George to think of me as "home." I knew it was a bit of a stretch to expect him to love me, but every time he landed on my shoulder or nuzzled up to me, I felt loved.

Sunday 10 June

I now let George find his own way out of his cage in the kitchen, instead of reaching in and taking him out of the cage myself; I simply opened the door and left him to it. I'd removed the cling film off the cage now that he was too big to escape any of the bars.

I resisted the urge to watch over his every move in case the dogs ate him. Time and again they had been fine together, and I had to trust them at some point or I was never going to get anything else done; the dishes would pile up, the paintings would remain as raw materials, my poetry column would die out, and I would have become a prisoner of my own concern. In the meantime, for my peace of mind, George was in his cage when I wasn't in the kitchen, which inevitably meant that I tried to be in the kitchen as much as possible . . .

George could now fly the length of the kitchen, and he made the most of it: he flew at full tilt into the creamy painted kitchen wall, bashing himself so that he fell out of the air and into a bewildered heap on the floor; he flew into one of the two closed kitchen doors. They were shut because I didn't want him skittering around the rest of the house, projectile-pooing as he went. Having bounced off several hard objects, he scrabbled across the floor in a fluff of feathers, little claws trying to get a grip on the polished floor-boards, and scuttled off around the kitchen island and between the table legs with the dogs in hot pursuit; they didn't chase him to catch him, just to watch what he was doing. When he stopped, they stopped.

He was also becoming more aggressive as he developed and used his claws to scratch and protest when I picked him up. He was snippier and more investigative with his beak around my fingers, the dogs' wagging curly tails, and the little vases of flowers on the kitchen table: I could see that letting him go would be the only thing to do at some point. If he became really obstreperous I determined that I'd be *glad* to let him go; if he became truly nasty then I could imagine myself tossing him out of the window with glee.

In the beginning he'd lived on my shoulder, and now there were times when he wouldn't come to me even if I waved food at him. He'd look at me, cock his head to one side (I could almost swear he was shaking it) and stay put, apparently uninterested. Magpies, I was discovering, are smart, funny, and appear to think out solutions to problems with better results than the average three-year-old child. But, like a teenager, George was rebelling, doing only what he wanted to do when he wanted to do it. If he did not want to do something, there were not enough doggie Schmackos in Wales to persuade him.

At times like this I felt rejected and I didn't like the sensation that he was now making a choice NOT to be with me all the time, although he did let me grab him when I needed to pick him up. I didn't know why he'd stopped thinking my shoulder was "the place to be." I later learned, from keeping other birds, that he had indeed reached adolescence and—like a human child—was now separating himself from me to prepare for another life.

George took to landing on top of my head sometimes, instead of my shoulder, which was now nothing more than a launch pad. It was very uncomfortable, because he'd initially grab at my scalp to steady himself. I wondered if this was because he felt my shoulder was too small for his increased size, but now his talons were forever getting tangled in my hair.

There was a certain air of companionship if George was sitting on my shoulder; I felt we were complicit in our proximity, as if there was a genuine bond between us. But if he was standing on my head, I was relegated to lamp post and he was only up there because he got a good view of his surroundings. My position as perch felt demeaning.

I could see that he had a sort of developing logic in his actions; he was clearly trying to work things out for himself and coming to conclusions of his own. He studied objects and how I lifted them and put them down and where I put them; he could always find and retrieve them—I hid various items that he liked to pilfer in the folds of the neat stack of tea towels beside the kitchen sink: small bags of dog treats or rubber bands or the sink plug. But George could remember exactly where in the pile the object was and pull it out at first attempt, which astounded me, because the fifteen or so tea towels were identical and folded in exactly the same way, like books with their spines facing outwards. This ability to memorise precisely where I put things meant that if I wanted to hide something, George could not be watching.

Esther Woolfson writes in *Corvus: A Life With Birds* about birds that "cache" being predominantly corvids, falcons, hawks and woodpeckers; the most intelligent of birds. They store items and food in numerous hiding places that they must then remember.

Birds that do this also steal from the caches of other birds and are conscious of the likelihood of being stolen from, which prompts their removal and repositioning of the item if they believe they have been observed. This is a clear understanding of cause and effect, in addition to demonstrating their resourcefulness and prodigious memories.

George was stealing from me even when I didn't notice. He watched me at all times in order to identify any item he might want to avail himself of when my back was turned. And, just as Woolfson writes, if he thought I'd seen where he hid something, he'd go back and move it later. It was a frequent occurrence to find scraps of food buried in the spines of large cookery books or stuffed under sofa cushions.

George's own resourcefulness reminded me of the tale of the smart crow in *Aesop's Fables* where the crow, gasping from thirst, sees a pitcher of water, but the water level isn't high enough for the crow to drink. So, the crow drops pebbles into the pitcher until the water level rises enough for him to quench his thirst.

In *Gifts of the Crow* John Marzluff and Tony Angell talk about the way corvids have been shown to do this, without training. To incentivise rooks in the absence of thirst, waxworms were dropped on to the surface of water in a pitcher. The rooks not only rapidly worked out that dropping usefully placed nearby stones into the water would raise the level so that they could get the waxworms, but also that the larger stones achieved their aim much more quickly.

Food is a great incentive for any of us feeling peckish, but sometimes, with the most intelligent birds, they do something for nothing for someone else: an online article for the *New York Times* on 17 March 2022, written by Anthony Ham, describes an Australian study of their own magpies (*Gymnorhina tibicen*) that established the fact the birds would help each other for no reward—except, perhaps, the expectation that they would be helped in return.

Australian magpies are a different combination of black and white to those in the UK and more closely resemble the shape of a crow, with a mostly white—rather than black—beak. Although they are not related to the corvid family as Eurasian magpies are, being a member of the *Artamidae* (a family of birds found in the southern hemisphere of which there are nine subspecies), they possess that extraordinarily quick magpie intelligence.

The article describes how Dr. Potvin and her team spent six months developing what they believed were almost completely magpie-proof tracking-device harnesses that could be attached to the birds without causing them discomfort or impeding their flight. Before they had even packed up their gear half an hour later, having attached the trackers to five magpies, the first tracker harness was off. One magpie had worked away at the harness on another until it found the only weak point and snipped it with its beak. Within three days, all the trackers were removed by the magpies. The total defeat of the scientists demonstrates their brain-to-body mass ratio must be something extraordinary for a bird.

George, meanwhile, hadn't progressed as far as water pitchers and stones; he was still working out size, shape and spatial relationships: looking behind things, into things, underneath things. He examined the surface qualities of the table, chairs and worktops, running his feet over them, sliding to see how slippery or rough they were. He tapped with his beak to test consistency; he eyed them sideways and straight on as if to get a sense of their three dimensions.

It was thus that he discovered the two cake tins had resonance; they became magpie-drums when he found out that he could make a noise on the surfaces with his beak. He tapped over and over again, exploring the tins for their musical value, and apparently, the difference in their tone—first one tin, then the other, then back again. The large plastic lids of some old glass sweet jars that I used for pasta, which stood beside the cake tins, became part of the percussion set, but were obviously not as much fun, being more muted; the cake tins were LOUD.

Small objects like cherries or matchboxes delighted him and he'd peck at them, turn them over, get his beak into them, hacking holes; his beak was like a machete, hack, hack! He'd propel his beak forward with all the energy he could muster, pushing from his shoulders.

Today, when I opened the kitchen door in the morning, I found that George appeared to be frantic in his cage; really crazy, terrifyingly manic. When I let him out he went skittering around the kitchen floor, and on to and off the slippery varnish of the kitchen table and satin paintwork of the chairs, cooing provocatively at the dogs as if trying to rile them into some sort of action. He looked to be actually *goading* them. He was as hyperactive as a child swilling an energy drink.

I felt that Snickers had to be watched because she *did* get excited when George ran across the floor; I was concerned she'd get carried away and squash him, although she was just playing. Having caught up with him in one instance, Snickers raised her front paw and brought it down on the bird to stop him running away from her. I reprimanded her and she withdrew her paw.

Standing upright, George slid across the floorboards, literally pushing his feet as if they were on skates, first the left, then the right. Then he did a sidestep sidestep routine that looked choreographed. Again, he pecked everything with his beak: the cushions, the sofa, pens, notebooks, newspapers—were they edible? Did they break? Did they taste of anything? He must have had questions that needed answering. A lot of questions, every day.

Inexplicably, he suddenly threw himself up at the sofa, bouncing off the back of it as if it were a springboard, on to Widget's sleeping form. He righted himself, then dug his feet into her thick, unruly fur, before leaping on to Widget's footstool beside the sofa. From there, he turned his attention to me, picking at the loose threads of my grotty old blue fake-velvet slippers, and pulling and tugging at the legs of my gardening trousers (mud-coloured and washed and ironed into cardboard subservience) while I sat there watching; he screeched at the dogs in a demanding way, as if asking them to notice him and react. He pecked at Mouse several times as she lay in her basket by the Rayburn; Mouse was always by the Rayburn and always quiet and unassuming—she didn't want to play or be part of anything these days, now that old age was creeping up on her. She grumbled and turned herself around to remove herself from proximity to George's beak.

During the day George found The Ex sitting at the kitchen table. Unaware of The Ex's questionable feelings towards him, he perched on The Ex's bare arm as he read the morning's paper, watching The Ex's face in fascination, or as if food might suddenly fall from it. I hoped this might help to win George some favour from that direction.

Tuesday 12 June

It now became my habit to open the front door of George's cage as soon as I came downstairs in the mornings. There were moments of peace when George perched and settled fluffily, surveying all beneath him from the vantage point of the kitchen table, the back of the chair beside the table over which my work shirt hung (to give him something to grip), or the pile of throws on one of the kitchen chairs that I keep to cover the dog sofa when people visit (so they have a clean surface to sit on).

George found Snickers curled up on a cushion on the arm of the sofa in the sun that streamed through the window, and sort of nested on her, fluffing himself out and hunkering down into her thick coat just beneath her chin. Snickers was too dozy to be bothered by this. All I could do was watch in amazement and be grateful for such strange and wonderful moments.

One morning I was reading the newspapers on the kitchen sofa and he unpicked my shoelaces, then flew to my shoulder for the first time in what seemed like ages, skinning my nose with a passing claw as he did so; he wasn't skilful at landing yet. His ability to fly wasn't as innate as I'd imagined it would be; it was clear that he needed a lot more practice, but he still spent an awful lot of time on the ground. He raced around the floor after Widget, pounding the boards with both feet together, leaping in a weird two-footed manner—jumping, really—while using his wings to balance as if they were ski sticks and he was leaping over snowy hillocks while wearing invisible skis. Occasionally he'd stop to scratch his head by lowering the wing on the relevant side and bringing his foot up behind it; it looked bizarre.

Wednesday 13 June

I watched Widget and George side by side on one arm of the kitchen sofa, both trying to get at moths that landed on the outside of the kitchen window; Widget tried to catch the fluttering specimens by batting at them with her paw, patting the glass over and over in her efforts, while George tried to neatly pick them off the glass with the tip of his beak, puzzled that his beak met with a flat and slippery surface that kept him and the moths apart.

My tiny world of garden, dogs and magpie gave me respite from the other elements in my life that were more painful, difficult or challenging. I wilfully buried myself in the simplicity of the tasks attached to them, because I was also working on the last edits for my autobiographical poetry book, *45*, for HarperCollins in the US, while fighting an attack of chronic fatigue syndrome (also known as myalgic encephalomyelitis, or ME) that I suspect was brought on by the challenges of raking over one's life in order to condense it into poems, resulting in a fair bit of correspondence.

Life with The Ex, however, was in a peaceful place for the moment, and moving back to Australia wasn't mentioned. Often, he cooked for us so that I could come in from the garden or the office and be fed, without having to take time out from my labours. But it was a role reversal that had a limited lifespan.

So, George was an anchor, consistently magpie-ish; needy, charming, attention-seeking, inquisitive and adorable.

Holding him, I noticed that after less than a month he was bulking up a bit—I loved to feel his warm feathery body and hot little feet; he no longer felt like a tiny bundle of straw. All that dog food was adding to the covering of flesh on his bones.

As he was getting on with the dogs so well, I eventually grew bold enough to let George out of his cage two or three times a day, certainly always when I stopped for a meal because I was there to watch him. I'd let him play around the kitchen with the dogs, hopping madly from one end of the room to the other, being licked off the arm of the sofa by Snickers or Widget after teasing them by dancing on their backs, or picking at their ears from the vantage point of their shoulder blades.

I was sketching him when he hopped on to the top of my sketchpad and stood staring down at my picture, cocking his head from side to side, because his beak was in the way of the view either to the left or the right, depending on which eye he was working with.

Then he tried to drag the lines that I'd drawn off the page with his beak, pecking and pulling, pecking and peeling, but finding nothing that gave any resistance. When he found that wasn't possible, he hopped on to my shoulder and made a necklace of hops around my head using my chest, my back and my shoulders; his burgeoning confidence was undeniable, and in the back of my brain, scratching away like a persistent beetle, was the worry that it heralded the end of our relationship and his departure.

Over and over, I told him my name to see if he'd ever try to imitate me. He'd listen intently. Again, one evening I heard him chattering in his human-sounding syllables as if he were having a conversation with an imaginary friend. I stood outside the kitchen door for several minutes and listened, fascinated, wondering what I was going to find when I opened the door; it sounded so much as if he was trying to communicate with someone.

As the days flew by, he became more reluctant to be caught and put back in his cage, and it wasn't hard for him to make it difficult for me to get him; he'd hop sideways, skitter across the floor, flap to the top of a kitchen wall unit, or nip in and out of the chair legs around the table. He knew how to stay out of my reach because he'd had plenty of time to study my many limitations.

I found that the best thing to do if George was being elusive was to sit on the sofa and cuddle the dogs, then he would come to join us; he didn't want to be left out. He'd land on the arm of the sofa and hop into the mess of doggy bodies wanting to know what was going on—wanting to be in the thick of it. Only then could I get hold of him.

One evening when I was sitting on the sofa and talking on the phone, he came and perched on my knee unbidden, which was lovely; not that it meant much to George, but I felt a real joy in his familiarity with me: I was part of his furniture. It brought to mind the way a child will sometimes clamour for attention when they see their parent focused on a phone call instead of them.

A friend sent me an email telling me to watch out because Louis de Bernières had adopted a crow, after which he was permanently covered in guano (although she wasn't strictly correct because guano, used in fertiliser, only refers to the excrement of bats and, apparently, seabirds). I replied, "Too late!" and sent her a picture of me and George: George, looking plump and glossy, was standing on my head.

There were things I had to be careful of, however, because being so curious George wanted to explore everything, which meant landing in places that he shouldn't, like the toaster when it had just been toasting and was still glowing, or the top of the Rayburn door when it was open. I must have terrified him with my howls of "nooooo" as I leapt towards him to scoop him off whichever red-hot appliance he'd chosen to land on. But he didn't seem to feel the heat in these things. He didn't flinch, he didn't squeal, he didn't appear to notice at all. I wondered what kind of nerve endings birds possess in their feet; maybe none that matter: after all, they sit on frozen branches in winter with nothing to protect their snakeskin-like foot-flesh.

Friday 15 June

George took his first full bath. This was momentous; he'd done little forays into the dogs' water bowl before and ended up with a soggy head, or wet toes, but this was a full-on fluid assault of his whole being.

First, he did his usual scampering turns around the table legs, sliding on the floorboards, and hopping about on his ever-growing feet, knocking his heels as he skipped (here, you have to imagine it in human terms—he actually skipped like a child skips, but his back toes, protruding as they did, caught the floor, so it appeared that he was also banging the floor with his heels), then he played in the dogs' water bowl. So, I filled it up when he'd finished. He saw me do this, and that's when he went back for a full-blown bath.

If I'd ever wondered about nature over nurture, this must have been a good example of nature: he fluffed, he splashed, he ducked and shook his feathers into the water; he skittered and got soaked from head to foot, making huge puddles all over the kitchen floor. Then he clambered out and realised he couldn't fly, so now he couldn't escape from the dogs. He ran around the floor with his wings out like wet, dripping sticks, with Snickers and Widget after him as if they thought that he was just as good as a melting ice lolly; their little tongues were hanging out and they lapped at him as they slid over the wet, slippery floorboards behind him.

Again and again, George tried desperately to get airborne without success. I managed to stop laughing long enough to rescue him; I wrapped him in a hand towel and kept his little body warm until he stopped shivering.

Two of the neighbours came over for a drink in the evening; I had got to know them when I viewed the house in 2004 and I knocked on their door to ask them about the neighbourhood and what it was like to live here. Bob and Sheila felt to be family now.

Eventually, after cheese, crackers, hummus, and a few glasses of wine, they expressed a curiosity to see George. I'd taken his cage out of the kitchen to begin with, and left it in the utility room, but brought it back in when we'd finished eating. Now I let the bird out and he jumped on to the table to investigate the spread before him. This was his first experience of *visitors*.

I managed to prevent him from scampering across the table between the stems of the glasses, so he danced around the floor with the dogs for a while. Then he flapped up to the back of my chair and just sat there, looking at my back. Eventually, he stepped forward and climbed up on to my left shoulder. He sat there for several minutes more, being totally charming. He observed the guests, nodded in their direction, nibbled my ear affectionately (or, more probably, in search of nits) and appeared interested in the conversation, which was all about him. I felt quite bad when I put him away for the night, as if I'd betrayed his trust. One moment he was standing on my shoulder, feathers brushing my cheek; the next, he was in my firm grip as I placed him back on his perch in his cage.

Saturday 16 June

This evening, perhaps remembering the rude treatment of the night before, George was very much more distant. In *Gifts of the Crow*,

Marzluff and Angell document the ringing of a crow (putting identification rings on its legs) and the way that crow then came to remember the man who had assaulted it, picking him out in a crowd and scolding him, warning other crows of the danger he posed. The crow also learned which people would feed him—until a new resident in the neighbourhood lured him into his garden and shot him. A fate that I feared for George when he left home. But it was the fact that the corvid held a grudge from a remembered incident that interested me in the story, although I didn't come upon it until years after my life with George.

He was attentive to imaginary fleas around my left ear when sitting on my shoulder having flown up from the floor, but he didn't stay there. I knew that I had to get him back in the cage while he was within reach at some point before the night was out. So, of course, like a good little mind-reader, he kept out of reach as much as possible and I had to outguess him. It was as if he could translate my predatory micro-movements—the tension in my back and shoulders—as I prepared to pounce.

He waltzed, he danced, he cooed and squawked; every movement appeared to delight him and appeared to cry out: "Look, look, I've got legs!" and "Look, look, I've got wings!" He teased the dogs by flying up to them, challenging them to chase him, then running between the table and chair legs until the dogs were in knots. He was very much harder to catch than ever before.

And he had a new game; he spun around on the kitchen table, around and around and around, until he was literally staggering and falling about, his wings out and down as if they were walking sticks to support him. He did it over and over again, obviously enjoying himself. I did the same when I was a child and discovered that I could make myself dizzy and fall over by spinning around on the spot. I just couldn't work out why a magpie would do this, except that he was playing, just as I had been. It meant that George had to have quite sophisticated thoughts in that tiny head of his. In disbelief, time and again, I'd watch as he spun round several times, staggered, then spun round a few more times, staggered, and spun again, until he was almost collapsing with dizziness.

Once back in his cage for the night, he fluffed cutely, and studied me intently when I talked to him. He looked more earnest. It was almost impossible to resist projecting on him the kind of thought processes a human being might have.

Another new game—apart from escaping my grasp when I needed to get him back in his cage—was that he'd take one of the dog biscuits from their food bowl and tuck it down the side of the sofa cushions; Snickers and Widget, having followed the bird's progress, would then dig the biscuit out. He liked to do this with some regularity, which encouraged Snickers and Widget to follow him at all times. And he jumped all over me, testing the fabric of my jeans, the ties of my shoelaces and the hairgrips in my hair with the tweezers of his beak. He was endlessly inquisitive. I would have loved him to cuddle up and be adorable, but, despite the fact that he spent a big bit of his brief youth on my shoulder or my lap, he didn't demonstrate any desire to give or receive affection. I was afraid that now I was just the person who put him in a cage.

When I had a nap on the sofa, George sat next to me in the brace across the back of the old dining chair I was using as an impromptu table for my mug of tea, and dozed off himself. Very cute and companionable. The trouble was, when he let me stroke him, I would eventually have to take an opportunity to catch him to put him back in his cage, thereby betraying his trust all over again. I reckoned that he was growing wary of me; if he was scooting around the kitchen floor, there was no hope of catching him and once he got among the table legs he knew he'd bought himself more time. This evening, he escaped my grasp as I tried to put him away, and I had to catch him by the leg; most undignified.

Monday 18 June

George was being foul-tempered and aggressive; I got hold of him a couple of times and just held him for a while. He screeched in such an ear-splitting and alarming way that I outscreeched him, imitating his little magpie voice to see how he reacted, and he shut up. When I stroked the top of his head, he wriggled and squirmed, whereas he used to love it. It was akin to a child becoming suddenly resentful of the public displays of a mother's affection in front of friends. Or, speaking from experience, a child recoiling from the ministrations of a heavy-smoker aunt, who reaches into a handbag that reeks of stale spilled perfume, to fish out a tissue into which she has, at some point, spat cigarette phlegm, which she now wets with her own saliva to wipe a perceived blemish off her niece or nephew's face. I had certainly developed George-like avoidance strategies thereafter; they were part of my survival kit as a child.

Some days George was a joy, but he hadn't been for the last three. He tugged at the dogs' tails so they yelped; he gathered fluff from the floor, tried to eat it, then spat it out again, only to have it get stuck to his tongue and beak. So then he wiped the sides of his beak on nearby surfaces, like sharpening a knife. (Eventually, I managed to divest him of the fluff balls.)

I wondered at the time if his dog-tail pulling was because the tail of a Maltese dog is like a bouncy, fluffy, curled-up spring, just the sort of toy any child (or corvid) might want to grasp hold of, or if there was more to it.

In the literature of corvids, innumerable incidents and examples of tail-pulling are described, usually of more powerful birds and animals; sometimes to tease them and play, sometimes to confuse them and steal their food, sometimes to torment them into confusion so they can be brought down.

However, corvids will work together as a team to achieve an aim and sometimes violence isn't necessary. One sunny afternoon I happened to look out of the window at the back of the house and saw an unusual number of crows flying downwards towards what appeared to be my back garden. I hurried up to a room on the first floor that afforded a better view, where there was a bay window through which I could see not only my small back garden, but the neighbour's much larger one. Her garden had various trees, and one tall, scrappy fir tree near the centre was thickly black with glossy crow bodies. Then I noticed that the ground, too, was littered with crows as if someone had scattered them evenly over the lawn. There was a deathly, eerie hush about them; they weren't screeching or cawing. Once they had landed, they stood, quietly, as if waiting for something.

I could see more crows in the sky, heading in this direction. I phoned my neighbour to see if she was in; she was terrified of birds—or anything flying: I'd once gone round late at night to rescue her from a very tiny, scared little bat, which had somehow got into her house. It was finally cornered in the kitchen, where it vanished. It was only when I noticed that she had what resembled a dead leaf in her basin that I found it. I carried the tiny creature to freedom wearing it as a brooch on my sweater, where it hung by the hooks on the upper side of its papery wings. It took a moment to register the chill of the night air, and then it launched itself into the dark.

Thankfully, on this particular day, my neighbour was out.

With a strange feeling that nothing was real, that I was seeing things, that there was some terrible happening that I hadn't yet discovered, I walked round the houses and into my neighbour's gateway. Crows were still arriving; I was counting in tens and there were over two hundred when I got there. They didn't move, and I had to step over them to walk through their mass. The garden was now thick with crows from edge to edge. I stood in the middle of them, puzzled, feeling rather giddy, and still in a state of disbelief because the crows ignored me. It was as if they couldn't see me. More arrived and fixed themselves to another tree, as the tatty bare branches of the fir tree were now fully occupied.

Occasionally a crow would ruffle its feathers and let out a strange little crow-grunt, and the low-key, almost muffled music of these happenings ran like a ripple through the throng.

Crows, I knew, had purpose. There was nothing lightweight about a crow's intention. I bent over to touch one; it shifted slightly but didn't fly away. What, I wondered, was the reason for this gathering? Looking around, there were crows upon crows upon crows; the tree appeared to be blossoming with an overabundance of silky black flowers, and the ground was covered with a gently rippling sheet of black satin feathers, but I could see nothing that indicated why they were here. Until there, in the centre of the gathering, I noticed a small heap of crows; a black carbuncle, as if they were standing on a tiny hillock.

Stepping carefully between the birds that shuffled around my ankles, I made my way to the heap and found three or four crows, guarding something beneath them, standing over it, heads raised, bodies alert. They shuffled aside as I peered down over them to see a female sparrowhawk. For a moment, I thought they'd killed her. Then she moved her head and looked up at me sideways to get a better view. I pushed a couple of the crows off her and they let me. But the sparrowhawk didn't move. Then I saw what had happened.

The sparrowhawk had brought down a crow. The crow was still alive, lying on its back on the grass, the sparrowhawk's claws pinning its wings to the ground. The other crows had come to help, but couldn't attack the sparrowhawk because it had the other crow in a death-grip with its beak at the crow's throat. Neither could move without risk. If the sparrowhawk killed the crow, the others might kill the sparrowhawk. And perhaps the same if it let the crow go. As long as the sparrowhawk had the crow in her grasp, nothing would happen. Stalemate.

I looked around at what was now a sea of crows engulfing the whole garden and thought how much like a scene out of Hitchcock's *The Birds* it was. Except there were many, many more birds here. Hitchcock would have been envious at such a thick, ominous spread of feathers.

Something had to break the deadlock, so I bent down, firmly grasped the sparrowhawk, which seemed to me to be the bird most at risk, and pulled her off the crow. The crow righted itself, looked around, staggered for a minute or two, then flapped upwards in a haphazard fashion. Having been spatchcocked for a while, it might have been a bit stiff. The other crows followed; two, three, four at a time, rising silently into the air. Then more, ten, twenty at a time; they dispersed over the roofs of the houses.

Now the sparrowhawk was struggling and squirming in my hands. I reckoned the crows would have lost interest, so I tossed her into the air and thought she would fly off, quickly, in the opposite direction to the crows. But she didn't. She flew to the garden fence a few feet away where she turned towards me and glared, watching as the rest of all those crows flew up into the cobalt blue of the sky. She didn't move until they had all gone, and I didn't move until she'd gone.

Tuesday 19 June

Today, I didn't let George out, except to make a fuss of him, which he now hated. He screeched, but I held him and stroked him until he quietened down before returning him to his cage. I felt wicked putting him back in there, but he was too hard to catch now. Whenever I had to chase him round to get hold of him to put him back into his cage, I worried that I was stressing him. It wasn't hard to see that

I'd have to let him go if for no other reason than because I couldn't bear seeing him shut up in a cage when he was so active and alive. The question was: would he be able to look after himself? Would he learn how to feed himself?

After cleaning George's cage, I took out the rubbish; a dark and terrible storm had begun, with thunder and lightning that rocked the house. It was times like this that my wish to release George was shaken; I imagined him getting cold and wet and dying in some shabby corner of a field, unable to fend for himself because some well-meaning human being had never taught him how to hunt and take shelter.

Wednesday 20 June

Ever since the night the neighbours came over, when George perched so prettily on my shoulder and I took the opportunity to shove him back in his cage, I felt he now associated my proximity with being returned to his prison. I could have been wrong—it could have been his developmental process, but as a human being it was increasingly difficult not to anthropomorphise him, and corvids do have long memories and can hold a grudge . . .

Despite the fact that it was becoming nigh on impossible to catch George to put him into his cage at night, where he couldn't cause any damage while I slept, I couldn't bear to keep him in the cage all day.

So, I let him fly around the kitchen while I worked in the garden for two hours. I shut the dogs in with him; they had lots of space. When I came back in, I had several poops to clean up, but they were now much smaller than his baby deposits. So far, so good; this boded well for the future.

During the evening I stroked him a couple of times, although he was wary, and I got hold of him twice to put him on my shoulder.

The second time he stayed there for a few minutes. I covered up the dogs' food bowls and left George's food in his cage, so if he was starving, that's where he'd have to go. He went into his cage for food just once, and so quickly that he dropped the piece of meat while making his escape in case I should shut the door on him when he saw me looking in his direction. I was certain he'd anticipated my intention to leap at him from micro-movements that I might have made in my preparation to pounce.

When I finally *had* to put him away, I cornered him by Mouse's dog bed, which was an old wicker shopping basket with a large stiff central handle. Before being chewed so it frayed at the edges, it was an impressive container in which an enormous bouquet of flowers was sent to me when I was in hospital following surgery a few years earlier.

If I can think of a single use for an item, even if it is twelve years in the future, I will hang on to it; sometimes it takes aeons to think up a purpose for something—but when I do, the satisfaction is enormous. Of course, it all becomes clutter until then, and I'd only just got rid of three sacks of wine bottles that I'd collected over the years for the fruit and vegetable wine I used to make, in the days when bought wine was bottom of the priority list and not accommodated in the budget.

Back to the basket: Mouse had been growling at George because he was sitting on the handle of the basket with his tail hanging down over her head; sometimes he'd crap on her and, unsurprisingly, she objected.

I'd been chewing my last mouthful of supper—a bit of beef, but with George squawking with indignation I did the first thing I could think of, and put the chewed meat between my teeth and he took it, swallowing it immediately, and was quiet when I put him in his cage. Then he let me gently stroke the top of his head through the bars, which he'd refused to allow me to do ever since that night when the neighbours came over, and he behaved so beautifully, and I took advantage.

Wistfully, I thought of a life where George didn't leave, but didn't crap on the dogs (which always required a mini-bath in the utility sink) and didn't dismember the kitchen when left to his own devices: if only I didn't have to put him into his cage at night; if only I could make his prison less of a prison and somewhere to go as a "home." But if I didn't cage him, in the morning the kitchen would be a disaster site after he'd picked at and pulled apart everything he could get his beak into. There was nothing, and I mean NOTHING that escaped his forensic examination.

On one occasion, he found a heap of used teabags in the bowl on the kitchen counter, and ripped one of them to shreds, emptying tea leaves all over the floor. I'd had no idea so few tea leaves could cover so many square feet of floorboards.

As for getting George back into his cage, I decided that I had to set up a ritual—we, as humans, brush our teeth and wash our faces or shower when we go to bed; maybe George needed some preparation too?

One night I told him sternly "bed" and pointed to his cage; I did it a few times. He was so intent on watching me that I was able to grab his unsuspecting little form in both hands and place him, screeching loudly, back into his prison. I also took his food out of his cage at night, hoping he would be happier to see me in the morning when I gave it back. But it didn't make a difference as his morning brain was entirely focused on freedom.

During the night, if I had to go to the kitchen, I was careful never to put the main light on, and I'd keep very quiet, tiptoeing over the bare floorboards in soft slippers to raid the fridge or make a hot drink by the light of a small lamp. That way George remained with his head tucked under his armpit, folded into himself like a little black-and-white ball. He could do that now; his neck was longer and more flexible. (Previously, he used to just point his head in the right direction, which looked odd, as if he had a stiff neck.)

My brainwave for magpie bedtime was to move George's cage out of the kitchen and into the utility room, so he couldn't see it. Instead, I put a cardboard box on its side on top of a chest of drawers in the kitchen, with a sawn-off broom handle through it as a perch. He didn't go in there himself, but that evening I put him in there and he stayed; he seemed to like it. What I hoped would happen is that when dusk fell and George looked for somewhere to roost, he would roost there, and then I could move him, when he was settled and dozing, into his cage. That way he wouldn't be so pissed off at being caught, and I wouldn't be pissed off at seeing how quickly he could destroy my kitchen before I got up in the morning. This ploy actually worked!

Saturday 23 June

A gorgeous day, but I was still smarting from yesterday, when a friend, Sue, someone I had known for years, brought her latest boyfriend to my house and I had my first actual encounter with the kind of critical person whose voice I had been hearing in my head since George first appeared.

George was sitting on the arm of the sofa in the kitchen when they arrived. "Oh, there's a magpie on the sofa," said the boyfriend with an offhand sort of grimace. I scooped George up and reluctantly put him in his cage in the utility room, so our guests didn't have to be assailed by his curious attentions. After all, they were city folk, not used to anything with feathers unless it was a budgie or a feather boa.

This man arrived with a contemptuous sneer and didn't change his expression for the duration of the visit. I showed them around my work in the garden: the circular rooms of plants, with the circular pathways, all meandering around the 40-foot-wide dough-nut of a pond, over which presided a gigantic Atlantic cedar tree. I bent down to show them one of the many hundreds of tiny frogs that had spawned in the pond that summer; it was no bigger than my little fingernail: a perfect miniature frog in every detail, every spot, every blemish, every minute toe on every tiny foot. Incredible. Inwardly, I marvelled at their lack of interest, yet they had never seen anything like it. To know that my garden was teeming with these exquisite creatures was a delight.

Then, just as I was setting out the food on the kitchen table, this oily weasel of a man suggested that someone should report me to the RSPCA for being cruel to a magpie. I was too astonished to tell him to leave, which I wish I had done. "What, for saving it?" I asked incredulously. Thinking that he would be less rude and judge-mental if he had a better understanding, I explained how I came to be fostering George. He didn't comment other than to give the sort of grunt a horse might make at a particularly tiny carrot.

My impression was that he'd arrived with some preconceived idea about me, and had decided that he was going to make no effort at all to be pleasant, which made me wonder what Sue had told him. He was boorish and rude, and it threw me completely, because my intention is always to be bright, sunny and welcoming to people who visit, whether I know them or not. I wasn't at all prepared to welcome into the sanctuary of my own home someone who was intent on making a critical attack on me.

Feeling stung, mind reeling, I completely forgot to serve the pies, pâtés and full cream tea that I'd prepared for them and left in the fridge, although we ate the cake my friend had brought, and some sausages I'd cooked.

After the verbal assault on my bird-rescue efforts, I remained rooted to my chair, no longer inclined to engage in any hospitable actions towards these two. My whole body felt leaden; I just longed for them to go. And Sue did nothing in light of her partner's rudeness except to talk over him for the whole visit, as if to prevent him saying anything else offensive.

When I confessed my still-present anger to The Ex, he reasonably asked why I hadn't brought it up at the table yesterday when everyone was listening. But that was the problem; I *had* tried to bring it up, it's just that no one took any notice—not him, not Sue, and least of all the unwanted guest.

In fact, I'd tried twice, asking the obnoxious man on what basis he'd made his magpie judgement, but he simply turned his back to me and began talking to The Ex, who, being a sociable host, took up the conversation on both occasions, not realising that he was interrupting my attempts to air my feelings about our guest's comments. I'd called it out and said pointedly, "You're changing the subject," but the man ignored me.

I'd have had to shout to make my point, and perhaps I should have. But anger—and humiliation—is like a stain; it has to wear off or bleach out. Time helps, but feeding that anger is counterproductive.

George made me feel better, but at the same time, I kept turning the boyfriend's comments over in my mind because they tapped into my gnawing fear regarding George; had I done the wrong thing in rescuing him? He wasn't a protected species; in fact, farmers shot the likes of him. The visit reinforced my reluctance to have friends over because no one wants to be judged in a negative way, least of all by a guest in their home. You have every right to expect manners, at least. And that they keep their counsel about rescue magpies.

When I opened the fridge and realised I'd forgotten the wealth of food I'd wanted to serve them, I was astonished at how the shock of the boyfriend's comments had driven all my preparations for their visit out of my mind. Might he have ameliorated his behaviour towards me if I'd had everything laid out on the table when they arrived? In hindsight, I suspect he'd have eaten more and been just as ghastly.

I was now in the habit of leaving George to his own devices much more: today, he snoozed on his perch then he stretched his legs and wings and flew around the kitchen. He hopped on to my crossed foot several times when I stopped for a cup of tea and sat on the sofa with the dogs. Then he took the sheet of a letter from the open mail on the kitchen table and flew around the room with it, which made him look as if he was advertising something on an oversized banner.

When I came in from working in the garden later, I found a scene of devastation; it was as if someone had busted a bag full of rubbish all over my kitchen floor. The plethora of magpie crap was expected, but he'd discovered the bowl of used teabags and hadn't just shredded one, but had taken the time to shred them all. He must have flown around the room with them to tease the excited, happy dogs who didn't like to miss a good party, because there were tea leaves and empty teabags on the chairs, the table, the kitchen-unit surfaces, the floor, the sofa . . . and there were tiny shards of wood everywhere, as if a very small log had exploded. At first, I couldn't work out what they were, then I realised—they were all that was left of two red pencils from the cup by the telephone. I noticed that George hadn't touched the dull colours.

When he'd dropped the pencils on the floor, the dogs had pounced and chewed them to tiny, tiny pieces and dispersed the bits among the tea leaves. It must have taken them a lot of effort to be so thorough.

George had also fought for the last bit of eraser from the top of my pencil. And there were red rubber bands from the mail that arrives every day, all over the floor—he'd left the brown ones behind in the bowl I kept them in. The dogs and the bird had been having a party in my absence, and everything George had taken was RED.

I gave George some bits of the pie I had for lunch; it was part of the spread that I'd forgotten in the fridge when Sue came over with her horrible boyfriend. George was hugely delighted. He sat on my shoulder while I ate; I could feel the soft pressure of his feet through my work shirt and the feathers of his chest up against my left ear. Balancing easily as I moved slightly every now and then, he stood there until I'd finished, taking the pieces of pie from me as they were offered. It made my day.

He also loved the string ball in the glass bowl on the sideboard, took the end, and flew around with it so it unravelled, the ball still remaining in the bowl that held it, bouncing around as it became smaller and smaller. It looked as if he was trying to weave some giant spiderweb across the kitchen. I was exhausted; I felt as if I was perpetually tidying up after an overactive two-year-old.

But, as destructive as he was, George made me laugh daily. Sometimes, as he did today, George landed on the large, round, varnished kitchen table, skidded off the opposite edge feet first, wings flapping for balance like the flailing arms of a novice skater, and fell on to the floor. Sometimes he'd scratch his head by dropping a wing and bringing a foot over the top of it; sometimes he slid sideways off the curved back of the chair that his remaining foot was clinging to. I had to keep the toaster covered so he didn't crap in it by accident.

When I first found him in the garden, George couldn't walk, or waddle or hop even two inches. After a few days he could skip and stumble; then, after a couple of weeks, he could walk a bit. After three, he could flap; after four (has it been that long?) he could fly a bit. Now, each day he flew higher. He began with the level of the kitchen chairs, then the table, then my shoulder. Now he used the tops of doors.

I noticed that George's tail seemed to have grown longer literally overnight, and I could see the black colour of it was actually tinted with green and purple and blue; it was quite beautiful, he looked suddenly very grown up.

When he was small he let me handle him all the time, but as he developed, he'd stopped that, so exceptions to the new rule were welcome. I couldn't deny that he was growing up, though, and when he sat in the window I wanted to let him out to fly, believing that he'd have such a good time. I just worried that he'd get killed by a farmer, or his parents (who wouldn't recognise him) or the crows. I'd mothered that bird, so now I had all the anxieties of a foster-parent. But I'd decided that tomorrow was the day I'd let him go. George's imminent departure hung over me like a bilious cloud, but I knew that to keep him prisoner would be cruel. If he wanted to leave, I had to release him.

Sunday 24 June

I'm ashamed; last night, after I'd written my diary, I went down-stairs and chased George around the kitchen until I caught him. His heart was pounding and he was protesting like hell, squawking and kicking. I held him gently, nuzzled his little black, shiny head until he calmed down, and sat and wept. I loved the bloody bird; I would miss him horribly when he went. Although I wouldn't miss the magpie shit all over the kitchen, which was a sort of test of one's endurance.

Of course, I overslept this fateful morning because I didn't get to bed until two, and I'd not slept for two days (bar one half an hour on the kitchen sofa with the dogs and the magpie) because I'd finally lost my patience with the accumulating paperwork in the office, and had a real blitz. So, I lay in until almost twelve. But I dragged myself up for George and the dogs. Working all daylight hours in the garden left only the night-time to catch up on paper-work and household admin—and in June, it got dark very late, so there was very little time for it.

George took a bit of getting out of the kitchen window when I opened it. (Only one of the two Victorian sash windows would open.) Then off he went. I held my breath as I watched him fly on to the bit of grass in front of the house, seemingly puzzled at this new outdoor space. Then he came back in again, landing on the arm of the sofa just inside the window as if to check that his "nest" was still available. Then he left again, this time leaping out of the window and into a soaring arch into the sky. My heart was beating so loudly that I could hear it thrashing against my ribcage making a thudding noise in my ears as if the sound was being carried in my bloodstream. It brought to mind the sound of rocks being pummelled in a wild sea. He was off! He was flying free!

But there was no getting away from the fact that I wanted George to come back and stay. Suddenly he turned in the air and swooped back in through the open kitchen window to land on the floor and skitter, slide and hop to a stop, before flying up, up and out of the window once more, which made me feel bereft in a way I'd not anticipated.

He disappeared for a while, then came back and sat on the car roof-rack in the heavy rain that had just begun; I could see he was puzzled by the wet stuff and how it felt against his feathers and skin; he looked up at the sky and shivered it off, and then got wetter. Rain was new to him. Later, when the rain cleared for a while, he sat on the garage roof. I kept going outside to check on his whereabouts, hoping that he wouldn't hang around in case someone shot him. But I fervently hoped he would come back; I was driving myself crazy with conflicting emotions, and trying to keep a lookout for him was distracting me from everything I should have been doing instead.

On one occasion when I went to have a look at George on the garage roof at the back of the house, he was right at the top on the ridge line, watching, looking, not moving. The young couple who lived on the other side of my garage had just come home and were parking in their front yard. I said "hi" and asked them jokingly not to throw stones at George if they saw him hanging around. I know magpies are not liked, I explained, but I've hand-reared this one, and I'm really very fond of him. Although, I added grimly,

I knew he might get eaten by something. That's life, they replied, making me wince.

Later, I saw George sheltering on the windowsill of my bathroom on the top floor at the back of the house facing the garage. I cursed myself for not being there to open the window and let him in. I tried to imagine how terrifying it must be for him, a tiny bird in a big open sky, with all these trees and buildings that he'd never seen before. He couldn't put those in his beak to see what they were made of or what they tasted like. And if he thought all humans were safe, he'd be wrong, and that's what worried me most.

In an effort to tear my thoughts away from George, I got to work in the garden, wheeling bags of topsoil chunks, which I'd dug off the existing flowerbeds to rid them of weed, to the edge of the big pond. There, I tipped it, grass-side down, on to the Butyl-lined shelf just below water level, so that I could plant into it later, and the grassy side below would die off. When I was a child my father showed me how to dig a neat earth row, turning each cubic sod over to expose the roots of the weeds and burying the tops, so they'd die, leaving the good brown earth to plant in. This was a variation on a theme.

During the late afternoon George was around the front of the house again. He was sitting on the top of the single-storey Victorian addition that jutted out from the ground floor. He paced to and fro along the parapet, doing his familiar "I'm a magpie" walk, where he strutted upright, but sticking his legs out in the front of him at right angles as he walked—or marched. I'd seen him dancing on the garage roof earlier—literally dancing, wings out, legs elastic, feet bouncing.

When he flew away over the trees, I felt such a profound sense of loss. But if he was OK, then I was happy; or so I told myself. I just wanted him to have a chance. In the kitchen, where he was familiar with every pot, pan, shelf, cupboard, table, chair and dog, he looked so bolshy and wild, but outside he looked scared and small, as if he thought the sky was going to drop on his tiny head and squash him at any moment; he was a minute pinprick in the vista of the garden.

And I had to remember that every single thing outdoors was completely strange to him; there was no inbuilt magpie-knowledge of what a tree was, or what a leaf looked like, or how big the air was, or whether he could reach a cloud. Other birds were going to be a revelation to him.

"Let him go," I kept telling myself, "he's only a bird." But he was so much more than "just a bird" to me; everything he did was linked to my thinking brain because I was conscious of his very existence even when he was out of sight. I constantly had images of George in my head, visualising him as he destroyed the kitchen, napped on the handle of Mouse's basket, tucked peas from my plate into my back pocket from a perch on my dining chair. He'd made a space for himself, and I'd let him.

I went back to work on the garden, digging, planting, planning a connecting path between circular flowerbeds (the last of the remaining grass was rapidly disappearing) until it began to get dark and I found George had come back to the place he was used to: home. He'd hopped through the window, which I'd left open because I couldn't bear to close him out, and into the kitchen. He parked himself up on the top of a cupboard by the window, which had lately become his favourite perch.

He let me pick him up, so I put him on his broom-handle perch in the open-fronted cardboard box, instead of his cage. I was filled with an overwhelming sense of joy and relief; my little magpie was safe again, and I hadn't kept him prisoner; he had spent an entire day flying free—and then come home.

It was wonderful to have him indoors for the night. I felt as if the household was complete, and, frankly, I was bowled over that after tasting freedom he wanted to come anywhere near me again.

I looked at him in his box, sitting on the broom handle that passed through it to form his perch, his little chest rising and falling, his head tucked firmly into the top of one of his wings, his breast feathers fluffed, and I felt such love for him.

Monday 25 June

I got up at eight to let George out of the kitchen window, but I hadn't bargained on the rain. It poured all day; the cellar was 3 inches deep in water, which had never, ever happened before; it pooled around the legs of an old pine worktable, bins with sawdust and wood bits in, and stacks of wood offcuts from working on the house: doors, cupboards, floorboards and all the boxes of tools, the legs of my bench saw and jigsaw, the boxes of unsorted oddments that needed filing into their own containers, like screws, doorknobs, curtain poles and anything that drilled or planed wood and metal.

Even the wide drive was flooded so the postwoman had to walk along the edge of the raised pavers that bordered the central flowerbeds to reach the door without getting her feet soaked. I watched her from the kitchen window in total admiration as she balanced on the narrow paving-brick strip, her boots squelching wetly, her waterproof jacket flying, her wide-brimmed hat directing water into a waterfall in front of her. It was a downpour of biblical proportions: I ate breakfast while George leapt about the table and chairs like a jack-in-the-box; there was no way he wanted to get wet again, now that he'd experienced rain, although I'd left the window wide open for him.

Every now and then he'd hop on to the sill, peer outside and shake his puzzled little magpie-head, before hopping about the kitchen some more. He plainly wanted to be free and fly outside, but he wasn't daft enough to compete with the weight of so much water, or the waterlogging he would suffer, which could flatten his only recent ability to remain airborne. As overjoyed as I was to have him home of his own free will, I rather dreaded his indoor attentions; it was impossible for him to keep still.

He was still in the kitchen in the late morning when our cleaner, Mary, arrived to do her weekly clean. After she'd got over the initial shock when George leapt on to the thick mop of her hair, she seemed fine. (I'd fibbed a bit and told her that this was a real honour, although she found the pecking of her skull a little harder to take and apologies were necessary.) George stayed on top of the corner kitchen cupboard for the duration of her cleaning efforts, watching her keenly. There was something about his interest in Mary that didn't bode well for the future; I could just feel it. I couldn't help thinking that her thick and wavy hair must have looked like a decent bit of hedge to him.

Nose twitching with disgust, Mary announced that she'd found two small pieces of dried-out dog shit beneath the cushions on the kitchen sofa. The dogs were trained to use a litter tray—like a cat—which I kept in a corner of the utility room, and so it seemed clear that the culprit was George; he didn't discriminate between items. He played with and hid whatever little morsel interested him. Although why tiny dried-out dog turds should be worth hoarding rather puzzled me.

By the time Mary left it was lunchtime and the rain had abated slightly. George ventured outside. Then came back in. Then out. Then in. Then out and back in through the wrong window, which was a silly idea because it was shut, so he almost knocked himself senseless on the glass. That's what he did all day, over and over again, although he avoided the closed window after his first encounter—at least he'd learned something.

There was now no doubt in my mind that red was his favourite colour: he pecked a stray red dinner candle to bits; the remaining red pencil was taken to be buried somewhere outside; the red bobble on the top of one of the dogs' toys vanished; and, now he knew where I kept them, the red rubber bands that I collected from the mail had been scattered across the kitchen floor yet again. The red mug (that used to hold the red pencils that he'd tossed to the dogs for destruction) was pushed on to the floor today, so it smashed. I wondered what it was about different colours that appealed to him, or whether the colours he saw weren't the same as they looked to me. I tried to tempt him to play with a ball of green string and he hated it, yet he'd been fascinated by beige-coloured string.

At quarter to nine this evening I shut the kitchen window and hoped he'd settle down inside, but instead, he tested every single one of the cooking utensils—long wooden spoons, spatulas, a potato masher, a pasta scoop, assorted ladles—in the earthenware vase by the stove to see if they were removable, but couldn't pull any out far enough because he wasn't tall enough. Then he checked the chewability of the top, bottom and sides of the little shade on the tiny lamp I kept by the microwave. Over and over he pecked at the gleam on the gold-coloured round metallic base of the lamp, attempting to strip it off as if he could capture the light itself.

He buried more dog biscuits down the side of the sofa cushions, which drove Widget and Snickers into a frenzy because they could smell them but couldn't get them out, although they dug for them frantically. (George had the knack of pushing the little biscuit bits forwards into a crack as if stitching something; he used force and his head and beak acted as a needle. The dogs, with their small wet black blunt noses and big rounded white fluffy heads, didn't have a hope of reaching the hidden snacks.)

I gave George a piece of cooked curly pasta—I'd tried some on him the other day, and he loved it—then I had to watch as he flew around the room trying to find a spot to secrete it. He stopped on top of one kitchen unit after another, tearing bits off and swallowing them as he did so. He perched on top of the door to the utility room, the pasta in his beak, checking out the crack between the top of the door where it met the hinges and the door frame. But for whatever reason that didn't appear to work for him, so he tried tucking it into the folds of the two work shirts that I'd hung on the back of the door; until I looked, I thought he'd tucked the pasta into one of the breast pockets, but they were buttoned up. Eventually I found it wedged beneath the collar of one of the shirts.

But as addicted as I was to having George as part of my life, there were definitely moments when I seriously considered wringing his little black-and-white magpie-neck. That night I didn't put him in his cage; he was too hard to catch. Thinking "How bad can it be? He'll be asleep most of the time," I left him in the kitchen with the dogs, with his cage door open.

Tuesday 26 June

I slung on a dressing gown and hurried downstairs, too anxious to even get dressed before I opened the kitchen window for George, so keen was I not to keep him indoors for one moment longer than necessary. In my mind, I conjured up his feelings of suffocation, his frustration at seeing the sky beyond the glass windows, and his fury at the obstacle between the sky and his little bird-body.

The largest kitchen knife was on the floor as if a would-be murderer had dropped it in passing, and a wooden spoon was out of the utensils pot and lying by the cooker—he'd obviously tried and tried again until he succeeded in dislodging these items; I noticed there was a cake tin near the wooden spoon container, which would have given him the extra height he needed to get the spoon out. There were also the usual spatters of bird shit here and there. Then

I found the dog shit. Ugh! It was very fresh. George had taken it out of the dogs' litter tray and spread it all over his old cage in the utility room—which was more than slightly disgusting of him; there was more of it on, and behind, the sofa in the kitchen, and under the cushions (which is where he hid the stuff he really liked). At that moment, if I'd had a tennis racket in my hand, I could have used George as a tennis ball in a fast serve.

Donning my black rubber gloves, I wearily cleaned it all up; using an entire kitchen roll and a strong disinfectant in a spray bottle, cursing his magpie playfulness under my breath.

George himself was like a crazed bat-thing. Before, he'd seemed totally wild in the mornings, having left his friendly magpie-head somewhere else the previous evening; each day it was as if he learned me all over again from scratch. But today, he was wild *and* maddened; he flew from one side of the room to the other above my head in a panic. I left him to it; he simply wouldn't get out of the open window, but just became more and more frantic; his panic made him blind to the exit that he normally used, and he kept trying to find a way out through immovable objects; he threw himself at walls and closed doors. I had to leave him to his own devices until he eventually bounced on to the windowsill as if by accident, and propelled himself into the sky with all the force of his frustration.

Then I gathered my reluctant willpower and shut the window, so George would be made to stay out and fend for himself for a few hours. It made me feel like a bad mother; torn between encouraging George to become independent and wanting him to stay and remain my bird-baby forever. But considering the dog-shit incident, his departure might be a blessing. I never wanted to deal with that again.

By the afternoon, George was hanging around the garage roof at the back of the house like a little waif. He seemed confused and lonely so I went into the tiny back garden and called to him and he flew down to sit on the fence next to me, but wouldn't get on to my shoulder. I sat with him for ten minutes while he let me stroke his beak and tease him; it is a strange feeling to call to a bird outside and have it come to you so you can stroke it.

As a treat for George I found him a couple of worms, but he wouldn't take them from me as he used to. I dropped them on the ground and only then did he come up to eat them by my feet. I felt a little miffed; he was keeping his distance—our relationship was more and more on his terms.

In an attempt to find him a really *huge* worm, I lifted a nearby pot and there was a whopper. George was very happy with it, but instead of swallowing it whole, he ripped it into smaller bite-sized bits, while I squirmed at my own presumption of the worm's agony.

I got indoors from the garden around nine thirty that evening to find George was nicely settled down in the corner on a kitchen cabinet. It was becoming such a happy pattern and I had adopted it just as I had adopted George—wholeheartedly. There was no sign of The Ex; he was in the bedroom watching TV having already eaten supper. It seemed to me that we were seeing less and less of each other despite living in the same house.

Gently, I picked George up and put him on his broom-handle perch in his cardboard box. He let me, giving only a tiny protesting squawk. This was the agreed halfway house—I'd move him to his cage later. It was very hard not to stroke all his fluff and cuddle him. He was so different half-asleep to his wide-awake cockier self. But he was still small. When I saw his parents outside, they were easily twice his size in comparison; well fed, slick and confident. It was a surprise to see them because I thought they'd gone for good after the storm that destroyed their nest. I knew it was them, because they appeared to have done a partial rebuild. As I watched them get on with their happy, ruthless, playful little magpie lives, I felt a stab of sorrow that their babies had all vanished, yet here was one that I had saved and they would never recognise him.

Wednesday 27 June

George was getting worse in the mornings; so was I. I was up very early again—for me, at any rate; seven o'clock. I felt fine to begin with, but for the rest of the day I felt as though I had slammed face-first into a wall, and my eyes felt raw—was I tired? Was it stress? Had I been crying in my sleep without knowing about it? Or was I coming down with something? I got downstairs to let George outside for the day before even brushing my teeth.

Oh, if he was like a wild thing yesterday, he was far worse now; I opened the right-hand window in the kitchen as usual (the other one didn't have window weights to keep it open) and George slammed straight into the left-hand window, which was, of course, closed. He knocked himself out, collapsing backwards on to the sofa, grabbing a clawful of the dog blanket that covered it as he fell, and landing like a stunned moth, upside down with wings splayed and head lolling. I picked up his small concussed body and felt how hot he was; he was burning up. I nursed him and cooed over him and stroked his little battered head until he began to come round; it took several anguished minutes, during which the dog-shit incident was suddenly totally unimportant weighed up against his tiny, precious life.

What if he did actually die? When he began to stir I put him outside on the windowsill through the gap in the open window, resisting the impulse to toss him up in the air to see if he took off. He stood up, stuck out a leg as if he was about to do a Monty Python funny walk, took one step and fell right off the edge of the windowsill on to the ground below, where he landed in a heap of feathers. Forgive me, but I laughed. At least he was alive.

Peering over the ledge, I watched him stumble to his feet. Still dazed; he was definitely tottery. But two seconds later he took off like a low-flying bomber plane, in a confident magpie way that had me impressed. He headed for the rockery garden and the oak tree, only one tree away from his unknowing parents.

When I got outside to work, planting and digging more flower-beds to feed my addiction to filling every part of the small field that was my garden with flowers and shrubs, George was hopping around the front of the house as he now liked to do, but keeping out of reach. He skipped in and out of the kitchen via the open window a few times. At one point he was on the ground when one of his parents flew out of the fir tree on the fence line by the house to have a look at him. The bird was plump-looking and glossy, with beautiful green-blue-black wings. It dwarfed George. As it flew down, George glanced up; his left wing drooped even further than usual and the little bald patches on his head made him look like a real scruff: he was so small and shabby in comparison. Oh, I felt a surge of pity for him.

Seeing the handsome magpie studying him, George suddenly took off in a panic, landing in one of the standard bay-leaf bushes that flanked either side of the front door as if he'd been catapult-ed by someone with no aim. Of course, George, despite sitting in front of the mirror in the kitchen for hours, didn't know he was a magpie, so the black-and-white monster must have given him a shock.

He hopped into the kitchen near dusk, and I shut the window when I came in at nine thirty. He was so calm, so unlike his morning self; this is when I loved his company. He was attentive and playful. He nuzzled the dogs and padded around the floor after them, then they padded around after him. He pulled at the biro in my hand when I wrote and paced around the notebooks I scribbled in on the table. Whether I was making cups of tea or frying courgettes, George was by my elbow watching my every move.

I wondered what I was going to do when we drove to London the following day. If I left him outside, he'd be out all night, and I was worried he would stay too close to the ground to be safe from prowling cats. And if I left him in, I had to cage him so he didn't trash the kitchen. I had an image of his frantic thought process as if it was me, looking at the bars of my cage, beyond which were toys, and space, and freedom. I felt the burning frustration of impotency, then the desire to test my confines to their limit and find a loophole through which to escape. I might bite and tear and hack at the edges of my too-small world. Then I might scream and shout for release. Finally, exhausted, I'd be miserable and sulk, and when I saw my captor again, I'd want to punish them for this incarceration.

Eventually I persuaded myself that it was only for twenty-four hours and at least he'd be alive when I got home, and, feeling like a furtive cheat, I moved George from his cardboard-box perch to his cage while he was docile, just to be prepared. This dilemma would afflict me every time I went to London; so, if George was going to be a permanent fixture, the temptation would be to avoid trips to the city altogether. But surely I shouldn't live my life around the needs of a magpie?

Thursday 28 June

The Ex and I were driving to London just for the day, so I left George in his cage, partly covered so he'd be dozy in the shadows; it was the only safe place for him. As we pulled out of the drive one of the neighbours' cats ambled across my garden as if to confirm that my decision was the right one.

We went to a very jolly *Times Literary Supplement* party after seeing Olwyn, only to get home and find messages on my landline answering machine telling me that my poetry column in *The Times*, which currently took a whole page, was going to be reduced to half a page. Instead of calling it "Poetry" it was now going to be called "The Monday Poem," which made me think of "The Sunday Sermon." I had an uneasy feeling that my column was now on borrowed time. This uneasiness amplified the chasm between my earnings and The Ex's; he was currently not earning at all. My job was what kept us going.

The Ex pointed out that losing my column would give me a chance to paint more and go back to exhibiting on a more regular basis. This would also mean that he'd get to exhibit too, as I would usually organise a joint exhibition.

George was asleep in his cage. Beneath his perch was the most incredible amount of magpie poo. I wondered how fast his digestive tract must work in order to manage such an enormously effective food-to-poop conversion rate in only a few short hours.

Friday 29 June

Having spoken to *The Times* about my column, I got more of a sense of my imminent termination than ever, and it left me feeling as if I was standing on quicksand. What are we here for? I asked myself. To live each day the best we can no matter what, is my rule, but what if it all gets too tiring? Sometimes I felt as if I'd like someone else to take up the slack and assume some responsibility so I could have time to catch my breath.

Tonight, I was sitting on the sofa on the phone to a best friend in California, sharing my fears for the future, when George flew over. He did a crazy magpie dance, spinning and pirouetting, sticking his little feet up in the air as if doing a goose-step, and raising his little head feathers. He strutted and spun as if he had music going on in his head, walked back on himself and did it again. He wanted my attention and he knew that a performance would do the trick.

When he roosted, it was on top of his cage. I picked him up gently, stroked his warm little body and put him on the perch inside. He was happy in his cage now; he'd fly into it when it was in the utility room, and hop about in it, so perhaps it no longer filled him with fear. When George was safely inside, the dogs settled down for the night.

I was working on poems for my book, *Out of the Ashes*, and the next time George perched in front of me, I wrote this for him as he performed:

GEORGE

He rifles his feathers
As if searching for socks
In the washing basket
Of his breast pocket and wing-pits.
Still sockless
He slides the split blade of his beak
Along each twisted-back tail feather,
Bringing them up almost to his ear
As his nut-cracker reaches each tip.
He's as thorough as a man
Who's lost his keys.
He shudders his skin
So his black-and-whites froth
And settle neatly.
An oil-slick glistens from his bum-rudder,
Which flicks up and down like a switch.
He pauses to examine his toothpicks
On the end of which are feet.
Experimentally, he slides one forward
As if pushing a small suitcase.
Step, skip, pivot, stride,
He's gathering speed; he turns again,
High-step, high-step, skip-skip,
And he's dancing a magpie dance
To his head full of magpie music.

Saturday 30 June

After mixing 25 tons of concrete and mortar to get me through the first two years in the garden, and using a hundred tons of stone and laying several thousand pavers, the garden was beginning to make sense to me, but the compulsion to create shapes and plant things didn't abate; I was going to keep going until I ran out of space and somehow, somewhere, I thought, I might have to build an aviary for George . . . just in case he didn't want to leave. But where? Quickly, I pushed the thought aside as too difficult. For now.

Today, when I let George out of his cage by opening it in front of the kitchen window first thing in the morning, I was persuaded by The Ex to shut the window after him, in the hope of discouraging the bird from coming back inside. He made it sound perfectly reasonable. But although it might reduce the indoor bird shit, I'd rather leave the window open despite the fact that the air was cool. However, the argument that I was encouraging the bird NOT to go back to the wild fed into my deep-seated guilt at wanting to keep him.

It poured with rain on and off all day, so George, who had left early, was soggy and wet by late morning, hopping around on the front yard and the kitchen windowsill, plainly wanting to come back inside. I felt such a sharp pang of pity so let him in, water dripping from the end of his beak and flattening his saturated feathers to his skimpy body.

Oh, he was *delighted* to hop indoors; he was soaked to his magpie-skin. He perched on the sofa by the window and shook his tail from side to side; it flicked and bent like a bunch of whippy little birch twigs. He wrung himself out and oiled himself at the same time, by sliding each wing and tail feather through his beak, forcing the water out of them. But the moment he hopped outside again,

I was obliged to shut the window; The Ex and I were going out to lunch and he was now far too frisky to leave in the kitchen. Since discovering that he could pull carving knives out of the knife block, he did it regularly and whatever he dropped on the floor the dogs got to play with.

When we returned around five thirty, George was quick to appear again; it was as if he'd been waiting nearby, watching for us. He hopped inside the opened window, leapt around the kitchen, ran across the floor with his wings out as if they were thrashing arms, and perched on the back of the chair next to me at the table to eye up what I was eating. He seemed overjoyed to see me, and in truth, I was overjoyed to see him. It is difficult to resist a magpie who skates across the kitchen table to your elbow, looks up at you, cocks his head to one side as if studying you, then does a little skippy dance.

At one point he landed on the table and slid to the edge at a leaning-back, almost impossible angle, then sat on the handle of Mouse's basket, and crapped on her, so I had to give her a bit of a blanket bath.

He explored the edible qualities of my shoes, socks, ankles, the gardening books that lay open on the table, pens, paper, newspaper, the car keys and the cooking utensils in the pot by the cooker. A bunch of house keys was entertaining; try as he might, he couldn't carry them, so he dragged them to the edge of the table and dropped them on the floor and attacked them from there, stabbing them with his beak as if he could kill them—he was nothing if not persistent: after he stabbed them several times he dragged them first with his feet and then with his beak, tried to lift them, and didn't give up until dusk fell and he was exhausted.

While I was being so amused, I didn't want to leave the room, but didn't have the time to simply sit and watch, so I did jobs that kept me close; I prepared food (peeled potatoes, carrots and parsnips, and marinated things) or worked through more poetry books for my *Times* poetry column.

As soon as George roosted on top of his cage, head tucked beneath wing, eyes shut, now very dopey, I was able to put him away for the night. I wondered how long it would be before he no longer came home in the evenings—but clung to the idea that he would ALWAYS come home. Unless someone shot him.

July

Sunday 1 July

Despite George's apparent affection for him, The Ex appeared to become increasingly intolerant and today he refused to let me open the kitchen window at all, once the bird was outside. But that might have had something to do with the fact that he was cooking some smoked salmon and Gruyère cheese mini-pies and nut tartlets because we were having three of the immediate neighbours around for tea—those pies were a treat George would have been unable to resist.

My back was painful and tender today, so I'd lain rather uselessly asleep in bed until noon, but managed to clean up the kitchen and change the dogs' litter tray before our visitors arrived. I also felt chronically fatigued and a subtle, deep sadness about the reduction of my poetry column, because I feared the end was coming. I wondered if the two were connected.

On and off all the afternoon George repeatedly landed on the windowsill and peered through the kitchen window as if wondering why I wouldn't let him in; it pained me to see his small, hopeful face wondering at the inexplicable rejection, his head moving side to side as if to make himself more noticeable, his little beak tapping, trying to attract my attention, his chest pushed up against the glass as if he could press through it, trying to see beyond the reflections on the surface.

The neighbours arrived at four. At one point George came by three times and pecked on the window demanding entry and I had to resist; there was too much food on the table for even me to risk his presence.

Around six, a blanket of total exhaustion—real bone-grinding, strength-sapping, speech-stealing tiredness—descended on me as I sat at the kitchen table with the others. This exhaustion pinned my feet to the floor and my arms to my sides. The need to go and lie down was irresistible—crucial—but since I couldn't, I fell silent until my neighbours left, letting The Ex do the talking for both of us. All I could do was try and smile wanly. I had noticed that since developing chronic fatigue, other people sometimes caused this reaction because there is a certain amount of energy required to engage with them, mentally and physically. My reservoir of energy was often easily depleted by visitors.

My chronic fatigue began when I was living in Australia in 1994, coinciding with the stress of being prevented from painting and writing for six months by (entirely self-inflicted) circumstances at the time: decorating to sell a house, house-hunting, packing boxes, moving house, and decorating another. I longed to get back to work with every fibre of my being; I craved my paints and computer and was counting the days until I could unpack my paintbrushes, but was persuaded to wait an additional two weeks to "go on holiday" with my then partner and his three children, and that did it for me: I genuinely believe that "not working" caused it. Something suddenly snapped—and I felt it.

HOW IT BEGAN

There was first the small sound
Of a metal wire snapping
Like a violin string inside my head
On a long drive south in Australia,
Me, a passenger.
The sharp, plaintive note
Snagged my attention;
It was followed by a sense of foreboding
That something was wrong.
When we stopped I found
That during our journey my feet
Had become welded to the floor of the car.
I tried to lift my legs at the knees
But the joints where my arms
Were hooked on to my shoulders
Had lost their point. My man
Stared in disbelief at my immobility;
With growing fury, he
Manoeuvred my limbs from the vehicle
And made me stand.
If I had to die in order to lie down
Right there on the pavement
I would have keeled over,
Soulless, immediately.
Weeks later when
This flu refused to cure
The blood tests began,
Followed by a CAT scan
And psychiatric examination
To rule out depression.

They found me sane as anyone could be
Afflicted by ME.
I could not read or concentrate,
Or walk more than a few
Dead-legged paces, or talk;
I found it hard with wooden tongue
To fix the words in place.
Inertia flooded my veins,
Set like concrete,
And immobilised my working brain;
It would be almost four years
Before I read a book again.
Now, a single question
About sugar, or not, in tea
Could render me senseless,
And sleep was not sleep
Of rest and waking, but a mud
Of the mind's making to wade through,
So that strength and cognitive ability
Were all used up
By the time my eyes opened.
The actions of a day were suspended
For as long as string. Despite my fury,
And all my efforts to resist,
My life as I had known it
Ended.

So, I need to keep working; answering the urge to write and paint and make and create things is akin to breathing for me. But, having developed chronic fatigue, I discovered that after I appeared to recover it was only a matter of time before stress of one kind or another caused it to flare up again.

*

Although the initial affliction lasted from February 1994 to October 1997, everything was more difficult afterwards—more of an effort—because my ability to concentrate never fully returned, and having both dyslexia and ADHD meant that I was already having to make huge efforts just to be "good enough." I was worried that my very much sharper, quicker, more agile pre-ME brain would never shine for me as it once did. (I declined the Ritalin I was offered for ADHD on the basis that the brain I know is the brain I can work with, and the energy that ADHD gives me helps to compensate for the exhaustion of ME, as long as I can work on my concentration, through sheer effort mostly.)

When I opened the kitchen window just after the neighbours had gone, and by which time The Ex had given up being intransigent, I called for George and he arrived in seconds. He hopped from the windowsill outside to the sofa in the kitchen. My relief was incalculable.

The phone rang, and I sat on the sofa to talk, while George perched on my knee as if to examine me more closely. He flitted around the sofa, wagging his magpie-tail, cocking his head from side to side, and allowing me to play with him by grabbing his beak over and over again. He was teasing me: "Look, I'm almost grabbable, but not quite!"

Then he flew to the central island where he rediscovered percussion: he jumped from lid to lid on all the pasta jars, then on to the two big, round cake tins, where he'd stamp his feet, as if loving the noise. There was no logical reason for his foot-stomping behaviour: it didn't get him from A to B, he didn't walk the lids in a straight line; no, he danced and jumped about on them repeatedly, bang, skitter, bang, bang, BANG.

Eventually, George settled on the edge of a glass fruit bowl, his little claws clinging tightly to the rim, his feathers fluffed and his head sunken into his chest, until I moved him to his cage. He felt to be gaining more physical substance; he seemed more solid.

He was a hectic, unprincipled bird, but it was impossible not to love him. There was no way I could truly imagine what thoughts passed through his little magpie-head, but it was interesting to me how his antics humanised him—he had a clearly defined character, recognisable idiosyncrasies and a very definite thought process.

Picturing all the lives of all the birds, tiny and otherwise, I thought how they must have to struggle through hatching, fledging, flying off to new territory, finding a mate, their little bodies driven by instinct and fed by the most minute blood vessels imaginable. I'd look at George's feet and wonder how small the capillaries were, then compare him to a sparrow.

Monday 2 July

Today I felt terribly tired again. Unbelievably fatigued. Yesterday, during the visit from the neighbours, the sudden blanket of exhaustion that descended on me had been crushing. But this morning I was far, far worse. Even after eight hours' sleep, I could barely scrape myself out of bed. When Mary arrived, I managed to keep my eyes open long enough to give her a garbled version of what to do and forgot to mention that the spare bathroom needed cleaning. Then I collapsed into instant unconsciousness on the sofa in the kitchen with the dogs. I'd already let George out of his cage and out of the window. I couldn't think, walk, talk, or do anything. I lay, cabbage-like, until Mary came down to clean the kitchen.

I repatriated myself to the office on the middle floor, with the newspaper and a cup of tea. I just managed to drink the tea before I had to sleep again, this time on the office sofa. (Maybe this is why I have a sofa in every room.) It was impossible to keep my eyes open and my thoughts were fishing-net weights. But I had learned that feeling guilty at my inability to stay awake under these circumstances only made me feel worse. So, I simply resolved to work harder, more effectively and with more focus, when I was upright and mobile.

When I finally woke, feeling as if I were waking up in a locked box without air, I decided to force myself to work my way through some of the mound of filing, emails and letters that had accumulated. Until now, I'd been concentrating on only those things that were absolutely urgent, because I was spending the rest of the time outside building the garden.

George interrupted by knocking on the window with his beak; the office is at the front of the house and overlooks the main garden where he liked to play. He flew off when I got up to watch him, as if saying, "Look at me! I can fly!"

He spent a great deal of the afternoon dancing on top of the five spidery black metal arches around the rock fountain I'd built in the front yard, which lies between the house and the main garden, over which I'd planted ivy and clematis.

George was fluffed up and looking gorgeous, despite his droopy left wing and little bald patches. He flicked his tail up, in a cocky way, at every opportunity; he swung his body from side to side and fluttered his feathers, posed and danced, and occasionally flew to the kitchen window which remained firmly closed by The Ex. Reluctantly, I was trying to be supportive about this, but at least George knew where I was and made sure that I could see him.

The paperwork eventually got the better of me, and, fed up and tired, I collapsed on the kitchen sofa during the late afternoon; the dogs cuddled up and George, having called at the window a few times during the day, was finally allowed in.

Once inside, George was frisky; he peeled strips of papery skin off the garlic in the bowl by the Rayburn, then tried to hide it in the crook of my bent knee as I lay on the sofa. Next, he placed it in the folds of my jeans, and tapped it further in with his beak, wedging it down as far as it would go. Having completed this one task, he hid a biscuit from the dogs' bowl beneath a corner of one of the dog blankets on the sofa, padding back to check on it frequently to see if it was still there; each time he lifted the edge of the blanket so purposefully, it was striking. Snickers watched him, and after George had checked the biscuit for the third time, she dug it out with her nose and ate it, so next time George checked he was puzzled as hell, looking around to see if it had fallen, or maybe rolled off somewhere, then checking the spot again in case it had reappeared, or he had been mistaken—to my amusement he returned to search for the biscuit several times. He cast his eye over the sofa itself, then ducked down to look beneath it, before going back and lifting the corner of the blanket again. Biscuit gone: magic.

When we had supper, George hopped on to the chair-back nearest The Ex, then on to his right forearm, then he sideways-walked up on to The Ex's shoulder—behind his head, and down his other arm, all the time peering into his ears, and pecking at the hairs that escaped The Ex's ponytail as if he would like to tidy them up. I was impressed that The Ex bore this examination of his person with equanimity.

George was like a playful child; he tried pulling the three little white toy dogs with magnetic paws off the side of the microwave (they are only about 3 inches long and remind me of the three real dogs). He'd succeeded before, and Snickers got hold of one; it was almost unrecognisable by the time she'd finished with it, having chewed off its tiny nose and eyes.

Tuesday 3 July

The good news today was that my half-page poetry column was going to receive the same pay as before. My relief was huge. My editor had phoned and told me they'd had to lose thirty people and needed to cut four pages, to save paper and ink, from each edition. I was very fortunate to have kept the same pay, and I knew that.

In the meantime, it was now impossible to ignore the fact that Snickers and George had some kind of relational awareness of each other: today, George spent the day outside as usual but came back a few times to crow at Snickers through the kitchen window, and Snickers sat on the sofa beneath the window in excited anticipation at the sporadic communication with her feathered snack-supplier. Since George was brought up with the dogs, having shared their food and water bowls, and played with them, he had no fear of them at all.

When George came in for the night he scampered and danced around the kitchen as usual, until he saw I had one of his favourite Royal Mail red rubber bands lying beside my elbow on the kitchen table; I was using it to hold the pages of the notebook I was writing in. I kept the rubber bands because they were so useful, but recently they had been disappearing; I assumed The Ex was using them for something, but I never thought to ask him.

George reached out his beak to take hold of the rubber band, sort of sidling up to it while leaning away from me. Then he tried to grasp it in his beak, so I held on to it, and he pulled and pulled, but his feet were on the glossy surface of the table, so he kept sliding towards me and eventually let go. I proffered it again when he had a firmer foothold and was standing on some newspapers; he yanked it out of my fingers with a determined and unexpected tug, then carried it to the arm of the sofa where he held it beneath one foot and kept pulling at it with his beak. Of course, it was elastic, so it kept snapping back to his toes every time he let go; he was beating his foot up.

Laughing, I ran for the video camera, which was in another

room, but by the time I got back he'd carried the rubber band to the top of the tall cupboard by the window. I climbed up on the sofa to have a look, and there I saw a significant collection of identical red rubber bands.

George noticed a bowl of grapes on the table, so flew down to steal one, working at it with his beak until he released it from its stem. Grape still in his beak, he flew back out of the window. Somewhere outside was a stash of grapes that were rapidly turning into raisins unless he was eating them.

When the window cleaner arrived, I warned him about George, but was panicked when I spied George out of the middle-floor study window as he was swooping for the open doors of the van. I raced downstairs, my feet hammering the bare wooden treads, and almost threw myself out of the front door. George might do something to put himself in danger and I was frantic; images of his thievery and mischievousness filled my mind. I arrived outside to find the window cleaner sitting in the driving seat of his van with the door open, enjoying his sandwich in the sunshine. George was perched on one of the man's work boots pecking at the silver sliver of toecap that was exposed through the worn leather. The window cleaner chewed at his sandwich thoughtfully, and regarded George as he furiously attacked his toecap.

Monday 9 July

George was exiled from early-evening entry to the kitchen again by The Ex because he'd stolen food while The Ex was attempting to cook our supper; first, a substantial bit of cauliflower went sailing through the air in George's determined beak, looking like a magpie bouquet, and was then followed by a piece of broccoli. Each time there was a gap of a few seconds while George buried his prize in one of the flowerpots in the front yard, or one of the new flowerbeds, before he returned to pilfer something else. Had it been me cooking, I would have been devilishly curious to see how far George would take his thievery, while I watched.

George wasn't aware of the ease with which he could become magpie curry; he was an opportunistic corvid, not a bird that could be taught manners. But I suffered when I was obliged to eat the parts of the meal that George had not stolen, while watching his little head banging his beak against the window, with Snickers hanging around nearby, peering out at him and looking for all the world as if she longed to be able to let him in. George kept calling to Snickers in a needy, high-pitched croak as if pleading for her to open the window.

Only once we'd finished eating was it possible for me to let George in without an argument with The Ex. While few others might object to the reasonable separation of meals and magpie, it took all the fun out of food for me.

This was when I noticed that George had a limp. I hoped it would pass, but he was holding his foot up all the time, and if he needed it to balance or land on something he'd use it, but would tuck it back up out of sight in his belly feathers the moment he had steadied himself. It didn't stop him leaping about my person (head, shoulders, knee, foot) when the phone rang and I tried to have a conversation with a friend while cuddling the dogs on the kitchen sofa. It fascinated me that he did this every time.

Saturday 14 July

Today wasn't a very useful day, although I was working with my energy levels while I had any, and today I felt stronger.

When I let George out of the kitchen window for the day and watched him soar above the trees at the end of the garden, I had a feeling that he was flying further and further away each time.

Although I longed to get out in the garden to prune, shape, plant and clear up, I ended up spending ages at the builders' merchants deciding on posts and fence-post spikes to aid my construction of a three-bay compost heap, which meant that I wasn't around as a playmate for George.

It was around three o'clock when I got home, leaving me plenty of time for an afternoon and evening out: The Ex and I were going to a fundraising dinner at Ludlow Castle and I was looking forward to an excuse to get out of my gardening gear and dress up, but I was also worried about George. I tried to shut out the pictures of his little black-and-white body waiting on the kitchen windowsill to be let into an empty house, where two puzzled dogs couldn't help him (I didn't count Mouse). I didn't let him in during the day, because I felt that then to turf him out of his "nest" for the night was back to front, and I feared it would only confuse him further. But he was absent anyway, as if he had things to do.

There was no sign of George when we got back because it was long-since dark. I called and whistled for him, but there was no beating of excited wings as he flung himself through the air and the open kitchen window. I tried to push away thoughts of him roosting on a branch that was too close to the ground, where a cat or a fox might get him. I wondered if I'd done the right thing; I wondered if he'd even come home tomorrow. What if he didn't? I didn't sleep well, wishing for morning to come, and thinking that if he didn't return, it would have been all my fault.

Sunday 15 July

The first thing I did when I woke in the morning was to throw open the kitchen window and call for George after his first night out. I called and called—and George came. If he'd been big enough, I'd have thrown my arms around him and hugged him. He seemed happy and alert and curious. I refilled the food bowl that I habitually left out on the kitchen windowsill with dog meat, and off George went again for the day. But my mind was put at rest: *he had come home*; he wasn't dead at the bottom of a hole in a muddy field. This brought me a feeling of great joy, and increasing confidence in the feeling that he would return. I was certain he'd be home when dusk fell—and he was.

On the phone again this evening, I sat on the sofa in the kitchen. George was very, very happy, it seemed, to be inside again. He roosted on my foot as I rested it on the opposing knee and preened himself. The weight of his body on my slippered instep was reassuring; in my anthropomorphising mind it was as if he really wanted to be near me. I felt less charitable, however, when I caught him with a lump of dried dog shit on top of one of the kitchen wall units; he'd obviously hidden it there some time ago. I chased him around and around the kitchen trying to get him to drop it, only to later find he'd tucked a much fresher piece into a corner of the kitchen sofa cushions.

Since spending the night outside didn't seem to have done him any harm, I felt that I could shut him outside again, but balked at that, because I was a foolish softie suffering separation anxiety. So, I left the window open and it was up to George. He was becoming stronger and livelier, which was good. I wanted him to be outside more. But then, I wanted him to continue to visit too. It's called having one's cake and eating it. Or, perhaps, having one's magpie, but not so that it tucks dried-up dog shit into all the kitchen crevices.

The following day a storm was brewing on the horizon. I left George outside for a while, but the clouds were drawing in and there were several claps of thunder that seemed to be growing closer. I opened the kitchen window and shouted for George in case he wanted to escape what was bound to be a deluge; it was already seven o'clock at night. He took almost immediate advantage and soared into the kitchen, and then the skies opened, the power went out for a few minutes—twice—and the downpour lasted twenty minutes. It was as if someone in heaven was emptying a bath.

George didn't go out again; instead, he ate the lentil mush off my piece of toast, pecking at it before working his way through a spoonful of fruit yoghurt that I put out for him. More and more often now, I fed George at the kitchen table when I ate, finding that if he was given a tiny glass of milk and a little dish of his own food, he didn't steal mine; he was, it seemed, developing a concept of ownership: a sense of mine—and his.

Snickers and Widget were desperate to play with him because he was now a fruit-flavoured-yoghurt magpie-lollipop. They licked him until he fell off the arm of the sofa. Then something in his little head reminded him of doggy Schmackos, and he stole one from the packet I'd tried to keep hidden beneath the tea towels folded beside the sink. He'd watched me carefully, and remembered exactly where I'd put them. Now he had an opportunity, he slid his head between precisely the right towels to produce a result, despite the fact the towels were many and identical.

Earlier, after making a piece of toast, I'd made the mistake of forgetting to cover the toaster with a tea towel again when I'd finished, so George stuffed a doggy Schmacko into one of the toast slots. Then I noticed his stash of dog biscuits behind the tea caddy. Perhaps he thought he'd filled up that spot, and was trying to find a new one. Yesterday he tried to bury a rubber band under The Ex's backside as he ate his supper at the kitchen table, while The Ex had simply watched in disbelief to see how far the bird would go. All the way, apparently.

Around ten o'clock in the evening I went downstairs having worked a few hours in the study, mopped up any little magpie puddles I could see, and tucked the dozing bird into the cage on which he was perched.

I noticed he was developing adult flight feathers. He had the black tubular coating of young feathers at the base of some of his wing feathers; they were new and lengthening. He had also gained confidence in his flight.

And so the pattern continued, of George returning nightly to be let out of the kitchen window in the morning. He was less manic in the mornings now, as if he was settling into a routine. I fervently hoped this routine could go on, and on, and on.

In the garden one day I'd seen what I thought was a familiar-looking magpie fly up into the huge Atlantic cedar. I call it "*the* tree," as if it's the only one, since all the other trees are no more than the size of one of its branches. It looks as if it has a whole other country up in its massive canopy.

The high-up distant magpie was bothered by a couple of crows that were taking too much of an interest. It hopped and skipped out of the way, in just the way that George moved. I was so certain it was George that I called out, and the magpie came down a couple of branches so I could see clearly that he had a droopy left wing. It *was* George; my heart leapt—the excitement that it was him, and that he was responding to me, made me feel as if I was about to meet my much-desired date on some fabulous evening out, who would open the passenger door to his Aston Martin so I could fold myself neatly into the leather upholstery.

George didn't open any car door but hopped back up to the top of the tree. I called and waved at the little bird. And then he *soared*, really soared, down, out of the tree, over the rock fountain (a little rough just there, he had to pull up a bit or hit something) and straight at me. He got really close to me, then he scooped into the air directly above me, to land on the roof of the house, three storeys up, looking down as if to say, "Look what I can do!" His landings still left a lot to be desired: they were bumpy, clumsy affairs; he'd bounce a few times on the ground, and a couple of hops were necessary to steady himself as he came to a standstill, but his new feathers continued to grow, and he looked a little less like a scrawny teenage bird.

Monday 23 July

The Ex wanted George to stay out for the night again, which left me with growing feelings of unease at an impending argument that

I could only avoid by capitulating. He was adamant and tried to convince me that it was for the best: "George is a wild bird, and he should leave now," he pointed out. George, I thought to myself, would make his own mind up in good time, but I felt the need to appease The Ex for now.

However, I let George in at lunchtime, at which point he seized the opportunity to make the most of his time indoors; he pranced around the table, danced across the floor, chased the dogs, pecked their retreating tails, and then let them chase him back. He then stole a grape from the bowl on the table before flying out. But I was persuaded by The Ex to resist George's tapping at the window all evening. His little head cocked to and fro as he peered into the kitchen, wondering why we wouldn't let him in.

I felt as if I was slowly killing something; it was unbearable to watch his growing desperation. Inwardly, I cursed The Ex, but I also wondered if he was right. The dogs leapt on to the sofa and panted at the window, and George sat the other side crying to them and tapping some more.

The pull between my willpower and heartstrings was so powerful I wanted to weep; but it was true: George was a wild bird, and if he didn't go out soon it would be getting colder and perhaps he needed to acclimatise.

Then, as the evening drew to a close, when he would normally be sitting on one of the two kitchen windowsills waiting to come in, he wasn't there. Instead, there was an enormous, fat, dark brown slug. The slug found a bit of dog meat and began to eat it. I filmed it, turning the meat around in its jaws and appearing to work away at it; I'd never seen a slug eat, and I'd never seen one so huge that it could be filmed eating.

I couldn't help myself and sneaked outside to find George. He was perched on next door's chimney, and I was so damn happy to see him; he appeared pretty damn happy to see me too. He flew down to play, pranced around me, jumping up from the tarmac and bouncing off my knees again. How could I ever bear him to leave?

Back inside, The Ex wasn't in the kitchen, so around nine, when it was getting very dusky, I opened the kitchen window and George landed on the sill straight away; he'd been waiting and watching. Smiling at his arrival, I left him on the back of the kitchen sofa in the gathering gloom, hoping he'd roost in his towel-covered cage before The Ex found him. But instead, he settled on the top of the door to the utility room, which is what he did when it got too dark to see his way to the cage. So, as soon as I thought he would stay quiet, I climbed up on a chair, took a firm but gentle hold of him, and placed him on the perch in his cage where he could remain, unobserved, until morning.

GEORGE EXAMINES

His quizzical black eye
Polishes its round gaze in its orbit
As it scans everything
To the left and to the front,
While his right echoes the trajectory.
I wonder if his two visions
Are simultaneous, or seen separately,
Each by one half of his magpie-brain
Which directs the careful points of his beak
Into the dog meat that I offer him.
He opens it up by piercing and separating
His scissors, and peers
Into the hole he has made
As if he might find something;
His way, his purpose,
A gold-coloured curtain ring.

Tuesday 24 July

The trouble with George was his adoption of one antisocial habit in particular, and it was becoming a concern that troubled me more, every time he came into contact with strangers—and pretty much everyone was a stranger; he jumped on their heads.

It began with the pacing of the ground around them, sizing them up as if judging how high they were, then he would nimbly flap upwards, land on their head, bounce, maybe once, perhaps twice, then drop down to the ground again or fly off, sometimes cackling as if laughing out loud. For anyone not prepared, it was a shock; there was a thud on their skull and a flap of feathers, or a bit of a cranial bump and scrabbling of claws.

Today, when my neighbour, Sheila, came over to give me a couple of telephone numbers for workmen who might be able to fix the leaking roof, George had been hanging around the entrance where two brick pillars support the pair of cast-iron gates. He flapped from one pillar to the next, then edged along the top of the gate, sliding sideways, one foot after another, watching me talking to Sheila for a while. I could tell that he was examining the top of her head, so I warned her that he might jump on her but would mean no harm. It wouldn't hurt, I assured her, hoping that I was telling the truth.

To begin with, I managed to keep George at bay with my hand, but eventually, like a footballer getting past a goalie, he flapped upwards and dropped, bouncing off her head as if testing her skull for firmness and consistency. Sheila bore this bird-foot assault with remarkable fortitude. He was never so happy, it seemed, as when everyone was looking at him: he scuttled up and down the top of the gate; he turned and slipped and turned and looked down at us, riveted. Then he jumped from pillar to pillar again, across the opening for the gate, dancing around the coping stone of each before jumping back again. The problem, I confessed to Sheila, was me, not the bird. The bird would be fine, I said, trying to sound convinced, if not convincing, if left outside for the night. The Ex had insisted again that George was kept out, since I reneged last night.

And I *did* leave George outside for a bit. I took the dogs for a walk around the garden and George came too, doing his two-step run in between short bursts of flight. When I came in at nine I managed to leave him outside, but in any case, he wasn't hanging around the windowsill.

In fact, he stayed away until nine thirty when the sky grew darker. It was then I relented and opened the window. I thought nothing would happen; I thought George was all tucked up for the night in a tree somewhere. But about ten minutes later, he flew in like a rocket, soaring, wings stretched, straight through the open window and on to the back of the sofa. He seemed genuinely delighted to be home and spent half an hour hopping around the chairbacks as I sat having a snack at the dinner table—without The Ex, who was off watching TV in the bedroom because we still didn't have a living room. I turned the lights down and hoped George would roost before The Ex noticed he was inside, like last night. And, for a while, he did roost on top of the door to the utility room, where I left him. I fervently hoped he'd stay there, because if he could resist the temptation to make himself known to The Ex, all would be well. But George's stomach was going to give him away.

The Ex was hungry and, appearing in the kitchen, wanted to make himself a salami sandwich. Everything was fine to begin with; I watched The Ex walk from kitchen to utility room half a dozen times, passing right underneath George without looking up. George remained perched atop the connecting door, head tucked beneath one wing, seemingly asleep. Stifling laughter, I watched until the smell of salami became too much for George to ignore, and his head emerged from his wing feathers and the glint in his eye followed

The Ex to the fridge. The Ex turned to find George standing on the floor behind him, looking up at him quizzically, wanting salami.

But it didn't stop there, oh no; George wanted some of The Ex's salami sandwich so badly that when The Ex, already exceedingly annoyed at the return of the interloper, sat down to eat, George placed himself on the kitchen table in front of The Ex's plate, legs akimbo as if he meant business, and watched the sandwich begin to disappear in instalments into The Ex's mouth. With his wings firmly folded, and his head cocked sideways, his eyes followed every movement of the sandwich: up to The Ex's mouth, down to the table, up, down, up, down. The Ex was adamant in his determination to freeze out the bird—so, no salami titbits were offered.

George waited to see if The Ex would change his mind. He didn't. On this occasion, perhaps realising how close to the wind he was flying, George did not attempt an assault.

Wednesday 25 July

This afternoon as I went around the garden with the lawnmower, I spotted George up on the roof. I called up to him and he flew down to me, and when I say "flew down" let me try and describe what he did.

He flapped about a foot up off the roof, which was three storeys above me, then dived. I mean, really *dived*, wings plastered to his sides; his body turned perhaps twice as he barrelled towards my face. He was like an arrow, and all I could see was his round body with his manic little head aiming straight for me. For a moment my eyes were so focused on his tiny face that I could swear he was grinning. I knew he wouldn't hit me, but I thought he'd surely crash into the ground and kill himself at such speed. But he didn't—at the last minute he opened his wings and was pulled up out into the air above my head as if he'd suddenly opened a parachute. He flew to a branch behind me, cackling and clattering his little noise. What a show-off, what a tease!

George followed me while I mowed, and when I cleaned the grass out from beneath the mower where it had become clogged and compacted, he was there, grabbing beakfuls and burying them underneath the tools in the open-fronted garden shed. He hopped around my ankles and knees and let me pull his beak—for some reason he didn't seem to mind that.

When I'd finished the lawn I got The Ex and the dogs outside, so we could sit and have a drink in what was almost sunshine. Almost. It was warmish, but grey, with the odd escaping ray. George was ecstatic: he romped with the dogs; he clambered all over The Ex's arms, shoulders, knees, feet; he bounced all around me; he stole the black rubber gardening glove I was teasing him with and threw it all over the grass. Then Snickers found where George had hidden a chunk of bread in one of the flowerbeds. She dug it out and sat chewing it thoughtfully. George saw her and went to investigate. I called her back to the table and Snickers brought the bread with her. I could see it was a rather large bit.

George followed, shoving his inquisitive beak into Snickers's face; then suddenly, he snatched the bread and flew into the trees with it. Snickers went in chase, but without wings there was no hope.

The Ex had made himself a salami sandwich, which he brought outside, and a sesame Ryvita sandwich for me, with Brie and Marmite. George loved my crackers and cheese, especially the Marmite, when I let him have a bit. We were back indoors around nine thirty and opened the window for George; The Ex didn't protest tonight. George arrived in the kitchen in a flurry of feathers two minutes later.

He watched The Ex making himself a cracker, cheese and Marmite sandwich just like the one I'd had. It was too much for him to resist; as The Ex turned around to put the Marmite away, George made off with the entire two-cracker contraption.

The Ex didn't see the funny side of having his food stolen, but it didn't matter: I saw the funny side for both of us. Still laughing, I rescued the crackers from the clutches of George's beak and fed the remains of the broken snack to the dogs, giving George only one small bit of Brie. That bit of Brie travelled the kitchen in his efforts to keep it away from Snickers, who loves Brie almost as much as she loves roast chicken. Finally, George wedged the cheese in the Victorian window catch. Very nice. When he wasn't looking, I took it out and put it in a bowl in his cage.

Thursday 26 July

As the weeks passed I was still struggling with the fact that I didn't seem to be able to shake my chronic fatigue relapse, and now my lower back was so painful I had to roll out of bed in the mornings on to all fours, then negotiate the pain in order to stand upright, dress, and strap myself into a stretchy back brace before I could even manage to sit at the kitchen table.

The pain in my back would ease the more I moved, although it would never totally leave me—I've had it for over thirty years, since I was a passenger in a car crash when I was seventeen. I was getting a lift in the back seat of a 1970s Mini (one of the old, tiny Minis, not the modern things that are the size of a proper car). The Mini was hit head-on by a Ford Cortina doing around 76 mph on the wrong side of the road.

Two firemen had to cut me out, as I had been thrown, kneeling and bent over, under the front passenger seat when my own seat was shunted beneath it as the car crumpled. When the occupant of the upturned chair slumped back into it from being catapulted on to the bonnet through the hole where the windscreen had been, his weight pushed the bar at the base of the seat across my lower spine. He then remained lying half on the bonnet because his chair was resting on top of my curled-up form. I found myself trapped, crouching in a space so small I didn't think a human being could fit into it, with two unconscious companions.

Pain began then and continued in various degrees throughout my life. I had found exercises to manage it, together with visits to osteopaths (very helpful) and chiropractors (very unhelpful) whenever I got stuck bent double, and occasional bouts of painkiller use, but I dislike taking medication that has its own side effects. At least if I managed the pain through exercise—and later, as arthritis set in, diet—I knew what my body was coping with.

However, if I had a lie-in because these two stones in my existence were grinding me between them, George would be pissed off as hell by the time I let him out of his cage; I had to find ways to get downstairs to release him, even if I collapsed on to the sofa afterwards, when he'd soared off into the sky outside. But today I couldn't get out of bed at all to begin with—it simply wasn't possible. I couldn't lift an arm, and lay there like a starfish, dazed and bewildered and scared. Chronic fatigue isn't like being overtired; it is like becoming inert, barely able to form thought, knowing that something is very, very wrong, losing the strength to move a limb, before falling into unconsciousness. Reluctantly, I had to rely on The Ex to release George into the garden.

Although my ability to concentrate or read had atrophied and I struggled through feelings of profound exhaustion on such a frequent basis (so often I could rarely be bothered to note it in my diary) that it had become all-too-noticeable, the joy in gardening and the joy in having George had given me a sort of borrowed energy.

And if I felt awake enough to work late, I had to use the energy while I had it. My energy could not be stored, and going to bed early did not mean I woke refreshed—often it was the opposite.

At nine forty-five this morning when a friend phoned, I'd normally be up and working on the house or the garden or my poetry column, but not lately and not today. I was fast asleep dreaming that I was at an awards ceremony where no one was dressed up in anything long and glamorous, they were just wearing trendy pussy-pelmet skirts and fashion-victim shirts. I was just deciding how to "customise" a supposedly fashionable dress that looked exactly like a hessian potato sack, when the phone rang in real life . . . After a brief conversation I went back to sleep and stayed that way until lunchtime, forgetting who I'd spoken to entirely. Then I still couldn't get up. When George was finally let outside for the day, it was good to know that the little bird could look after himself.

I stayed in bed with a pile of poetry books and my poetry file, which I eventually managed to carry up from the study on the middle floor below, when I unstuck my limbs from the mattress. The act of will required for this simple excursion almost had me asleep on the landing. I read a bit, then slept, read, then slept. This, I thought, is not good.

In an attempt to use each waking minute for some useful purpose, I began making a list of new poems that I wanted to write about for my *Times* poetry column, so the newspaper could clear permission from the publishers of the various collections that the poems were chosen from. I'd been making the list for weeks, since the last list was about to run out. To be paid to read other people's poetry and write about it was a real privilege.

Life is unpredictable, I thought; yesterday I had been mowing the lawn, today I was bedridden. I finally managed to get up around five in the afternoon. The Ex had not been much in evidence, but we crossed paths in the kitchen to eat.

While I began in my dressing gown, when I needed to clean

out the dog litter tray it became impractical, so I got dressed. I had intended to go back to bed afterwards, but instead I managed to keep going. I cleared out junk from the chests of drawers and a wardrobe in the little spare room, so it would be easier to move the furniture the following day when the carpet layers came. I was, at last, after three years, going to have one small (tiny) room on the top floor finished, just big enough for a double bed, a wardrobe and a chest of drawers; it was the guest bedroom. Friends were going to be able to come and stay, if they could tear themselves away from the city.

Still struggling through the unexpected chronic fatigue relapse, I found myself sitting with The Ex in the kitchen early this evening, preparing to eat the supper he'd cooked; George was at the window, locked outside because of his habit of stealing food. Now George was desperate to come in; he twice flew up at the window in a demanding way, pushing his little head up against the glass, beak turned left, then right, his eye peering in. Then he sat on the sill, right up tight to the glass so he could see in past the reflection on the surface, and gazed at us, as if trying to work out if we'd seen him. It was such an urgent series of movements that I tried to reason with The Ex, who thought it was high time George was kept outside permanently, whereas I felt that his presence was something to be enjoyed and marvelled at, and I didn't want to waste it.

The bird was fine, but I suffered terrible separation anxiety, and resented The Ex for keeping him out. Seeing George's desperation to come back indoors made me realise that I could refuse him nothing. But I was making an effort in trying to accommodate the fact that two of us lived in this house and one of us only tolerated the magpie under sufferance.

In the meantime, my exhaustion dragged on as I attempted to plough through the proofs of my poetry book. Oh, I loved this book; I'd titled it *The Book of Mirrors* and it had everything from aspects of my childhood to a pheasant trilogy. I felt less self-conscious about writing in the first person now, and my poems were becoming increasingly personal.

George, however, was still the most entertaining element of my introspective daily life, beyond even the all-consuming garden. Every tilt of his head, every flap of his little wings, was somehow bewitching.

I'd felt the same kind of magic when, as a child (I think it was 1971—I'd have been eleven), my father, with his friend, the poet Richard Murphy, had taken my brother and me to an island called High Island off the coast of Ireland. And it was indeed high—and tiny; it rose out of the sea, its cliffs of slippery rock repelling all comers. It could only be reached at high tide.

The sea was choppy and the rowing boat we arrived in, rowed by my father and Richard, had to be hooked on to a sharp point of the rocks up which we then had to climb to reach the coarse grass above. And when we did, it was Eden! Rabbits and baby seagulls dotted the island, which was probably no more than an acre, if that, and, having never seen humans before, they had no fear. It was an extraordinary feeling to be able to walk up to a wild rabbit and just stroke it, or a baby seagull in its nest, and just slide my fingers gently over its feathers without it being the least bit concerned. Their lack of fear gave the whole island-top visit a dreamlike quality and I wished I could stay there forever and never have to deal with the egos and temperaments of human beings again. I put my hand down a rabbit hole and felt a rabbit inside; I gave its rump a little rub then left it in peace.

The idea of vanishing from populated areas and living a more animal-oriented existence had been a very solid desire when I was a teenager; I found people too often judgemental, critical and difficult. I wanted to disappear into a cottage in the middle of Dartmoor with a load of pets, pen, paints, paper and canvas. Now I'd rather done just that in Wales.

We had to leave High Island in a hurry as the tide had turned and was rapidly going out. Climbing down the jagged, wave-smashed rocks, and back into the lurching rowing boat, now terrified me, because the newly exposed rocks below were wet and slippery and the thrashing waves threatened to drag us into the wheeling currents. It was a longer way down now, and the boat was almost hanging from its tether.

The memory of that wild fur and seagull fluff helped carry me back to the mainland, pulled tightly around me like a life jacket against the sea spray and the lurching of the little rowing boat in which we were tossed. I never forgot how it felt to have wild animals and birds totally trust me, as if I were one of them. I wanted to be one of them, or at least to sit among them, accepted, peaceful, getting on with life without other human beings and all their clashing demands and ulterior motives. I also never wanted a rowing-boat trip like that terrifying excursion again. I decided that I didn't like being cold, wet, and more than a little scared.

Eventually, The Ex relented and agreed that I could let George back into the kitchen. The bird was jet-propelled; he shot through the gap I opened at the base of the sash window like a feathered bullet, as if he feared he'd be shut out again in a minute. He'd become much, much more agile on the wing; he'd been getting a lot of practice.

Tonight, he was in and out of the kitchen window several times from not long after six, until he came in for good around nine thirty as dusk deepened. He ate a bit of food off my plate; in fact, he took the biggest of the pieces of salmon that I'd cooked up, with spinach on a bed of mashed potato, and flew out of the window to hide it somewhere. Whenever I gave him mashed potato, which he loved, it stuck to his beak, so then he'd wipe his beak on the magazines I kept on the table. (One of my greatest pleasures is a really good meal with something to read—almost anything will do, but an interesting article on the Hadron Collider or the effect of gut bacteria on a person's mood and sense of well-being is pure joy.)

I gave George a cashew nut, and Snickers, who would probably kill a magpie for a cashew nut, followed him around all the places in the kitchen where he tried to hide it. Except that George was flying from kitchen surface, to top of wall unit, to top of shelves, to pile of drying dishcloths; he no longer scuttled around the floor where Snickers had a dog's chance of food theft.

I found George had stuffed a half-burned white candle, that so attracted him a couple of days ago, under the protruding plug sockets of the kitchen island. I put it back on the table in its squat, leafy metal holder, but tonight he saw it again, pulled it out of the holder, his beak grasping the sides of it as if closing a pair of scissors around it—albeit with some difficulty and considerable effort. He carried it away and buried it between the gardening books on top of the shelves.

Sitting with the three dogs on the sofa, I watched George with the now empty, leafy lightweight metal candle holder. Well, George had that candle holder all over the table; using his beak and claws he rolled it, he turned it, he tried to carry it and even managed a short distance, before he realised the dogs were getting cuddles. While he didn't want an actual hug, he did appear to want to be around a hug. So, he came and sat on my knee and my foot and my elbow. He tugged and pulled at all the little pocket tops on the front of my trousers. I tweaked his beak and teased him; he appeared to love the attention.

I was waiting for the day when George might meet another magpie and, instead of feeling terror at the sight of a strange bird, find himself emboldened by curiosity, and a better knowledge of his outside environment, which might give him the courage to make a friend or find a mate.

As I cleaned up the spare room ready for the carpet layers, I saw it out of the window: a wild magpie, looking bigger and fitter than George, flying into the fir tree on the fence line outside the kitchen window. George had been on the front lawn, and, as if he knew the magpie was coming, flew off into the trees in the other direction. The wild magpie shuffled out into the edge of a branch, so I could clearly see it, and it stared down at the kitchen window for a while, as if contemplating possibilities, before shuffling out of sight again. I half-expected to go into the kitchen and find an altogether strange magpie instead of George.

Tonight, George flew through the kitchen window to roost on the door to the utility room again and, later, put himself to bed in his open cage, which astonished me. As I shut the door after him, I saw what looked like a horsefly. It sneaked sideways beneath his feathers in an oddly slow and furtive manner. I'd noticed it on him earlier, just sitting on his back as he hopped around in the kitchen. I made a mental note that I must look for it, and kill it, when there was daylight, because if it was living on George, then it was feeding off George.

In an attempt to normalise my day, I managed to keep going until eleven at night, then collapsed in front of the TV in the bedroom with The Ex, who was watching *The Matrix* again. He watched the film often, but I hadn't watched TV for so long that I found the adverts unbelievable; I had forgotten that so many were stuffed into each programme it was hard to remember a storyline. I'm not sure what shocked me more: the number of ads or the length of time I'd managed to avoid any meaningful telly.

Friday 27 July

The fly that I had seen on George last night bothered me. First thing this morning, I reached into George's cage, took out his wriggling form, and found it. It was a creepy-looking thing, and behaved as if it were aware of what might happen to it. It had made a home in the ruff of feathers on George's back; it tried to slip under first one feather, then another, but as it moved strangely slowly, I was able to get hold of it in a piece of kitchen roll. It was a secretive, nasty, biting fly and killing it made a large and gruesome spatter of George's blood on the white paper towel.

Saturday 28 July

Today I was able to get up briefly. On the way to the kitchen around seven thirty in the morning, I stopped by the study and got out the file of a children's novel that I was working on and read a few pages. I decided that I must rewrite it, but I was in no shape to stay upright; my head felt clogged and thoughts half-formed themselves before falling to the floor with exhaustion. My arms and head felt too heavy to carry around and my legs were difficult to swing forwards; I had to go back to bed again and it took all my effort and willpower to get there. It was annoying and debilitating. The Ex was still sleeping, none the wiser.

When I woke again at eleven thirty, still feeling chronically fatigued, I slowly climbed into my gardening clothes, thinking that perhaps if I could put myself in front of the cement mixer and shovel sand into it, if I could just move a little at a time, if I could just string small efforts together to form an actual achievement, I was sure I'd feel better.

The willpower required was phenomenal, but if I could accomplish something in the day, it always had a positive effect. I had a bit of toast and a cup of tea, then had to lie down on the kitchen sofa when unconsciousness descended like a thick, heavy smog numbing all my senses. Experience had taught me that my anger about it only exacerbated the chronic fatigue.

The dogs, however, thought it was marvellous. They lay all over me and it was deeply comforting to have three small white animals curled up on top of me, their relaxed little bodies weighing me down and keeping me warm.

When I got up an hour or so later, I could still hardly move. Everything I did had to be done carefully. I began by wearing my back brace, but took it off as the back pain eased down from an eight out of ten to around a four. It didn't go, but it's hard to move in the brace, and when working outside, I needed to be flexible. Besides, when I moved the pain reduced—if I could have kept up perpetual motion my pain levels would, I thought, be manageable.

The pain in my back did not appear to be made any worse by manual work; it was just that I felt it as I moved. But then, when I didn't move, my back would seize up and became a brittle thing that felt about to snap at the slightest provocation, and the pain in any movement became too much to bear. Standing still was the most painful thing of all; I could only do it for seconds before the pain increased until I could no longer hear whoever was talking to me or think clearly. My smile would become a fixed, plastic thing as I wondered why I was too polite to simply find a seat.

There was no escaping the pain, but at least in trying to manage it I could be productive. To this end I doggedly kept my strength up with the manual labour that I did: the shovelling of sand and cement, the wielding of my angle grinder when cutting pavers, the digging; it all contributed to my core strength.

Everything I did made me feel better in myself—made me feel as if I was useful, creative, heading for the distant finish line.

On one of my tea breaks George joined me in the kitchen; I'd left the window open this afternoon so he could come and go as he pleased. The Ex was elsewhere, and I was making the most of it. George was making the most of me being up and about; he was so very frisky. He'd been outside with the jackdaws that had flown en masse down to the front lawn to pick up the brown bread I'd left earlier. It was as if he wanted to play with them, or perhaps he was just making his presence felt. Three weeks ago, he would have flown in the other direction. In any case they all flew off, leaving him alone, manically flapping from one bench to the other beneath the garden table, so fast I could hardly keep up with him, as if looking for his little friends—or seeing off the interlopers—I couldn't tell which.

He brought that same manic attitude indoors, skipping around the table legs, perching on the backs of the dogs and walking up and down Snickers's spine as she simply stood there patiently. She didn't bat an eyelid. When George danced it was like a quick two-step, and he danced on her rump. Snickers didn't flinch. Odd, I thought.

He took green beans from me as I was eating a lunch of leftovers from last night, so I had to give some to the dogs too. At least they're all getting their greens.

When working with the last load of mortar, shovelling it into the narrow trenches that I'd dug for strips of pavers along the edge of pathways in the garden, George came to join me; I tried to shoo him away because I feared he'd eat the mix, but he wouldn't go. Then he jumped in and out of the wet mortar in the wheelbarrow, perching on the side in between jumps, while I cried "nooo" each time and leapt forwards to chase him off. The mortar squelched between his toes. Then he took a big beakful of it and looked at me with a defiant expression, cement mix oozing out of the sides of his smile. I found a couple of worms under a nearby pot and tried to get him to eat those instead, but no, he wasn't interested, he wanted the mortar and flew off with it, leaving an odd little pile of nesting material just inside the holes of an old milk crate that I was using to sit on as I worked. I had visions of his beak being cemented shut, or the mortar solidifying in his belly, but surely, surely, he was smarter than that?

Then, just as I bent over, George hopped on to my back and climbed all over me, walking up and down my spine as I cleared up bits of debris from the hedge-cutting that the The Ex had done that day. My neighbour, Bob, walked past the gateway with his Dalmatian and saw me; he kindly pointed out that I had a magpie perched on my bottom. When a robin did the same thing a few days later, I wondered if maybe I was spending too much time in the garden; I had become a fixture and even the wild birds weren't scared of me.

George took several pebbles out of the mortar in the wheelbarrow and hid them somewhere. He also shifted the item that looked like nesting material, which he'd stashed in the milk crate, when it seemed I was getting too close to it for his liking. I wondered if he was afraid that I'd take it from him.

I was in the process of collecting the half-dozen heavy wooden lengths that I had planned to use to mark out car spaces in the yard, George in hot pursuit. I laid one of the sleepers in its new position and smelt something nasty and rotting and dead, but couldn't see anything. George appeared in the air off to my left; he dived into the plastic crate by my feet and took out the nesting material I'd seen him with earlier; now I could see that it wasn't nesting material at all, it was a putrid mouse carcass and he'd been trying to hide it from me, plainly fearful that I might steal his treasure.

When Mr. Brown, the man who might fix the hole in the roof, came round, I showed him where I needed him to replace some missing tiles. He was a man of few words, so I found myself talking too much. Mr. Brown listed to the left like the Tower of Pisa. I asked him if he was OK to do the roof and he said he was. Neither of us mentioned his leaning angle. I just hoped he wouldn't fall off the roof. He had an oddly gentle handshake, as if he were afraid of crushing my fingers.

George couldn't be kept away. He pranced around the ground behind Mr. Brown, gazing up at his flat cap. I knew what George's intentions were; he wanted to land on the man's head. He made a few passes at Mr. Brown's shoulders, skating through the air just past him, then landed on the roof of my car. He took some doggy treats from me, but it didn't take his attention off his intended goal for long enough; I had a palpable sense of the tug on George's attention coming from elsewhere. Thankfully, however, Mr. Brown managed to leave without being trampolined—saved, perhaps, by his flat cap.

I worked with the last load of mortar, laying edging pavers on the narrow foundation, until I'd finished around nine o'clock, George coming and going about his business. But when I packed up for the night, George followed me indoors, flying in through the kitchen window just as I walked in through the front door. He was standing on the table waiting for me when I stepped into the kitchen, his legs akimbo and his imaginary magpie hands on his hips. It made me smile.

Monday 30 July

George came for a walk with me around the garden with Snickers, Widget and Mouse, as he so often did. He ran alongside and lined up for a snack with the three of them. But today there was something different about him, although I couldn't put my finger on it. He was just ever so slightly unlike his usual self.

When I gave him and the dogs a doggy nibble each, he buried his in some nearby shingle on the pathway, then went frantic when the dogs unsurprisingly sniffed it out immediately. He jumped up and down and danced about with his wings out, chittering accusingly, rather alarming Mouse. As I walked the dogs back to the house, Widget hesitated by the gates, as she often does, and looked across at Bob and Sheila's where we sometimes walked to say "hello." George watched her standing there for a moment, then jumped on her little round head, but her head was so tiny and he had grown larger and heavier, so she dropped her head down and he slid off the end of her nose, landing on the ground with a couple of hops.

When she didn't walk away, he did it again, and she, having lifted her head, now dropped it again, so he slid off the end of her nose—again. And when she still didn't move, he did it a third time. When Widget took a few steps, he ceased. I have no idea what the purpose was, but it was unusual for him to pick on Widget, who was the smallest and gentlest of the dogs.

He still took his usual HiLife doggy nibbles (a kind of dry dog food that was a perfect magpie snack, being small tubular shapes like chopped-up worms, each about half an inch long and moist enough to be slightly malleable) from my fingers, but he was skittish and excitable as if preoccupied with important thoughts that distracted him. I found it mildly disturbing. He didn't come to play around me when I was moving the stones that morning as he usually did. When he came indoors after The Ex and I had finished supper (through the open kitchen window as usual, although he'd tried to follow me through the door sometimes, getting waylaid in the hallway by all the boxes of things to undo), I left him to play with the dogs and settle. He hadn't put himself into his cage for a couple of days, so I'd had to catch him after turning out the lights, but that night he did, jumping out when he saw me coming to close the door. So I left him to hop inside again when I wasn't there, and go to sleep, before I sneaked back to tuck him in for the night. I sensed a growing distance in him.

Tuesday 31 July

Today, when I was working with the cement mixer again, building more of my retaining walls for raised flowerbeds (a visible achievement that spurred me on to more planting), George came to play around me, stealing more cement-covered pebbles from the mortar and drinking out of the water bucket I used to wash the cement off my rubber-gloved hands. I uncovered a nest of ants with eggs, which I had to get him to look at by waving one of my gloves at him—he loved to play with those gloves. I dropped the glove by the nest and he saw the ants. He landed on them with gusto. He couldn't abide woodlice and their crispy armadillo-like coating, but ants really delighted him. Having scooped up as many as he could until the last ones had scuttled into cracks and gaps in the ground to escape him, he spent some time perching on my back, nibbling my right ear as I worked; his balance was perfect. I just hoped no surviving ants might crawl out of the corner of his mouth while he was in such close proximity.

When The Ex and I ate supper outside this evening, sitting at the garden table on the lawn in the centre of the turning circle in front of the house, George performed: he perched on top of the bottle of wine, hovering like a hummingbird to keep his balance. He then flew from one side of the garden to the other, swooping and cutting in close to our heads, and turning sharp angles in the air, as if to demonstrate his increasing flight skills, and he stole a sausage off my plate. *A whole sausage!* I'd given him and the dogs a little bit each, but he'd uncharacteristically ignored his—he obviously had his eye on a larger prize. He'd watched me and my sausage and worked out the most opportune moment to pounce. I chased and caught him with it while he was still running along the ground, because he couldn't get into the air quickly enough with all that extra weight. I was laughing so much that it was almost impossible to get him. Then Snickers grabbed one end of the sausage and I had to snatch it off her; I wasn't going to let her eat a whole sausage on her own: her doggy waistline was already large enough as a result of cleaning up after George.

Working in the garden every day, and then indoors on my *Times* poetry column in the late evenings, had created a pattern with George; he knew where I would be at any given time, and would come to play. I had my little trusty companion. At the same time, I swear he spied on me; on one occasion he appeared from nowhere when he saw me working in a secluded corner of the garden. We stared at each other while I chatted to him about anything and nothing, then suddenly he darted forwards beneath my hand and snatched a gigantic spider that I hadn't noticed crawling around my knees. George stood looking up at me for a moment, our eyes locked. The spider's legs stuck out like broken twigs from either side of his beak. Then he tilted his head at me just slightly, and squeezed the spider. Its belly exploded out of the sides of his mouth, spattering an egg-yolk-yellow goo all over the stone nearby. He quickly swallowed the spider by tossing it back, then beaked up the goo from the rock, snapping his beak sideways against it and scraping his lower beak upwards to clean the mess into his mouth.

Later, I found the red candle he took outside a few days ago; it was hidden at the foot of one of my fence posts in the front yard.

August

Saturday 4 August

Everything is fine of course, until it isn't, and sometimes we don't know it isn't until someone tells us, and today one of my neighbours told me that she would open a bottle of wine to celebrate the day George left home for good. George's presence was making itself felt among the neighbours; he had no fear of them, so teased and bounced and played around, stealing small things and making people nervous.

It was explained to me that my elderly next-door neighbour, Jean, for whom I had great respect and affection, was apparently terrified of George—and I'd had no idea. She was too polite to tell me herself, but her fear had been noted by others.

I now knew that the issue of George had to be addressed, and his freedom would have to be curtailed, or I would have to take him on a very, very long road trip.

And what, asked my neighbour, if the magpie bothered young children when they came to visit? I didn't mention how George bounced off Mary again as she was leaving yesterday; I just didn't know what to do to stop him. That particular habit would certainly mean the end of his freedom if he hung around.

I telephoned a friend who possessed many acres and asked him if he knew of any local woods or places that might be suitable in which to release my magpie safely. Nowhere near his land, he said, because his gamekeeper would shoot it. In fact, they kept a magpie in a cage to lure the others in order to kill them. This wasn't what I wanted to hear.

I left a message for another friend who lived in the sticks near Carmarthen, asking if he would like a semi-domesticated magpie. When he called back the answer was an emphatic "no."

If George were any better behaved, he would be more manageable, and if he were any wilder, I wouldn't have to worry. I almost persuaded myself to take him somewhere the following day and leave him with a pile of his favourite HiLife doggy nibbles. But the idea upset me so much that I actually cried; losing my little feathered companion by depositing him in a strange place, where he had no references and no ready food supply, seemed as bad as doing the same with a dog or a cat. The very thought created a sense of profound loss for me. Besides, corvids have territories— around 12 acres apparently. I'd have to take him far enough to think he wouldn't come back. I had a vision of my bewildered, lost and hungry little magpie and it made me terribly sad. I am pathetic, I thought; all this for a bundle of feathers, a beak and a pair of claws. Ah, yes, said the voice in my head, but think about the blood flow and heartbeat, and the magpie-thoughts that bring him home to your side. All those cognitive rationalisations from an active brain that was still learning. Did I want him to learn what it was like to be deserted?

I tried to console myself that George wouldn't starve, and remembered a day when I'd had a local lad helping me in the garden; he wasn't wearing gloves and had voiced his concerns about spiders as we shifted stones, bags of compost and lumps of wood; he didn't like them one little bit. George flew in to join us and I pointed at a couple of large, fat spiders on the bags of compost. He ate them both, picking up bits and pieces of other insects around our feet, scavenging, being thorough. The young lad couldn't believe his eyes as George cleared up, ruthlessly leaving no creepy-crawly crawling.

Beneath one bag that we moved, lying in water that had pooled on the clay soil, was a putrifying mouse. I knew I'd have to get rid of its festering little carcass and wondered if it was so rotten that it would fall apart if I touched it. The lad stared at it in disgust, and then suddenly, George swooped in, scooped up the entire mouse without even landing, and flew off with it. Corvids get bad press, but primarily they are scavengers cleaning up roadkill and carcasses in general. Still, I feared that one of my neighbours might find a rotting mouse hidden in their exhaust pipe or tucked under a plant pot, because George would want to secrete it somewhere in a place where it would just fit, so he could eat it later.

George vanished for the late part of that afternoon and I had horrible thoughts that he'd finally encountered someone with a gun or a car. Then I saw another of my neighbours working in his front garden and asked him to tell me if George had ever been any kind of a nuisance. George, he said, had perched on the boot of the car when it was raised. He'd realised it must be George, because his wife had talked about him; his wife, who'd had her head jumped on by George. He was fine about George, though he didn't mention whether or not his wife was. I begged him to let me know if George became annoying in any way. I wanted as many people as possible to know that this magpie was a pet, not a pest that could be eradicated.

Leaning out of the bedroom window, I noticed George was outside on the garage roof. I opened the window and called to him, and he immediately flew up to join me, landing on the windowsill, and let me stroke his beak. I tried not to think about having to find a way to get rid of him, but I could see that it was an unavoidable issue now.

He'd become my identity: The Ex and I were at the pub down the road when we were served by a woman who lived nearby. Oh, she said, you're the woman with the magpie! Oh dear, I replied, heart sinking, I hope he's not being a nuisance. Not at all, she assured me. She told me that she realised he must be someone's pet because he was so tame. This wasn't good news. How far did he go? Who else had he introduced himself to? My magpie had another life that I had no inkling of; it appeared that he knew more people than I did.

I also discovered that George recently joined a friend of ours in the village—and his dog—for a walk; he hopped and skipped along the road with them for quite a way, showing no fear at all (of course not, he thought he was a dog); it seemed he was rapidly becoming known by everyone, but the fact that there were others who would drink to his departure made me eye some of my neighbours with a growing sense of unease. I wanted everyone to love him, but . . .

Sunday 12 August

I had a couple of girlfriends over and gave them tea at the table on the lawn in front of the house; George's curiosity was piqued by my preparations. After eating the petals off the red roses in a small vase on the kitchen table, he saw me replacing the spent kitchen roll with a new one, and he grabbed at the empty cardboard cylinder. There ensued another tug of war between him and me—somehow, he won, slipping it out of my fingers (perhaps I wasn't trying hard enough?) and flew out of the window with the cardboard kitchen roll sticking straight out of his beak and dwarfing him. I had to go and retrieve it from the front yard. As I returned it to the kitchen, I noticed the plug from the utility-room sink half-buried among the cushions on the sofa, then had to chase George around the kitchen several times trying to get him to drop the pink kitchen sponge; if the dogs got hold of it, they'd turn it into pink confetti.

When, feeling slightly harassed, I rejoined my friends outside, George followed me; he was in an investigative mood, and these were new subjects. He pecked their feet from time to time, and, as they were both wearing dressy summer sandals, it hurt. He appeared fascinated by the sight of real toes with nail varnish. He kept eyeing the hair of one, which was cut in a fluffy white bob and looked gorgeously thick. I could tell that George really wanted to get his claws into it; he paced the ground by the bench where she sat, gazing up at the crown of her head as I grew increasingly apprehensive. Eventually, he hopped up on the back of the bench behind her and tried to access her crown from a more convenient take-off point. Each time he tried, I waved him away, as if shooing a gigantic wasp.

The woman with the wonderful hair got out her camera and George really turned in a performance: he hopped on to my head and my shoulder and pecked at my eyelashes. I was unnerved when I felt his beak against the side of my eyeball. He shuffled along the back of the bench and played around me, nibbling my ear and catching the stray hairs that caught the breeze. He knew all eyes were on him and was very happy with the attention. He stood on my head again, and nuzzled and danced; he was adorable, and he knew it.

My friend looked at the photos she'd taken some days later: "But he's just a little bird," she complained. And he was—she'd tried to photograph his enormous personality, but all that came out was his tiny size in comparison to his surroundings.

After George put himself to bed, I found a Caramac wrapper in pieces hidden under Mouse in her basket—poor little dog— together with some screwed-up tissues and the plug from the utility-room sink.

Monday 13 August

I left George in the kitchen with the window open and in the company of the dogs, while I worked in the middle-floor study on my poetry column for the following week. But The Ex shut the kitchen window while he cooked supper. This meant that when George desperately wanted to come in for the evening, he couldn't, and I didn't know about his exclusion as I was still occupied. It was only when I came downstairs to eat that I discovered George was nowhere to be seen because he had no means of entry. He didn't appear at the kitchen window even when it got to eight o'clock, which was way past the time he now usually came in.

Keen not to break the pattern of his bedtime, and seething at The Ex, who was on another one of his sporadic "keep the magpie out" missions, I took the dogs for a walk around the garden, calling George and doing the double-whistle I habitually did to get his attention. But there was no sign of him. Then, just as I got the dogs back to the house, I could hear a magpie cackling over the road somewhere by the neighbouring properties. I stood in the doorway and called again and again; I could hear the desperation in my own voice. Suddenly, George came soaring over the flat roof above the kitchen window, then down to the windowsill, ready to be let in, his little bird-face pressed up against the glass. When I opened the window, he was in like a shot, as if he was terrified of being shut out again. I was going to have to be more watchful of The Ex, I thought, as I poured George a magpie-sized glass of milk, which he guzzled greedily, tipping his head back to swallow each time.

Wednesday 15 August

I found myself apologising for George again, this time to the husband of the gardening partnership taking care of Jean's garden next door. Standing by the gate in the old iron rail fence that divided our two properties, I could feel the gardener's stinging disapproval in the delivery of every word he spoke to me.

George had unfortunately jumped on the gardener's head, bouncing off it as if it were a cushion. He'd put me in a position where I had to apologise to the gardener in order for him to know that George was not a magpie he should level a shovel at.

"Well," he replied in a taut voice, which made me think of thin fronds being stripped from a metal palm tree so that they twanged, "when it jumps on your head it's not nice." He appeared to be devoid of any humour which might have softened the critical tone.

"George does that as a greeting," I explained, "and if he bothers you, please squirt him with water from the hose that I know you have handy."

"Oh, he's all right really," he told me then, suddenly appearing to relent.

"George," I said, as the bird perched on the arch over the little gate, "you'd be perfect if you didn't jump on people's heads." I stroked his sleek black beak while the gardener looked on, and insisted that he and his wife must let me know if George bothered them again.

It seemed that by treating George as I had, I had inadvertently created a half-tame magpie, who—because of his confidence in interacting with other humans—was perhaps more at risk from them than he would have been otherwise.

My thoughts turned to the mole that had been decimating the garden; I felt bad about the mole. I'd gone through a lot of trouble to get hold of a humane mole trap, because most mole-catchers simply kill them. It was a see-through plastic tube that had to be inserted into one of the tunnels (with gloved hands so the moles don't detect human scent) and covered over. Then checked daily, because once the mole is trapped it can't move, so it can't feed.

Yesterday was the first day that I didn't check it, because when I glanced at it from above, there was a tunnel clearly dug around the side of it—a noticeable ridge of earth, so I didn't bother to dig it up. But today I dug it up to move it and the mole was inside, dead as a doorknocker. I buried it in one of the burrows, although I toyed with the idea of leaving it somewhere for George. I was annoyed with myself for a long time, because I hadn't wanted to kill it, not least because I had never seen a living mole. I still haven't.

The same day, I found out why the dogs have been barking at night. It wasn't a hedgehog as I'd suspected, which is what had disturbed them once before when I discovered one secretly living in the house (the little creature must have slipped in through the front door one night, when it was left open). The hedgehog was so weak that I found it staggering down the hallway, unable to muster the energy to hide among the boxes of flat-pack kitchen units and forgotten belongings that were still stacked against the walls, three years into our occupation. I'd fed it for a few days until it was strong enough to release, but this new nightly disturbance was caused by something very much bigger.

It was dark when, in the lights from the kitchen window, I looked out and saw what appeared to be a lost Labrador gazing up at the dog food on the windowsill that I left out for George every afternoon. It stood, tall and leggy and blond. I quickly grabbed a piece of ham from the fridge, quietly opened the front door, and threw the ham out to the creature, and was astounded—amazed—aghast—to see that it wasn't a dog, but a fox, like no fox I'd ever seen. We stood and stared at each other for several seconds.

It was the biggest, rangiest, palest-coloured, long-legged fox ever, and it didn't seem scared of me. I tossed it a bit more of the ham, and it backed off, returning a few moments later to eat the meat. It was so tall that it seemed unnatural. I wanted to keep it there so I could stare at it longer, so fed the fox pieces of ham until it had eaten it all, astonished at the length of its legs.

I still felt bad about the mole.

As I watched him that night, George coughed up a pellet of indigestible bits, just as an owl does. Even as a corvid that eats small dead mammals and birds with bones, fur and feathers, it hadn't occurred to me that he needed to dispose of the indigestible bits. I wasn't used to it, because until recently, he'd been living on dog food, and there was nothing in dog food that wouldn't pass out of his rear end. This meant that George was successfully foraging for himself.

Thursday 16 August

Only a few hours later, as the sun rose, George was noticeably different: more frantic, more impatient than usual. After taking the towel off his cage, I spent three minutes sorting out food for the dogs, and in that time, the time it took to walk around the kitchen for one extra revolution, he became manic. By the time I held George's cage to the open window and tried to let him out, he was scrabbling and panicky, trying to force his head through the bars over and over again, which was very unlike him; he's not normally a stupid bird.

Upon release he immediately flew straight out of the kitchen window to the back of the bench just outside, and, instead of turning to take a couple of doggy nibbles from my outstretched hand as always did, he flew off. Holding out my hand with the nibbles in it, I felt rebuffed. How, I asked myself, could I let such a feeling engulf me for nothing more than a sodding magpie?

From an upstairs window at the back of the house, I saw George strutting his stuff and exploring the half-built house on the building site at the end of the cul-de-sac where I lived. I think he was looking for the workmen who, I guessed, would be feeding him scraps.

There was an evolutionary process to George's development. His flying skills had improved to the point where he could dart, corner, wheel, spiral, and barrel roll out of the sky; he had developed a taste for creamy substances and had his own little glass of milk always available now at mealtimes, together with a little plate of whatever The Ex and I were eating, which appeared to discourage him from stealing off our plates—except for the time he flew out of the kitchen window carting half The Ex's salami sandwich.

He appeared to have given up trying to make what sounded like parts of human speech, but listened to me intently, then sometimes opened his beak as if he was trying to respond, before snapping it shut, suddenly, as if thinking better of it.

During the afternoons, he'd come to join me outside on the front lawn when I took a break for a cup of tea. That was when I could watch as he collected insects from the flowerbeds. He pouched everything in the saggy base of his beak, then he tried to find hiding places for these delicacies. Of course, some of the insects were still half-alive, so when he spread them out on to a paver to rearrange them and put them back in his beak (as if to pack everything more neatly and so fit more in), a couple of winged ants tried to crawl off, which prompted him to gobble everything up again.

Once, he spat the insects out on to one of the supports under the glass garden tabletop, hammering them into the 90-degree angle with his beak, so if there was any life left in one of his victims, it was squashed out of them.

Of course, it wasn't quite so cute when he had a mouthful of something with legs, which wriggled out of the sides of his mouth. One time, he tried to tuck a dying leggy thing up my trouser leg, which prompted my cry of protest.

Every day, I noticed little things about him, like when he shut his eyes a thin film of a lid—a transparent nictitating membrane—closed from the inner corner to outer corner of each eye, beneath an external eyelid that closed from above to blink. To sleep, a third lid closed upwards. This is the same arrangement as owls.

One night he almost fell off the lower perch in his cage when I'd put him to bed; he'd seemed oddly unsteady when he nodded off. He shuffled closer to the adjacent higher perch, rested his beak and his head against it, and shut his eyes again. I'd never seen him do that before: using a headrest to keep himself upright.

He developed a mantle of browner feathers just beneath the black feathers of his back, which he'd shake out and spread like a cape over his shoulders for the duration of his sleep; these feathers emerged from beneath the outer, shiny black layer like a soft, hidden blanket. It is hard to describe something like that, but think of it as an exchange of feathers to effect the transformation.

His feelings for the dogs seemed to approach sibling rivalry: I gave the dogs each a bone one evening, but of course, when George came in for the night there was no bone for him. So, there ensued a battle. Mouse and Widget refused to give up their bones and snapped at him, although he managed to keep his body parts out of the reach of their sharp little teeth. He found Snickers had left her bone—the biggest—unattended, and actually managed to grab it in his beak and fly—or perhaps stagger on the wing would be a better description—out of the window. I retrieved it from him outside in the front yard. Eventually, he found the cast-off bits left by the dogs when they couldn't get their tongues any further down the bone shafts to get the marrow out; George's beak was long enough.

The three dogs sat on my lap on the sofa and George tried to join us but there wasn't room for him; he snipped at Mouse and Snickers, then wedged his beak just under Snickers's back as if to prise her off my lap. Each time I covered them up with my hands and said "no." George had watched me caution the dogs, always with a simple "no," and he'd watched the dogs stop whatever they were doing. He listened now and backed off. I tickled his beak and wondered if it would be possible to train him like a dog. Maybe then he wouldn't be so terrifying for Jean next door.

Friday 24 August

My dreams that George could live an untroubled life with us were not to manifest. Today, the issue of an aviary, in which he would be permanently confined, reared its ugly head and I couldn't ignore it.

The window cleaner arrived and told me that he'd already seen George a couple of times this morning; George had been doing his rounds of the neighbouring houses again. This worried me.

During the afternoon I paid Jean a visit and picked up the courage to ask her, face to face, how she felt about George. George frightened her, she told me; she didn't want to go outside if she thought he was there, because birds in general scared her, and the idea of a bird landing on her head was enough to make her think twice about opening the door at all. When she did go outside to get into her car, she had taken to wearing a hat.

Worse was to come; Jean confessed that there was no way she could tell the difference between George and the wild magpies that lived in the trees in her own garden—there were at least three of them, so now she was scared of them all, in case they were George . . . I felt my heart sink. He was going to have to go into an aviary.

I refrained from telling Jean that, while I was working in the garden that morning after a stint in the office, George had jumped from the roof of the summerhouse and literally used my head as a springboard to leap off into space. It wasn't unpleasant, just a strange squishy feeling like being assaulted with a squash ball at slow speed (any faster and it would hurt). I had a vision of a sign on the gate with the caricature of a gleeful magpie bouncing off the top of someone's head, a delighted grin on its face, saying BEWARE, BOUNCING BIRD.

Saturday 25 August

Today I set about collecting the materials necessary to build a very, very large aviary on the back of the house; the biggest possible, given the space. It was the perfect spot and would take up almost half the small back garden, which was riddled with ground elder in any case. And one day I'd knock a door through from the utility room into the aviary.

If George had to go into an aviary, then it would be as huge and heavenly as I could make it, with flowerbeds, a pond and a little fountain. Although, in my mind, it was a task too enormous to contemplate: who could build it for me? How much would it cost? How would I feel, trapping George, just so that he didn't bother my neighbours?

George was free to leave, and he hadn't done so. The alternative to an aviary was a very, very long drive and the hope that he didn't have the instincts of a homing pigeon. And I simply couldn't bring myself to do that, and besides, Jean still wouldn't know if the wild magpies were George, because he might find his way home and could land on her head at any moment. So, unless he departed of his own free will, the aviary was the answer.

George flew off with his customary two doggy nibbles in his beak. It had become a pattern for him to fly out of the kitchen window from his cage, which I'd rest on the arm of the sofa. He'd perch on the back of the bench in front of the window, turn, and take two nibbles from my outstretched hand—he always looked for the second one once he'd grabbed the first.

Then I began my search of the building merchants for the aviary uprights; I could get them almost 12 feet long. And then there were rolls of welded mesh, joist straps for the cross beams, and staples for the mesh—to be used in the staple gun I could attach to my large air compressor . . . I realised that I had to get everything organised quickly if I wanted to make the aviary happen before matters got much worse.

My problem was that, although I'd landscaped the whole garden (with 125 tons of stone and having mixed 65 tons of concrete by the time I finished), I had no desire to build the aviary. I was tired of building stuff. But I got chatting to someone who worked part-time for the Derwen Garden Centre and discovered he used to be a professional carpenter and still had all his tools. After looking over a sketch of my dream of an aviary, he agreed to build it for me.

It was going to be about 18 feet by 30 feet, and over 11 feet high; then I would make a garden inside, with more raised flowerbeds and natural stone walls.

George came to have a look at John when we were out the back discussing the aviary, but he kept his distance to begin with. I found a worm beneath a stone and tossed it in his direction. He swooped down off a telephone wire and took it. It was a large worm, so he strutted around with the ends dangling from his beak for a short while, stretching it every now and then by trapping one end beneath a foot and dragging at it with his beak so it bounced back like a rubber band, as if to quieten its wriggling until he could find the perfect paving stone to dismember it on, which he then did. John was gobsmacked.

Wednesday 29 August

There was much grinding of hedge cutters from next door, and the thought that George—who had continued to find heads irresistible as landing pads—might find himself minced didn't appeal. As soon as I heard those hedge cutters, I opened the kitchen window and called him, and magically, he appeared, hopped on to the sill, then on to the back of the sofa. I shut him in for the rest of the day and resigned myself to the fact that I'd be clearing up puddles of bird shit every time I went into the kitchen.

George didn't complain; he didn't hammer at the window to get out, he didn't sit by the glass and stare wistfully at the sky; on the contrary, he made the most of being inside, playing with the dogs, and exploring every aspect of the tools and cleaning items that I kept in the utility room. Oh, he was so happy with his little feet in the boxes of screwdrivers, spanners, drill bits and dusters.

Then I found the plug from the utility-room sink hidden beneath the folds of the covers on the kitchen sofa again. This time I got a short length of *very* heavy chain that was lying around and attached it to the plug; half a dozen links of chain strong enough to drag a truck out of quicksand. I doubted very much that George would be able to shift it now; that plug had been flown out to the garden pots outside the window so often that it was collecting frequent-flyer miles, and I didn't want to lose it for good. It wasn't possible to find another plug to fit this particular old sink.

A little while later I heard a *THUNK* on the kitchen floor, followed by the sound of something metal being slowly pulled across a rough surface. It was George; he'd managed to get the sink plug down from the drainer, but could no longer lift it because of the six enormous metal chain links I'd attached to it. So he was dragging it across the floor to the window, his little feet digging into the floorboards for leverage. When he got to the window, he tried to lift the plug several times, but the chain kept him rooted to the ground. With the windowsill in his sights, he tried over and over again, and only gave up when he was exhausted.

But it was the vanishing lightbulbs that puzzled me most. George didn't always steal red things or things to eat. Sometimes he maybe thought something was useful; it was like an obsessive compulsive disorder. He saw an item, was interested by it, picked it up, then had to put it somewhere he'd remember and where it would fit. Long things went into long spaces, big things went into big spaces, and so it was with the lightbulbs. Life, for George, might have been simply about finding a place for everything and putting it there; perhaps he thought of this as "tidying up." I identified with this in a fundamental way; I have been trying to file my life since I was a child: letters, diaries, pay slips, tax demands, marriage and divorce artefacts.

One night I was in the kitchen when the dogs began barking at the big hole in the floor by the new boiler in the utility room, over which there were half a dozen little temporary boards so it was possible to step across, although part of the hole remained visible. I peered into the hole and under the boards to see if there was a mouse or a rat, but all I could see were lightbulbs. Lots and lots of lightbulbs.

When we'd moved into the house I'd put all the bulbs that were still good, which came out of all the old, discarded light fittings that had now been replaced, into a plastic bowl at the top of the stairs to the cellar. Every time I needed a new bulb, that was where I would get one. George had obviously spent a considerable amount of time emptying the bowl—there were only three lightbulbs left. He'd tucked about twenty lightbulbs beneath the pipes at the bottom of the deep hole, and he'd even included one tiny bulb still in its packet.

September

Monday 3 September

There was no denying the fact that George seemed to have it in for Mary, and it was honestly very hard to stop him when he had set his mind on something: he would remember what it was that interested him (or annoyed him) and work out how to get a closer look when possible. Or, in Mary's case, attack it. I knew that corvids were prone to holding a grudge, and so wondered if Mary had threatened George when I wasn't looking—maybe she had thrown something at him? It was strange that he picked on her with such ferocity without a reason. He was so specifically aggressive towards her—and only her; it was a source of bafflement.

One morning when Mary was leaving after a couple of hours' cleaning, he hopped up to her foot and tried to bury the bit of cardboard he was carrying between her heel and the sole of her sandal. He was pecking it in HARD. Then he dropped it, and just kept trying to get at her feet—hack, hack—and it obviously hurt since she squealed. I escorted her to her car, but he continued to flap around and around her as if he were a bee and she was covered in honey, gazing up at her head as he does when he's considering an airborne assault.

He leapt up and bounced off one of her shoulders. So, I put my arm around her and herded her to the car, shooing George off all the way, but he wouldn't leave her alone; he was as clingy as a wasp. She climbed into the driver's seat and he sat on the top of her car door so she couldn't close it without crushing his feet. She tried to push him off and he landed on her roof. Then he slid down her windscreen as if he were skiing and perched on her window wipers. He turned to face her through the glass like a creature in a mini-magpie horror movie. He was hounding her, but why? Why Mary?

Even as she slowly drove away, he ran, dancing and skipping, in front of her car as if to stop her—I chased him off over and over again, but he kept coming back and having another go and I feared she'd run over him. Out in the street Mary had to stop for him again, and I tried to grab him; but he just ran round and round the car on the ground until finally I got him to fly back over the hedge to the garden where he perched on the top of one of the gates and glared down at me. I kept an eye on him for a minute or two, but no sooner was my back turned than he flew down the road looking for Mary's car again. The aviary had now become even more urgent; this kind of harassment couldn't go on.

In an effort to get George away from his fixation with Mary, I called him to join me when I took a break for a cup of tea and a slice of sponge cake in the garden. I sat on one of the granite stools at the little round granite table I'd placed beneath the cedar tree. The three dogs and The Ex joined me, and George eagerly followed for fear of being left out. I gave everyone a bit of cake, leaving quarter of the cake on the plate. George ignored the little bit I offered him, hopped on to the table and flew off with the entire remaining piece. The Ex just sat and watched, too surprised to stop him. "He took the rest of the cake," he said, amazed.

I ran after George, leaping over flowerbeds and between bushes; he was flying low (the cake was very heavy) and I cornered him behind the garden shed. He was already tucking the cake beneath a bit of thick black plastic sheeting I had laid down to cover some weeds there (hoping they'd die). I rescued the cake, then George went back to check and see if I'd actually taken it.

That night I got out the sample of the thick welded wire mesh that I intended to use for the aviary, and, while George was roosting, much to his indignation, I took a firm hold of him and tried his head through one of the 2-inch-square holes. His head just about fitted through, but his shoulders didn't. It should be fine, I thought.

Saturday 8 September

It was while I was working in the garden that I heard shots from a nearby field. A sense of panic descended on me; I called for George and was incredibly relieved to find him hopping about beneath my garden trolley like a playful child. He danced around me most of the day, and I was happy to be able to keep him close. I left the kitchen window open too, so he could go inside when he wanted to. He came in when I stopped for a snack lunch and relieved me of a couple of bits of my cheese sandwich.

Supper was on the tiny bit of front lawn that I hadn't dug up yet. George flew to the table and did something very strange; he walked up to me and deposited a red berry—one of his favourite things in the world to play with—by my plate, stood back and looked up at me. He actually GAVE it to me. He'd never done anything like that before; usually he was a taker of things. That berry stayed there for the duration of the meal while he hopped around at the edge of my plate wanting to steal big bits of food, rather than the little bits I gave him.

When I'd finished eating, I handed him back his berry. He wouldn't take it until then. But once he had it back, he tried to find somewhere to place it.

He even tucked it—for a moment—in a fold of The Ex's shorts, by his crotch. George pulled the fold over the berry so it couldn't be seen. But he was then not happy with it, so he took it back again and tried to bury it in between the laces of The Ex's trainer. When that didn't work, he tucked it between two slats of the bench.

After supper he played with the antenna of the car, bouncing up and down on the end of it as if he were an aerial toy attached to it, then hopping off to try and pull it out of its socket before returning to bounce up and down some more as if trying to dislodge it.

Thursday 13 September

Predictably, when Mary arrived to clean again this morning, George was ready and waiting. She rang the bell when I was in the study on the first floor, so it took me a minute or two to get to the door, hurrying as quickly as I could. Puzzlingly, Mary kept on ringing and ringing the bell in a sort of mad frenzy. When I opened the door, I found her with her back pinned to it; she almost fell in on top of me. At her feet (although today she wore shoes)—glaring up at her—was George; he'd herded her neatly into a corner of the doorway and she was petrified.

As she cleaned the windows in my office upstairs, I stood in the yard and watched George follow her from window to window, flying up to the glass so he banged against it, pecking and flapping at the pane, trying to get at her. I tried telling Mary it was "unrequited love" but she wasn't fooled.

While attempting to bribe George with some dog food to leave her alone, I noticed he had a tick on his neck; I'd never seen a tick that big. It hung from the side of his neck just below his beak like a jowl, so that it would affect his jaw when he pouched food. It hadn't been noticeable the day before; maybe it hadn't been there, or wasn't big enough to be noticed. I tried to catch George in a towel, but he wasn't having it; he flew into every shelf, corner and other hiding place. I realised I'd have to wait until he settled down to sleep at night.

But that evening I ended up stalking him around and around the kitchen as he hopped ferociously ahead of me; we did twenty rounds of the central island before I doubled back and trapped him beneath a shirt. Oh, that bird could bite if he didn't want to be caught. The only way to achieve anything when holding him was to simply bear the pain, and it hurt.

I sprayed his backside with a tick and flea spray, then tried to get hold of the gigantic blood-bellied tick on his neck with tweezers. But while George was trying to take my fingers off with the scissors of his beak it wasn't possible.

With a piece of kitchen roll, I firmly gripped the tick between my fingertips. George was struggling with such ferocity that I feared he might snap a vertebra. It was a shame he wasn't so tame any more that he just cocked his head to one side so I could divest him of parasites more easily.

Carefully, I pulled the tick off, certain I got the head. The tick was easily the size of the top of my little finger. I could see black legs as thin as hairs, and so small that they were barely visible, dangling from the pointier end. I needed a magnifying glass to see its bits, but oh, the sac was massive. I popped it in the sheet of kitchen roll and squeezed; it exploded in a puddle of George's blood.

I held George to try and calm him down, but he screeched and snapped. Thinking on my feet, I dispensed three tiny drops of peach schnapps down his throat with a pipette and it seemed to calm him. I reckoned that after sipping white window paint, wood preserver, wet cement and waterproofing agent, a bit of peach schnapps wasn't going to kill him. It was a minute bit; literally drops. Honest.

When I put George back in his cage I wondered if he had squealed at being picked up because he hated it, or because I was messing up his now immaculate feathers, because he then spent ten minutes reorganising every strand of plumage afterwards. He also kept scratching the sides of his head, first one side, then the other, dropping each wing to scratch over the top of it, and wobbling only slightly, perhaps as a result of the schnapps. Anyway, he seemed much happier after a thorough preening, and let me stroke his head without snapping at me, as if we were friends again. Before I went to bed, I touched up George's neck with a bit of disinfectant on an earbud, thinking that, at this rate, he might become very keen to leave home.

*

September was racing by, and I had no idea how much longer I had with George if he was ever to fly free for good. But I promised myself that if he was still here when the aviary was finished and hadn't flown off, then that would become his home. Deep down, as much as I wanted to keep him, this was NOT the future I wished for him.

Friends came to stay, kept their opinions about my feathered house guest to themselves, and left, some never to be heard from again. One friend told me, years later, that she'd thought my house was disgusting. A live, native bird as house guest was beyond her tolerance level, despite the fact that any droppings were immediately wiped up with a spray of disinfectant. Of course, I was also still living on a building site, which may have coloured her judgement. She hasn't been here since.

Sunday 16 September

The garden was beginning to exhaust me; every week it seemed that I needed to mix another ton of sand and cement to make another rough stone wall. So, I forced myself to work steadily out there all day, not daring to stop or I wouldn't be able to get going again. Except for sitting on the kitchen sofa with a cup of hot tea, while it pelted with torrential rain outside for just fifteen minutes. Of course, the ground was soaked when it stopped, but the earth smelt fresh and fragrant, and the plants glittered with translucent droplets.

While I sat with the dogs, George unpicked both my shoelaces with astonishing intent. When he'd undone the first one I did it up again, then filmed him going back to repeat the job, and undo the other shoe too. I noticed how the dogs were increasingly wary of him now, because he was a bit snippy with that beak of his.

It seemed to have become much sharper at the point and the edges were like knives.

Thursday 20 September

By now, although I had made real headway in the garden, I felt quite depressed. I thought that maybe I was mentally overtired, because in addition to my aggressive back pain and being physically exhausted from the daily labour, I was writing a newspaper column and various other articles to keep the money coming in, as well as running the massive ramshackle lump of a house. I was the one to plan out and draw up the diagrams for everything that went into it, from the electrical layout and the plumbing layout to the heating layout, as the house was slowly renovated in the background of my life with George.

Although I was delighted when the *Daily Mail* agreed to publish a series of four articles I'd written about building and planting my garden, and I'd finished two more articles for *The Times*, sometimes I felt overwhelmed; I needed to be three people to keep on top of everything. I was stretched to breaking point—and then there was the secret that I had been keeping from everyone who knew me, with the exception of one friend in the States in whom I confided by phone . . . the fact that, as happy as we often were, my marriage to The Ex was slowly crumbling.

Every small success I had seemed to push him away from me because he had no equivalent, and the financial disparity between us had become a chasm. This only appeared to exacerbate his desire to return to Australia "when he got old," which was increasingly "now." In Australia he had history, connections, relative success and an artistic base. Here, he felt dependent on me for all that, and I couldn't supply it; he had to craft his own.

*

This morning George was ripping shreds out of a newspaper, while the dogs were tearing around with their lifesize grey dead-cat toy; the three of them carried it together, tugging at its limbs, sharing the cat in their sharp little jaws as if it was too heavy for just one of them. The rest of the world seemed less important when I saw them playing like that, but often, now, I just wanted to sit and weep, because I knew my relationship with The Ex had changed and that there was nothing I could do about it. I knew that the more I succeeded in anything, the bigger the rift, and I strived to succeed even when I didn't feel to be getting anywhere. I had to keep trying; it's in my nature to do so.

My marriage would only thrive—and it would only be on borrowed time because it would mean I wasn't paying attention to my own work—if I arranged art exhibitions for The Ex, and if he sold paintings. But I'd already been through that in London, and his paintings, as marvellous as they were, hadn't sold; he didn't have a history here, no one knew about him.

I wasn't, however, ready to shatter the illusion of our happy coupledom—which had once been so true—and damage whatever social life we had by sharing my problems. It was going to remain my secret for now; the thing I couldn't fix.

It was possible, of course, that I could still fix things for George. The idea of his little heartbeat, the warmth of his body, the grip of his feet on my shoulder or knee, filled me with happiness. But every day that passed dragged me nearer to his incarceration.

I made the overripe bananas, which had been going black in a bowl beside George's cage, into a banana ice, with three tins of evaporated milk. Even as I made it, I doubted the recipe because evaporated milk was something I never used. I didn't even know why I had tins of evaporated milk!

George flew in through the window and perched on the toaster to watch me; I'd covered the toaster with a tea towel just in case.

Then I tested the banana mix on him by giving him some on a spoon. He couldn't get enough of it, so I guessed it was all right. Because he was there, with me, I thought that he was less likely to get himself into trouble today. But I was wrong: he flew at Bernie, the plumber, as soon as he arrived. Bernie was slowly working his way through the house, putting in radiators, boiler, showers, baths and basins . . . for years I'd collected second-hand basins, along with second-hand light fittings and curtains, and had half a dozen beautiful marble basins from a display in a shop in London. (The pack-rat renovator in me had come into its own.)

Bernie came indoors to complain that George was attacking him. George, however, having bounced off his head, had now lost interest in Bernie because he'd found a new toy—the entire contents in the back of Bernie's pickup. All day George lived in those open boxes of tools of Bernie's; all the things he could possibly want to steal were in one place, packed and ready for transport. All he had to do was learn to drive the truck.

The only thing that distracted him was Mary's arrival and departure when she came to clean, and I had to closely shield her to and from her car as George launched a concentrated assault on her person, trying to get past my arms and legs to get at Mary's.

The post holders for the aviary arrived today and would be closely followed by the posts and the mesh. George's days of freedom were numbered.

We'd had gigantic ravioli parcels for lunch, and I couldn't finish mine, so covered my dish with a towel and left it by the kettle to finish later. But George helped himself from beneath the towel, sliding his beak in first, and pulling out one enormous ravioli after another. I found him hauling a huge one around the floor with the dogs in ever-hopeful pursuit. When I looked to see what was left, George had taken *all* but the very last piece.

And when finally I came in from the garden and sat down to glance at the newspaper on the kitchen table, I found George had tucked a dog biscuit into the pages, and I noticed a shredded bit of ravioli tucked into the collar of an old work shirt that hung over the back of the chair next to me.

The trouble was, George was a joker and he encouraged others to join in his games.

Saturday 22 September

We were going out for the evening, and I went to check on George in the kitchen and shut the window. I found the kitchen in a terrible mess. As well as the usual magpie shit, which required immediate removal, George had found the matches I'd hidden in a little pot on some kitchen shelves—he'd destroyed the box on a previous occasion, so I'd saved the matches; now he'd tipped the pot all over the floor and there were matches everywhere, then he'd pulled all the tissues out of the tissue box, one by one until the box was empty, so the dogs had shredded them and the kitchen looked as if it had been hit by a snowstorm. George was standing on the middle seat of the sofa, legs akimbo, and a whole doggy-snack Schmacko as long as a pencil in his beak. Snickers and Widget were pawing the sofa from their positions on the floor, surrounded by tissue-snow in anticipation of George's better nature (only I don't think George had one of those). George seemed fascinated by the fact that he had the dogs' undivided attention and appeared to relish the power he held over them by being the possessor of one of their favourite foodstuffs, which he refused to share with them. Quickly, I divested him of the Schmacko and cleaned up the magpie poo, but I had to leave the rest until later. I couldn't catch him so knew I'd have to leave him to roost at dusk when I'd be able to get hold of him.

But there was more chaos when we got back from our evening;

an unopened packet of mini-CDs for the camcorder lay on the floor and was now fully opened, because the dogs had chewed off all the cardboard. Two big kitchen-size boxes of matches that were weighted down with a tin of beer on another shelf (to stop George dismembering them) were on the floor. The can of beer had rolled to the other side of the room and both boxes of matches sported capacious beak holes. One of the boxes was slightly open and several of the matches had been taken out and sprinkled around the floor amongst the shredded tissues. The loaf of bread that sat in its plastic wrapper at one end of a kitchen unit had moved to the other end. George flew to the spade-handle perch that rose from a wooden block beside Mouse's basket, and sat there as if butter wouldn't melt . . . the cape of feathers that lay beneath his wings was shuffled to spread over his back in a fluffy, blotchy cloud as if to say, "I'm not in, don't bother me." Cleaning up seemed to take me forever. He watched me for as long as it took.

And I had to clean up thoroughly, because an art dealer was coming to look at my paintings with a view to giving me an exhibition. I would have liked to have a clean kitchen and polite dogs, but instead I had a magpie that led them astray, dragging chaos behind him like a train. At least I had finished paintings for the art dealer to look at.

Sunday 23 September

I took The Ex and the art dealer to supper at the pub down the road, and the barmaid told me that her daughter had a six-week-old puppy, and that George had paid the pup a visit this morning while it was romping in their back garden. This worried me further, because George was becoming part of other people's lives, and he seemed to have a righteous sense of entitlement that might get his little head bitten off by a dog that didn't give a damn.

When we returned home, I wanted to let George back inside because it was raining hard. I called and called until he came, and when he did, oh, what a soggy little creature he was. He hadn't sheltered at all, and seemed overjoyed to be indoors, hopping around and perching by the Rayburn, playing with the dogs and skittering around the floor like a wringing-wet black-and-white rag. When he settled on the back of a kitchen chair, he systematically ran every feather within reach—tail, wing, chest—through the blades of his beak, getting rid of as much water as possible until there was a puddle beneath him.

Wednesday 26 September

Today I was seized with the urge to get the aviary for George under way no matter what. After all, I'd planned it out and arranged a man to help me build it. I'd also ordered and received the Metpost concreting spikes, so all I now had to arrange was the delivery of the wood, the welded mesh, the nail plates, screws, a brad gun and cement. George, being extremely intelligent, treated me differently when I had to shut him in his cage for longer than normal (or perhaps he could tell I was up to something), or if I kept him in the kitchen during the day without opening the window; he ignored me, wouldn't come when I called, wouldn't play with me, and doubled his attention in every other direction.

I'd recently bought the biggest dog cage I could get, so I could put his little dog cage inside it. Then, when I let him out of the little dog cage in the morning, although he wouldn't be going outside, he would have the run of the bigger cage. That way I wouldn't feel so guilty shutting him up if I went away for the day, and didn't want him loose to trash the kitchen. He was now too dexterous and creative to leave loose in a room full of potentially dangerous objects without supervision.

But when he found he was in a cage within a cage, he hated it. He opened his beak slightly, which I'd come to learn was a sign of panic. He jumped around in the cage and tested the bars, sticking his head through to see if he'd fit. Fortunately, although his head did, the rest of him didn't no matter how he stretched, pushed and craned his neck. He sat on top of his small cage; then, from time to time, dropped to the newspaper-covered floor of the big cage, making a tremendous bad-tempered metallic thump. He was very, very angry.

I put some plastic spray-paint lids and a kitchen-roll cardboard tube into the cage, so he had something to destroy. And I hung an old pair of safety goggles on the inside, so he had something to hack at. And he did. He attacked those goggles as if Mary was wearing them.

Thursday 27 September

Just before I left for London with The Ex, I put George's small cage, still covered in a towel, in the new big cage (I'd chosen one big enough for a St. Bernard) with the door open. But he was so active and frantic to escape that I couldn't bear it, so I covered the big cage up with a blanket, because he's much calmer in the gloom. I consoled myself that he had more room to hop about, with food, water and the objects I'd thrown in for him to play with.

When we got back, I saw that he was roosting inside the little cage inside the big cage. I shut the door of the little cage, pulled it out and put him back on the sideboard. George actually seemed interested to see me, sticking his head through the bars inquisitively to have a look at me. I folded the other cage away; it took up a vast amount of space.

Friday 28 September

The wood for the aviary arrived. I made tea and coffee for the driver and his mate as they unloaded, and Bernie the plumber, who was standing knee-deep in a muddy trench working on the new water pipe to the house, which ran right through the aviary.

The skip on the back drive was the table, full of rubbish as it always was. Its position afforded a good view of the back of the house and we all stood there in the sun, drinking our steaming mugs of tea and surveying the muddy pit now measuring about 21 by 28 feet. Before, it had been a large, paved area, with ugly flowerbeds full of ground elder and brambles. Somehow, this rectangular quagmire was going to become an area of raised flowerbeds, with garden fabric to separate the new soil from the old weed-infested dirt.

In retaining walls of smooth river stones, I would plant a forest of bushes and little trees for George to play in; I wanted to create an oasis for him. There would be a pond at the far end and the aviary would be an impressive 12 feet high. I would grow ivy and clematis up the support posts and turn it into a leafy green room.

George flew over and landed on the edge of the skip. He eyed the truck driver intently: a middle-aged Welshman in a flat cap. The truck driver stared back, somewhat perplexed at the proximity of a magpie. I explained that George was a pet, and then had to apologise in advance for George bouncing off his head, as I noticed George's beady eye fix on top of the man's hat; that bird was so predictable. George hopped down on the ground from the side of the skip, his gaze still directed at the flat cap. Then he jumped up on to the neighbours' green post-and-rail fence, before hopping back on to the edge of the skip, as if deciding that this was the best situation to eye up his opportunity.

Then he had it; he jumped to the ground near the truck driver's feet and stood for a second, before flying up to the man's cap. Having landed, he pushed his feet like pistons out from his body, launching himself off the back of the man's head. The truck driver stood there with an inscrutable expression on his face. Once the jump had been completed, George left him alone. The truck driver expressed surprise, however, that a magpie, a notoriously wary bird, was sitting there staring at him from the back end of a 6-yard skip.

My days now vanished in the push to cage George. Every day I had to tackle the stuff that was in the way: pots, rocks, and bags of rubble.

October

Monday 1 October

The first day of the week and the first day of a new month. I resolved to try and organise myself better, because I felt I wasn't focused enough to be as effective as I ought to be when I was working either in the office, study, studio or garden, and writing my diary was taking far, far too long, because I wrote so much about George in it, recording his baby steps, playful actions and inspired aerobatics.

When I let George out at eight o'clock this morning, he didn't just take a couple of HiLife doggy nibbles from my hand as usual, he took as many as he could stuff into the pouch of his beak until his jaw was bulging like a carrier bag full of tin cans. He was back tapping at the window when I was chewing my way through a bit of toast for breakfast, but I couldn't let him in because Mary was going to be here, and I thought that one more attack from George would persuade her to hand in her notice.

He flew down to join me at the back of the house when I was digging in the mud where the aviary would be. I'd point out some tiny spider or bug with my black-rubber-gloved finger and he'd take it in the pointy tip of his beak, as if picking up beads with a pair of tweezers. Then he turned his attention to my wheelbarrow, rummaging among the cuttings like someone in the bargain bin at a knicker shop, tossing clumps of earth from one side to the other in his search for hidden insects and worms, hopping between the handles of the wheelbarrow and on to the handle of my shovel. Eventually he disappeared and I felt suddenly lonely. His absence left a palpable empty space.

However, when Mary left I opened the kitchen window, and when I came down to the kitchen to make a cup of tea during my "office time" in the evening, there he was, sitting on his spade-handle perch above the dogs' beds. He must have been in for a while because the five tatty grapes that The Ex was going to throw out, which I saved for him, were gone from the little dish on the table. I hoped he'd buried them somewhere outside, or I'd be forever opening gardening books with rotting grapes stuffed into their spines.

I poured him milk in his tiny, narrow, magpie-size glass, and he drank from it, wiping his beak on the toaster afterwards.

I had just finished reading a newspaper article at the kitchen table, when George hopped on to the folder in which I keep notes of the work I'm doing on the back yard; it lay on the chair beside me. Fascinated, I watched as he tugged at the bits of A4 paper and newspaper clippings that I had heaped on top of the folder. They were too heavy a pile for him to shift all at once, and I was surprised that he didn't take just one bit and fly off with it as he sometimes did. Instead, he got hold of all the papers and cuttings and lifted them in his beak to the full extent of his neck and looked at me accusingly. Then he stepped forward, his feet and body pushing the wedge of paper in his beak towards me, and looked right at me as if to say, "HOLD THESE FOR ME."

So I did: I took hold of the edge of the wedge of papers and held them up for him. He dived back down under them to the top edge of my folder, slipped his beak beneath the cover, and pulled out a big chunk of the cheesy toast I'd given him last night: the added weight of the sheaf of papers that I'd put on top had made it too hard for him to reach in and get it. I could feel my jaw drop slightly at the calculated manner in which he not only retrieved his food but requested my complicity, having remembered where he'd hidden his snack several hours ago.

I was further impressed when he flew outside during the early evening as we were getting ready to eat, and *brought back* the packet of 3-amp fuses that he'd stolen earlier from the utility room. He also took out a dog chew that I'd given him a couple of days ago, which he'd hidden in the folds of some rags.

I was outside later, stealing time from my "office hours" to spray-paint lines in the back-yard aviary area to mark out where I wanted to build raised flowerbeds. I could see George inside, standing on the sill of the window in the utility room, watching me as I got wetter and wetter in the pouring rain. He was shaking his feathers and preening; I swear he was laughing. It was incongruous: me outside getting wet, and George, the magpie, inside keeping nice and dry.

The rain was torrential throughout the evening but huddled in the kitchen with me were The Ex; Widget, Snickers and Mouse in their baskets; and George on his perch between them. The pounding of water against the two enormous sash windows was relentless and made me grateful that the leak in the roof had been fixed—and that George hadn't managed to scare off the roofer.

Tuesday 2 October

For the time being I managed to keep the bubble of my life intact: my job with *The Times* seemed safe; George was still with me; my autobiographical poetry collection, *45*, had been published in the United States and was selling; and my new collection, *The Book of Mirrors*, would soon be published too. My chronic fatigue relapse seemed to have abated, although my back pain was getting worse. But if I rested and didn't move, it made life even more painful— again, it seemed that if I could be in a state of perpetual motion I could keep the pain at a lower, more manageable, level.

This morning, after getting to bed very late, I slept like a log, which meant that I didn't move during the night and had stiffened up. I had to drag myself out of bed, and roll on to the floor before I could eventually stand; everything ached: back, legs, shoulders. I managed to get dressed and let George out of the kitchen window.

He soon joined me in the little back garden where I was digging out what would become flowerbeds inside the aviary, having finally got my joints working again. Once I'd got going there was no stopping me; I felt as if I was in a race for time but wasn't able to work out what caused that feeling. I lived with a sense that time was literally whistling past my ears and the sooner I achieved the thing I aimed to achieve, the sooner I could stop. I still feel that way. But at the end there is always another challenge—and another (all self-inflicted)—so there is no end to the race against time for me.

All day I worked on filling potting-compost bags with the ground-elder-infested earth, so it would be ready to chuck in the skip when it had been emptied.

Every time I sat down for a minute to catch my breath, George came and sat on my knee, or hopped around me, picking up little spiders and bugs, and pecking bits out of the wall of the house that he thought might be interesting.

As soon as I'd climbed out of my mud-encrusted boots at dusk, I spent a couple of hours going over the last draft of my poetry column for the following week's Monday *Times 2* section. (John Donne's "The Flea," where the speaker appears to have pseudo-sex by means of a flea drinking blood from both him and his beloved—I couldn't resist it.)

Marke but this flea, and marke in this,
How little that which thou deny'st me is;
It suck'd me first, and now sucks thee,
And in this flea, our two bloods mingled bee;
A sinne, nor shame, nor loss of maidenhead,
> Yet this enjoyes before it wooe,
> And pamper'd swells with one blood made of two
> And this, alas, is more than wee would doe.

Oh stay, three lives in one flea spare,
Where wee almost, yea more than maryed are.
This flea is you and I, and this
Our mariage bed, and mariage temple is;
Though parents grudge, and you, w'are met,
And cloystered in these living walls of jet.

How to write about having sex, without having sex.

Being dyslexic, I have to check everything I do over and over again, never certain if I've missed something that needs attention, so everything takes longer than I would like it to. This need to work was in direct conflict with the unshakeable feeling that the sooner I finished the aviary, the sooner I could stop worrying about George's safety and the wrath of my neighbours.

In order to build George's aviary, I'd had to anticipate any work that might need to be done in that area later on—and get it done now, such as the new mains water line. The other big thing was putting in a new power cable, so that the four electricity meters in the house, left over from its life as four flats, could be replaced by one meter. Then there was the need to repair the very handsome and capacious brick Victorian sewage pipe, some parts of which were broken, and the installation of new inspection hatches. And finally, the removal of several tons of earth riddled with ground elder. George's cage was pushing me to resolve all kinds of issues with the house that I'd have preferred to leave until later. Much later.

Thursday 4 October

When I let George out today, he disappeared and didn't come home until late; there was none of his usual playing around with me outside. He returned just before dark, flying in through the open kitchen window, and settled down for the night. It lent me a sense of unease, because all-day disappearances weren't normal. Did he have "rounds" he had to do now, visiting various neighbours who had become part of his expanding territory? He certainly spent a lot of time with the workmen building the house at the bottom of the cul-de-sac.

I don't believe in jealousy—it is a destructive, futile emotion and we should be happy for the success and happiness of others— but I felt pangs of it when I imagined George paying the kind of attention to strangers that I'd like to think he reserved for only me.

Friday 5 October

So, I was watchful when I let George out today. I observed how he stuffed his face with doggy nibbles from the palm of my hand as if he were packing for a very, very long journey. Then he vanished. He didn't come back in the late morning as he usually did. He didn't come back at lunchtime as he usually did. He didn't come back all afternoon or come for a walk with the dogs around six, as he usually did. I called and called to the open sky, but in my heart I felt he wasn't going to come; my mind kept going over the way he'd literally stuffed his face with food as he left. I sensed a disturbing absence in the air; the space he left in my day was huge. I carried on working out the back, digging holes in the yard ready for the uprights of the aviary, but every now and then I'd stop to whistle for him. He didn't come, and my sense of foreboding intensified as the hours passed.

I hoped that when I got indoors George had put himself to bed as he usually did, but he wasn't there, or anywhere in the kitchen. I took the three little white dogs out for a walk around the garden, to see if the sight of them could tempt him out of the branches of nearby trees, but George didn't join us. I imagined his little head bobbing at the kitchen window wanting to be let in, but he didn't appear. I fervently hoped that he'd come home the following day; I remembered he had returned after being shut out for one whole night in the early days. If he didn't come back this time, then I'd really believe he was dead. It was too sudden a break for him to make otherwise; surely he would stay away just now and then, like a teenager going off to college and coming home in the holidays, breaking me in gently, until finally he stayed away completely?

That night I was heartbroken. I feared George was dead. I cried while I watered the pots in the front yard, I cried while cuddling the dogs on the sofa in front of an open kitchen window. The dogs and I waited for George, but he never came; there was no familiar thud on the window frame as he landed, peering into the room to see where we all were and where to fly next. Sometimes he'd simply soar straight in through the narrowest of gaps, to land on the toaster or the microwave.

The dogs window-watched until I closed it long after nightfall. Dismally, I ate some turkey soup that I'd defrosted from the freezer—so I knew how old *that* was. I cuddled the dogs as usual, but there was no George to perch on my foot or to pull Widget's tail. I wished I could stop weeping; my eyes were raw.

Earlier, I'd asked a neighbour who had recently moved into the street with his wife, if he'd seen George today. He hadn't. But he did say that George had once jumped on his back. Oh dear. But he insisted that he hadn't minded. He told me about a magpie he'd had when he was fifteen. He'd kept it for two years in an aviary. But it used to bite when people gave it food (George didn't) and was always bad-tempered. I smiled inwardly; magpies, I think, are so smart that they grow furious when they realise they're prisoners. Something chewed a hole in the aviary one day, and his magpie got out. He tried to tempt it back with food, but it flew away and never came back. I think his magpie got out the wire cutters.

Saturday 6 October

I'm ashamed to say that having gone to bed in tears the night before, I woke up in tears. If George was a little shit, I'd be glad for him to go off all of a sudden without even a goodbye. If he trashed the kitchen daily and pecked me, and grouched and spat, then he could stay away. But he didn't; he'd sit on top of the kettle and drink milk from the tiny glass that I held up for him. He took food from my fingers; he watched me cook from the top of the storage jars; he sat on his perch among the dog beds when the weather was horrible outside. He was a member of my little family, and I felt his loss in ways I couldn't explain.

I got up and opened the kitchen window first thing and left it open all day but there was no sign of George. It was really cold too, but I didn't care; the dogs kept close to the Rayburn, which took the chill off the kitchen.

Tears were an intermittent problem as I worked in the office. I felt as if my best friend had died. Every day George had played with me, been a companion with the dogs, and kept me company in the garden. He even visited me when I was upstairs, flying up to the window of whichever room I was in; there's something very endearing about a little buddy who can do that. The dogs were gorgeous, constant friends and I loved them dearly, but George was a wild creature that I brought in to live with us, and who had, until now, chosen to stay. If only I knew that he was still alive.

In the early evening, I asked The Ex if he wanted to come out in the garden with a cup of tea. Although cold, the sun was lovely.

In the beginning, we had been a real team, working for a future life together. But I was once asked by a friend, who is a psychologist, what state The Ex and I were both in when we met in Australia. We met the week I was diagnosed with a twisted bowel that required emergency surgery and had been starving me for months as it prevented me eating—a simple sandwich would land me in hospital—and I was already in my second year of chronic fatigue. But I was happy—if somewhat skinny—and loved life, and painting, and writing, and my little single-storey home on the edge of the bush in Western Australia.

"You were seriously ill, then," observed my friend, "and so you were equal. Then you got better!" It was true, the roller-coaster Frieda wasn't something The Ex had been expecting when he moved in with the Frieda afflicted with chronic fatigue and a stapled abdomen following bowel surgery, although the fact I was landscaping his garden with a pickaxe, and moving blocks of sandstone to build him a raised lawn before they took the staples out, should have given him a clue.

We'd paint together in his studio; he was the only person who knew about my chronic fatigue (apart from my American friend). Whenever I passed out with the sudden closing-down of all my senses, falling on to a mattress beside my easel that he'd kindly supplied, I'd wake up to find he'd taken the paintbrush out of my hand and put it in white spirit for me, often leaving lunch of a ham roll at my elbow.

Now I longed for the camaraderie we'd had during those early days before everything became unequal. So, feeling deeply sorrowful about George's absence, The Ex was the one I turned to, and there were moments like this when the inconsistencies in our union fell away.

My father once told me that a woman should never be more successful than her man. Despite my protestations of equality, he insisted that evolution had decreed that the man must be the provider. Of dead bison many years ago, and now, of a living wage and a roof over the family heads.

The Ex and I sat at the bottom of the garden by the summerhouse, in a circle of small shrubs that surrounded two wooden garden chairs. This spot got the last of the afternoon sun, and I thought it would be comforting. The warm air softened everything and seemed to slow down time itself; for a moment, I relaxed. Until I heard the dogs bark frantically from the kitchen. The Ex went inside to find out what had disturbed them, while I tried to control the surge of hope I felt that it might be George. Reluctantly, I followed, and, on the way back to the house, potted up a couple of cuttings; I desperately didn't want to go into the kitchen and be disappointed. The Ex came to the front door and beckoned. Is George in? I asked, trying to quell my fear that the commotion was for something else entirely. He nodded. It was six thirty and getting dark fast; we were losing daylight every twenty-four hours as we hurtled into winter.

My mouth was unbearably dry as I approached the house. I found George sitting on top of the water-purifier jug in the kitchen, legs splayed, head cocked to one side. I almost cried with relief; I wanted to fling my arms around his tiny frame. I got his little glass of milk from the fridge and held it out for him. He guzzled. I made the dogs sit for salt-free cashews, and George lined up too, snatching at them as if he was starving.

Because George hadn't been in all day, I'd left a bowl of stuffed olives out, covered only by cling film, which was no defence against George's incisive beak. He helped himself to a massive olive, then tortured the dogs—who tracked his every move—by burying it in one of the dog baskets, before digging it out again when he thought they'd actually find it, and trying to hide it here, there and everywhere. Tonight, he was really keen to take food from me. It was so interesting to note how he, smart bird that he was, took the HiLife doggy nibbles, which had got a bit dry, and dropped them in the dogs' water bowl so they softened, then took them out to dismember them on the edge of the bowl before swallowing them.

I offered him the milk again, when he was down by the microwave. He leapt on to the storage jars and pat-patted down the whole row before coming to a halt on the handle of a metal kettle that sat on top of the cooker. I put the little glass on the countertop, but he didn't want to jump down for it; he tilted his head (which made me think he was shaking his head) and looked at me meaningfully until I lifted the glass to his beak so he could drink from his perch. He had me well trained.

Sunday 7 October

I let George out first thing and prayed he'd come home that night. Once out of the kitchen window and perched on the back of the bench there, he turned and again stuffed his beak with as many doggy nibbles as he could from the heap in the palm of my hand as if he were taking a packed lunch on a long journey. It was the same on Thursday, when he was out all day and didn't come back until six. And on Friday, when he didn't come back at all. Today he didn't come back during the day, but arrived in the kitchen at about ten to six—I came in to find him perched on the toaster with his right foot tucked up. For one awful moment, I thought he'd lost a leg, but he'd done something to his foot that made him tuck it away when he wasn't actually using it to balance or land. He was rather distant, but happy to take cashews from me—which he snatched, eagerly—and he lined up with the dogs to have doggy snacks of cheese or ham.

He pulled the tinfoil lid off the bottle of milk that I'd forgotten to put away (we still had deliveries of the old-fashioned kind at this point) and raised himself to his full height to get his head into the top of the bottle; to my horror, his entire head slid down inside the wide neck, squashing his eyeballs up against the glass in a grue-some way, and I had to grab the bottle and gently pull his head out, fearful of him getting stuck with the suction and having to smash the bottle so he could get air.

George
24/3/20

Then I filled his usual little glass with milk and left it for him, but no, that wouldn't do; he perched on the toaster again and waited, looking at it, then me, meaningfully, just like last time. It seemed he would only be happy if I held it up so he could guzzle it; he was like a little vacuum pump, sucking it up then throwing his head back so it ran down his throat.

I took some more footage of George playing with the dogs, teasing Widget by flying at a low level so that she could get him if he were any slower on the wing, with cheese in his beak that Widget wanted to take from him. He flew off to the sofa with it, with Widget pounding her tiny legs to catch up with him, then trying to lick the cheese out of his beak. George stood on the arm of the sofa making little cooing noises like a pigeon, then he dropped the cheese, pecked at Widget so she leapt off the sofa with a shrill squeal, picked up the cheese again, and leapt on to the floor with it, his feet already running. He scuttled across the dark oak floor-boards with Widget in hot pursuit.

She chased George as he flew around the kitchen island just above floor level. George disappeared to the far side of the island, then there was a moment's silence during which I have no idea what happened, and Widget emerged triumphant, chewing George's cheese.

When George had roosted in his cage, I plucked him off his perch to examine his foot. There was nothing wrong with his beak, and he could just about crack bones with it; I had dents in my finger flesh after I examined him to find that he had a little blood by his back claw. But the rest of the foot seemed OK. Maybe I should have just dunked the foot in diluted disinfectant; that would have woken him up! He must have spent half an hour readjusting his plumage when I put him back on his perch. I stroked his obstinate little head gently, so I wouldn't knock him over or upset his hair-do.

He was back, but now so were my concerns for his safety—and his new-found independence only underlined my grinding reluctance to put him in the aviary, which was now well on the way to completion.

Monday 8 October

George flew out on to the forecourt this morning, instead of racing back over the top of the house and away. I realised I was watching for warning signs of his possible desertion.

He played outside in the front yard for a bit, and when I got back from fetching the newspapers, he came and sat on a rock by the car and preened himself, fluffing himself up like a little feathery balloon. Then he suddenly vanished.

I didn't see him again until quarter to six exactly. I called for him, and he came to the window within a few minutes, but I suspect it was a coincidence. He bounced in and took the piece of well-cooked spiral pasta that I held out for him. Then ensued a feed-or-flight game between George and Widget around the kitchen floor, the sofa and the dogs' beds. George took food from me all evening and stuffed it everywhere. And when I toasted a sandwich he was ready and waiting; he snatched at it eagerly until I gave him bits of it.

He also drank milk from his little glass on the kitchen table, and took some of the last grapes from the bowl there. I filmed him, even though for some time he'd just sit and let Widget try to eat whatever he had in his beak. It struck me as odd that Widget had taken Snickers's place in this favourite game. Dusk fell quickly. George finished playing and sat on the sofa looking out of the window. It was such a poignant sight; George, sitting motionless among the cushions, his little beak upturned, gazing up at the sky above as if with some deep longing, watching it change from clouded blue, to violet-grey, to inky Prussian blue. This, he'd never done before.

The dark drew in very fast, and it was only a couple of minutes before George was harder to see in the gloom—I still hadn't put the kitchen lights on. I felt as if he was pining for something that called to him from very far away.

Then, when it was really charcoal-grey outside, he turned, hopped off the sofa and on to the floor, and pat-patted across to the sideboard where his cage was. I could just see him peering through the gloom, upwards. He hopped in front of the cage's open door and stood there for a while, as if wondering why he was doing this. It was as if he answered some compulsion that he was now beginning to question. Then he stumbled forward on to the newspaper-covered floor of the cage and hopped on to his perch. I heard the comforting sound of the rapid scratching of his head, followed by the whirring ruffle of his feathers as he fluffed his under-feathers out over the top of his wings like a shawl.

In the dark, I stroked him oh, so gently, then I shut him in for the night, and covered his cage. I had an unshakeable sense that I was about to lose him for good.

Tuesday 9 October

Despite my fears, George came back inside for a while during the morning, because he didn't like the pelting rain. It was almost enough to lull me into a false sense of security. I gave him little bits of my toast and marmalade, but he had other ideas: he flew out through the window with an entire marmalade soldier flapping out of the sides of his beak. I was laughing too much to rescue it. Two minutes later he was back to try and steal another one, hopping about the side of my plate, waiting for a moment when my guard dropped and I was distracted long enough for him to leap forward for his prize. When I ate the last marmalade soldier he watched every mouthful as if in disbelief, until it was all gone.

Pelting rain meant a day in the office for me. When the weather cleared up a bit after an hour or so, I found George had vanished from the kitchen. I didn't see him again until I went back down for a break from the office at six fifteen. He couldn't have been home for long, as there wasn't much bird shit. Six fifteen at this time of year seemed to be his trigger for sleep, because it was dusk so early.

Again, I filmed him for a bit, because he was trying to bury a dog chew the size and shape of the sole of a shoe, in the gap between the front of the sofa and Widget's little brown velvet stool, which was pushed up tight against it. Then he taunted Widget with pieces of leftover toast that he took from the bowl I'd started leaving out for him. He killed a couple of grapes on the top of the kettle, then pulled a candle (from the latest power cut) off its little wax fixing in a dish on the table, and carried it all around the kitchen trying to find somewhere it would fit. He tried to find a slot in the dog basket Mouse used, then beneath a cushion on the sofa, then beneath the old T-shirts in a little basket I'd put on the floor for him to play with, and finally behind the woolly padded work shirt that hung on the back of the door to the utility room, where there is a set of three parallel hooks; the candle nestled neatly in the cradle of the hooks behind the collar of the shirt.

When I'd filmed him for half an hour, I spent another half an hour doing a series of quick sketches of him, because I felt that time with him was limited. He loved being sketched; he pranced and danced and played, he tried to pull the sketchbook out of my hands, he peered quizzically and cutely at me, he pulled the tea towel off the toaster, and all the time he got closer and closer to me. He was much more at ease and much happier when my attention was focused entirely on him.

Then he put himself away in his cage like a good boy. But only after he'd taken my teabag out of my tea, which was brewing in a mug beside the kettle. I looked up, and there he was, staring at me from the toaster, with the hot, steaming teabag hanging from his beak by a corner, dripping back into the cup. He dropped the teabag on the counter beside the cup and hopped off to bed.

George
4/9/19

Wednesday 10 October

I was shattered when John finished working on the aviary at five. I'd
mixed six full barrow loads of concrete for him to fix the Metposts
in for the uprights. Then I spent the late afternoon rewriting my
Times article over and over again to get it perfect. I waterproofed
the four 2-foot-tall terracotta pots that I'd had delivered with the
marlin fountain (three leaping marlin that spout water), which
I'd just bought from the Derwen Garden Centre. I'd wanted that
fountain for three years, and my patience had been rewarded. (I got
a good deal as one of the marlin had lost 6 inches off the end of

its nose.) It was going in the koi pond that I intended to build in the aviary using river-rounded stones set in smoothed concrete to form an undulating wall on the outside, with a rectangular shape of Butyl-lined brickwork on the inside. The image that I had so clearly fixed in my head was hugely motivating.

When I took a break to walk the dogs around the garden, I called for George. He didn't appear.

If he left and was alive then I was happy for him; that's what I kept telling myself. I had already decided that I would still build the aviary anyway, even without George, because it's the perfect dog run for tiny dogs, and I wanted to make it a true wonderland by growing clematis up and over the welded mesh. It would feel like a room on the back of the house, and it would be somewhere to keep the koi safe from the heron that visits the pond in the front garden once a year, to pilfer my goldfish. So, I owed George thanks; I would never have thought of putting mesh over a gigantic pergola otherwise.

George didn't come home that night. But I wasn't inconsolable as last time; I was more prepared. And when I woke the following morning, I had a sense that George wouldn't be around during the day, although I hoped he might come back in the evening. I felt OK about it, because when he didn't come home one night, he did on the next.

When she was cleaning, Mary found a candle beneath the plug socket on the kitchen-island counter, and I rediscovered the candle that I'd seen him tuck behind the collar of a woolly work shirt hanging from the back of the utility-room door, cradled in the three side-by-side hooks, and which I'd forgotten about. I also found doggy nibbles buried in one of the cleaning cloths in the basket.

I found myself gazing wistfully at the big box of kitchen matches that was wedged beneath the two cans of beer that I use to kill slugs. (I don't squash the slugs with the cans; I give them the beer with sugar and they are attracted by the sugar but the beer kills them.) The other night when I was sketching him, George dragged the box from beneath the not inconsiderable weight of the beer cans and flew around the kitchen with it. Then he managed to open the box on the floor in front of me, hacking a hole in it in the process, and pulled out matches, tossing them to the waiting dogs. Life was going to be a lot quieter without him.

I took the dogs for a walk around the garden at five thirty (they were desperate to go out, their little eyes all bright and hopeful, their little tongues lolling) and I felt George's absence; he was always the fourth dog.

We got down to the bottom of the garden and, as I was bending down to pull up a weed, the familiar wingbeat blasted by my ear as George swooped in and brushed my shoulder, alighting on the huge horizontal cedar branch that I use as a seat beside the chimenea. He perched on the branch and gazed at me. I crouched down to be on his level, and he let me rub his beak; he seemed to be exhausted. Then, flying low through the bushes, he followed us to the house and soared through the open kitchen window. He had found a perch on the kettle even before I'd opened the front door.

He sat on the kettle staring at me expectantly, before feeding himself from the tinned meat in the dogs' bowls and drinking deeply from the bowl of water on the windowsill just outside. I was concerned that he might fly away again, but no, he came and squatted on a sofa cushion, pecking Snickers's heel to get her to move and make room.

I sat beside him; he let me rub his beak and stroke the top of his head. He was too tired to protest. And when he put himself in his cage for the night, I felt a surge of affection and wonder.

Friday 12 October

When I let George out of his cage this morning, I didn't carry the cage to the kitchen window as I usually did. Instead, I let him out into the kitchen. I thought he might leave immediately because the window was open, ready for him, but he didn't; instead, he played around a bit, helping himself to doggy nibbles which he dunked in the dogs' water bowl, before tearing into tiny pieces to eat. This morning he wasn't like a wild bat-thing, he was like a curious five-year-old.

I telephoned my elderly neighbour to tell her that George is usually away all day every day now, and that the chances of him bouncing on her were almost zero. I'm not sure "almost zero" was enough of a reassurance, but it was surely an improvement.

Then I felt guilty because George hung around the house all day, inside and outside, although mostly indoors.

There was a definite change in his behaviour, because the builders at the back hadn't seen him for days, nor had the neighbour across the road. I liked to imagine that he was off exploring, maybe marking out boundaries of a new territory.

Coming into the kitchen from working in the garden to make a cup of tea later in the afternoon, I heard noises in the utility room. I followed them and found George at one of his favourite pastimes: sorting through the loose lightbulbs in the plastic bowl there, lightbulbs that I'd already retrieved once, from where he'd hidden them in a hole beneath the floorboards. I later found one he'd tried to tuck into a hole in the skirting board, and another, still in its box, on top of the fridge. When I opened the fridge several doggy nibbles fell to the floor; George had tucked them in the folds of the rubber seal at the top of the fridge door.

*

By the time I'd finished in the garden and worked a few hours in the office on emails and paperwork, George was nowhere to be found. Then I heard noises in the cellar—the steps are adjacent to the utility room. A light had been left on down there. George had only ever ventured down a few steps before, but now he was having a magpie's holiday with all the nails, screws, screwdrivers, hinges, bits of locks and door handles . . . I may never find some of them again. I called to George and he followed me back up the dusty, dirty, concrete stairs, one hop at a time, looking about him at each jump as if he might see something interesting as he ascended.

I had to finish mowing the lawn, by which time The Ex had George neatly shut up in his cage before disappearing upstairs to the bedroom to watch a Schwarzenegger movie on Sky TV. For some reason he was angry when I joined him; he'd been stewing. We never go anywhere, he complained, his expression one that brooked no discussion. He told me that we didn't have a life and he felt like a slave. I was dismayed, I reminded him of all the times I'd tried to get him to go somewhere with me: Lake Vyrnwy, Lake Bala, the west coast. I wanted to explore Wales—it is so beautiful—and I'd have loved it if we'd gone together. We could take sketchbooks—something he never did, and that I used to do before I met him. But he'd always refused as he had no interest. He wouldn't even come on a picnic or to the theatre. Apparently the destinations he was talking about were Paris, Venice, New York and Rome.

I saw the improvements to the house and the garden as a means to an end, creating a beautiful environment in which to work and live, and from which to sell our paintings. He saw it as a barrier between him and the kind of life he craved, which appeared to be very different from the life I wished for or could afford. This morning he had been a loving husband; this evening he was an angry man who wanted to move to the other side of the world.

Saturday 13 October

While working in the garden, I noticed two magpies flying from the top of the cedar tree down to the silver birch by the roadside. I didn't think for one minute that one of them was George, because I'd never seen him relate to another bird, but before I could stop myself I called out, "George!" and one of them peeled away from the other, and plummeted to my feet from his high spot in the sky. I was speechless; it *was* George; he stayed with me for hours, perching on my back, or my head, or a nearby rock or branch.

At one point I was kneeling, pulling up weeds, when he came and pecked the grass and mud off the sole of my boot. Then he hopped on to my back. For a moment, I thought that he was going to tuck a beakful of mud down the back of my collar. But no, he skipped around my shoulders for a few moments as I was leaning forwards; then suddenly, my hair cascaded around my face and neck: George had pulled out the biro that I'd used to hold it up; I had twisted it into a tight rope and skewered it with the nearest sharp, pointy object.

He flew off to the top of the garden shed with the pen, where it became an object of fascination for ten minutes. No amount of cajoling could get it back; I had to wait until he'd lost interest, fetch a ladder and retrieve it.

He noticed that the ponds were filling; I was topping them up with a hose, so the 2-foot-square pond between the raised oval pond and the long rectangular pond I'd built was brimming. He stood on a jutting-out piece of slate in the wall of the pond, which I put there for frogs to make it easier for them to negotiate the otherwise steep sides. Then he bathed, flapping his wings and his chest feathers forwards into the water.

At the top of a tree stake sticking up next to the garden shed he perched and preened. He wrung out each of his wing feathers by running them through the clamp of his beak; then he puffed himself up and shook himself violently, so his entire crop of feathers whirred and aerated, flicking his tail from side to side so it whipped like willow shoots.

He was in his cage in the kitchen looking immaculate before The Ex and I went to some friends for dinner. What joy to have him home again.

It was an interesting evening until our host wanted all his guests to join his son's more hippyish party after we'd eaten. It was being held in a large yurt in the middle of a muddy field in the pitch-black.

The Ex and I began walking across the field with the others, unable to see our hands in front of our faces. The high, spiky heels of my leather boots sank into the mud and The Ex and I clung on to each other for support. Suddenly, we both had the same thought, turned, and ran for the car. We were home by 3 a.m., laughing like children and, for a moment, on each other's side again.

Monday 15 October

This is absolutely true: The Ex took Mouse to the vet for her booster jab, while I was working in the office on the middle floor, overlooking the front yard. As he pulled away in the car, I saw George through the window soaring after him. He flew over the gateposts as the car passed through and, as The Ex slowed down to check for traffic, he grabbed on to the middle of the front bar of the roof-rack, flapping furiously to keep himself balanced and upright, the force of the wind pulling his little head back on his shoulders. Then he hung on to that roof-rack as The Ex turned right into the road and drove off to join the main road through the village. Wings spread out, George looked as if he was surfing. He was still attached to the roof-rack with his wings akimbo as the car disappeared from sight.

When The Ex came home, having noticed nothing untoward, there was no sight of George. With a sense of momentary panic, I ran outside to check if George was anywhere to be seen, and called, but he didn't come. I returned to the kitchen to find him already sitting on top of the cake tins.

Suddenly, he appeared to have remembered something: he flew back outside the window for just a second or two, then returned carrying a tatty object that drove Widget and Snickers wild. It took me a moment to work out what it was, and it was only when I saw two little black shapes bobbing that I realised they were the dirty feet of a rodent; he had brought in the rear end of a mouse. He flew around the kitchen with the tiny legs and stumpy tail flapping through the air, and Widget and Snickers going crazy trying to reach it. He retreated to the top of a cupboard, surveyed his pursuers, then hid the half-mouse behind a stack of magazines beside him. I retrieved what were the sad remains of a field mouse when he wasn't looking.

Wednesday 17 October

John was progressing with work on the aviary.

My daily bargain with myself was: "If George is here when the aviary is finished—then he's going in it, and there he will stay." Yet the idea of his imprisonment still filled me with dread. I kept trying to remind myself that truly loving anything (anyone) sometimes meant letting it (them) go, to be happy elsewhere. In the forefront of my mind, that included The Ex.

The Ex helped John and me lift some of the 11-foot-long uprights into the cemented-in Metpost holders near one wall of the house and I realised how huge the aviary was really going to be. Measurements on paper do not give a real sense of physical scale at all. After digging more earth out of the aviary site in the back yard and chucking it in the skip on the drive, I ordered more wood to put finishing touches to the structure, and a portable scaffold to help John when he put up the cross beams.

George came and played around me in the back yard all afternoon. When I stopped to talk to the builder who was putting up the house at the end of the cul-de-sac, just feet away, George flew over to sit on the arm of his digger, which towered over me, while the builder explained that I could have their leftover sand, since they didn't need any more. I was delighted; I had a lot more cement to mix yet. George watched him intently and I prayed he wouldn't disgrace himself, which thankfully he didn't. I was reminded about *why* George had to be incarcerated.

When John had left for the day, I sat on a rock in the little back garden that was now a building plot, feeling dejected. Looking around me at the mess of weedy dirt, I could see that I still had bags of earth to shovel, but I was worn down and fed up. I wanted the house to be a home and not a worksite, I wanted my possessions to be out of the packing boxes where they had sat for three years already; I wanted a kitchen that wasn't flat-packed in the hallway where it had been for three years gathering rubble and dust so that the dishwasher, which was already out of warranty, could be plumbed in. I wanted someone else to mix the concrete, move the rocks, build the walls. But I needed to do all those things myself to save money to go towards more plumbing and wiring.

One of the bricks from a pile I'd been moving had big holes through it; it was an engineering brick, harder and more water resistant than a normal house brick. It had been used before, so the holes were full of old cement and dirt. Feeling as if I wanted to give up and pack away my pickaxe forever, I watched as George flew in and pecked out the mud and mortar from the brick holes. When he couldn't get the cement out of one of the holes, he hacked at it before trying to lift the whole brick in his beak, over and over again, without success. I watched for a few minutes, wondering why George thought he could lift a brick, but I was impressed with his refusal to admit defeat until everything had been tried. He was my lesson in determination.

As if he could sense that I was feeling dejected, George came and sat high up on one of the ladders that leaned against the wall of the house near me (for lack of anywhere else to put them), fluffed himself up and kept vigil for a while, not leaving me. When, eventually, I went in through the back door, he flew after me via the kitchen window at the front and met me at the kitchen table. The Ex and I ate together with the dogs, George picking bits of food off the little plate I'd given him at my elbow: cheese, Schmackos and broccoli.

Thursday 18 October

There was no sign of George at all once he'd flown off this morning. And there was no sign of him all evening. I thought he was going to have another night outside. When it got so dark that I couldn't see where I was stepping among the rocks in the garden (I was still repositioning the boulders), I gave up and went indoors. That was when I heard The Ex calling George's name. George had followed him in from the garden and down to the workshop in the cellar. The Ex thought George would follow him back upstairs but George was having a holiday with boxes of screws and bits of old metal, moving screws from box to box, and bits of wire and oddments to other boxes. He was like a child in a toy shop. He'd decided he was going to roost down there.

But Snickers was our secret weapon; The Ex carried her down the steep, grotty cellar steps until she and George were within eyesight of each other. Then he carried Snickers back up again, and George followed. He might not come upstairs for us, but Snickers was a different matter entirely.

I was pathetically happy to have him safely inside; it was a bitterly cold day, a real winter's day, and although he was a bird that could sleep outside, he didn't have to.

Friday 19 October

In the morning George flew out of the kitchen window as usual, but came in, went out, came in, went out, so many times (four, five, six times, maybe more) that I began to grow uneasy: I sensed he was uneasy too, as if he was trying to make up his mind about something.

It was as if he couldn't leave but he couldn't stay. He fluttered on the spot in the air in what seemed to be a froth of indecision and was making some quick turns in short distances as he wrestled with the dilemma that appeared to be gripping him.

In the hope of distracting him, I took the dogs out for a walk in the garden and George joined us; he flapped alongside the dogs on the ground, then suddenly took off over the silver birches by the hedge at the bottom of the garden and vanished into the sky. He didn't come home all day. Or that evening. It was the third time he'd stayed out for the night, so I tried not to worry, but the days had drawn in and the nights were becoming icy. I'd left the window open all afternoon and well into the darkness of evening, so the kitchen was like an icebox despite the Rayburn. But no George.

Saturday 20 October

Today I went out to see friends, and on the way home, on a road flanked by farmland over rolling Welsh hills as far as the eye could see, almost at the turning to my road, I drove past three men who had just got out of a Land Rover. They each had a shotgun broken over their forearm. I feared for George.

George didn't come back that night, or the night after, or the night after that. I realised how every day had revolved around him, because his needs were the least negotiable; they had become the pivot of all else that happened in the house. I had truly fallen in love with my little magpie.

Sunday 21 October

The Ex and I were invited to a lunch today, and I forced myself off George-watch to go. I reasoned with myself that I still needed to meet more people.

One of them was an artist, all white hair and beard, producing fabulous woodcuts of birds, so intricate and detailed that it was almost impossible to imagine they were given life by a block of wood. He told me he'd kept a magpie and that it had flown when grown up. But until then, it would steal £20 notes and shred them at the top of a tree in the garden. I couldn't imagine having a life where £20 notes were left lying around for a magpie to destroy; George only had newspapers to play with. But I was just a little envious when he described how there would be five magpies in a field and he'd call, then four would fly off and the fifth would fly to his shoulder. Then it left. They all leave.

I wondered if the artist was hiding the resounding sense of loss that such a departure leaves behind.

My days continued and dragged; even the dogs couldn't console me. I occupied myself with helping John work towards finishing the now pointless aviary. It was almost as if George had known the means of his incarceration was almost ready. Feeling bereaved, I found it increasingly difficult to concentrate; I harboured a sense that there was nothing I really wanted to spend any time doing— except to wait for George.

One day when I was walking the dogs around the garden, I noticed there was half a fried egg on the tarmac in the front drive; had George stolen it from somewhere and dropped it in passing? Magpies like eggs, but George really preferred his cooked.

Day after day George didn't come home. Every night I finally shut the kitchen window when it was too dark to see anything and it was too cold to stand the draught any longer.

Of course, I wept for him; I missed his little head bobbing up and down by my shoulder as he stood behind me when I sat on the kitchen sofa, the tug of war we'd have over shoelaces, the milk he liked to drink out of the little glass I gave him; the way he'd stand beside my plate at the table, waiting for titbits. I missed his little face at the kitchen window, when he pecked at the glass, asking to be let in, bobbing this way and that to attract my attention.

Day after day I tried to work, either in the garden, office or the study; I staked and tied the circle of crocosmias, so that they didn't fall all over the place as they died back, and wandered around the garden in the gathering dusk in the evenings, noting jobs I had to do: dig out the spiky plant by the stream and replant it in the centre of the hosta bed in the fernery, tie up all the vines, plant the clematis I'd just bought . . .

I constantly hoped that I might get back to the kitchen and find George had come home. But the truth was that I was also happy for him if he'd gone, and was still alive. I'd actually got what I wanted so I had no cause for complaint; he hadn't just gone off and stayed away that first time, but came back twice as if to prove that he was still all right, and that his absence wasn't because he'd been shot. All I had to do was assume that he was still alive and doing what he wanted to do. It was a thought that relieved me of the uncomfortable guilt I'd feel if I had to shut him in the aviary; it would have pained me terribly to imprison him and at least now his proximity to the house was no longer a threat to Jean next door. The danger was over, for George and for anyone who'd ever feared or experienced his little feet on their scalp.

The aviary was at a stage where it looked like a gigantic pergola and was actually attractive. I asked myself: did I still want the structure covered with welded mesh as was originally intended to keep George in? Yes. I did. At the back of my mind I thought that one day there might be another bird in need, and I'd like to be prepared.

One night, I was sitting at the table in the kitchen when there was a loud crash. The day before, I'd washed up the little glass that I kept for George's milk and I'd left it on the plate rack beside the sink; I hadn't the heart to put it back in the cupboard right away, just in case . . . But somehow it fell on to the floor and smashed into hundreds of pieces. It was odd that being safely contained in the dish rack it could leap out and fall. I was surprised, too, that such a sturdy—and tiny—little glass could make so many bits. It seemed to be a sign that George wouldn't need it any more. The more I thought about it, the more puzzled I was.

Friday 26 October

I noticed that my back pain was escalating.

On this particular morning, when I finally managed to roll myself out of bed, I found myself checking various rooms in the house on my way downstairs, in case George had wandered into one of them having flown through the kitchen window without me noticing and been trapped. Of course, he wasn't there; it was just a forlorn, desperate little hope.

Once in the kitchen I found myself crying again, and wondered if my feelings about missing George were simply exacerbated by my back pain, and perhaps my back pain was exacerbated by the tensions in my marriage? Perhaps I was really upset because my distraction—George—having departed, forced me to face what I found most difficult.

While trying to distract myself by tidying up, I found the blue sponge that he'd carried out of the window last week; he'd brought it back without me noticing, and buried it in the yellow plastic basin that I kept the bags of dog chews in. That made me weepy all over again.

At the first opportunity, I watched some of the last film I took of George on the camcorder. He was playing tug of war with shoelaces—it was a film taken less than a week earlier. Then he flew up to the microwave to watch the warming-up of food for supper. He was so present in the room, and so integrated in what was going on in my life. I scolded myself for being so smitten. But I still opened the kitchen window at four o'clock every day, day after day, just in case he came back.

The garden was filled with reminders of George's absence; I found his side-by-side footprints in the concrete I'd poured into the channel that ran down the side of the tarmac of the drive: a perfect little magpie jump. When I noticed it, it made me cry again. I'm pathetic, I thought to myself; get a grip!

I just wished he'd visit. I tried to persuade myself to pack up his cage, except that I didn't quite get around to it straight away. Every day I still looked up at the sky and whistled. Just in case.

Going through old photographs, I found a couple of pictures of George sitting on my shoulder as a small chick, where he spent all his time in his youth. A sudden wave of nostalgia washed over me, catching me off-guard and bringing tears to my eyes.

Saturday 27 October

Today marked a week since his departure, and George's cage still sat in the kitchen with the towels over it, and I still carried a bag of his favourite HiLife doggy nibbles in the breast pocket of my work shirt when I was outside. I called up at passing magpies whenever I saw them, but they always ignored me; they were not George.

Unhappiness is natural, and sometimes necessary. I believe we need to feel miserable about something truly sad, like a loss—even if it's only the loss of a much-loved pet; but it doesn't mean I enjoy the misery, and it shouldn't be indulged or it will grow like a wart and become incapacitating. I knew that if I didn't function, then nothing would change, and if nothing changed then I would remain miserable.

Now George had gone, there were the realities of life that I could no longer ignore.

Sunday 28 October

Today was the ninth anniversary of my father's death. I don't mourn death dates; in fact, I try to forget them because they cannot be undone and compiling death dates, other than for historical purposes, seems rather a grim task. Especially as we age and end up knowing more dead people than living ones.

My maths and biology teachers, who married while I was still at school, were coming to lunch. While I was getting everything ready, The Ex announced that he was leaving me. This was becoming a frequent and emotionally exhausting pattern of behaviour on his part.

He went for a long drive, leaving me to clean up the kitchen.

As I tidied up in preparation for my guests' arrival, I wondered why he had to tell me now. Couldn't it have waited? But it was somehow a relief; he was negative and difficult so much of the time, now, and it was wearing me down.

I also decided that I had given up on George. I put the towels that covered his cage into the wash with the covers from the sofa, which still had faint bird traces in the corner. His water bowl got washed up. I revitalised the sofa with fresh covers, cleaned out his cage and put it outside in the hallway with the stacks of flat-pack kitchen units and other assorted boxes of our possessions.

George, I hoped, was soaring happily somewhere. If, one day, he came back to visit me, however, I would be overjoyed. In the meantime, I tried to push thoughts of him into the furthest, darkest recesses of my mind.

When my teachers left just after three, I cleared up and stacked the dishes at the sink, putting all the leftovers in bowls and covering them ready for the fridge. With a stab of regret, I realised I didn't have to think about magpie-proofing them any longer.

The Ex returned to tell me that no, he wasn't leaving me. Not today, anyway. Maybe tomorrow. The idea of his departure had been more of a relief than he would have ever guessed, and now even that had been taken away from me. He loved me, then didn't; he was leaving, then wasn't. He was no longer my friend, and that was the part I found devastating.

I got back to work. I was trying to get a second newspaper column and was writing a series of sample articles under the banner headline, "Another Week in Wales." It was in the early hours when I got to bed, after retyping the drafts of my first three samples. Life carried on without George, and a new "normal" was evolving around his absence. I didn't know if the same could be said for the state of my marriage.

At the end of October, a jackdaw came down the chimney in one of the rooms used as a studio, the seventh so far. This time I painted its tail yellow, so if it came back again, I'd know if it was the same one. If not, I'd paint the next one blue, or red, or crimson. I resisted the temptation to keep it and got Mr. Brown to put a wire cage over the top of all the chimneys to prevent any more visitations.

November

Thursday 1 November

Mary, who had come to clean, found cashews and doggy nibbles tucked neatly into all the folds of the cleaning flannels stacked in the utility room. George had left something to remember him by almost everywhere.

One night I had a horrible dream just before waking: I was passing a rooftop of some buried-in-the-ground building that was ankle-deep in fallen leaves, and there, foraging, was George. But he was scabious; his white feathers were so filthy they looked black and his cheeks and the sides of his neck were raw with huge, pink, fleshy blobs that I realised were oddly-coloured ticks. He was accompanied by a female bird, but if she was a magpie she didn't look like it; she was brown like a female blackbird.

I called to him. He hadn't seen me because he was so intent on what he was doing, but when he heard me he raced, simply raced to my lap like a dog. I was able to examine the foul mess that his little face and body had become. I took him (and his bird companion) home—except this was a different home to my real one. His cage was there, however, but I had to find another perch for him, since I'd thrown the old one out (in real life too). I put him and his girl-friend in the cage and he was so happy. I sprayed them both with flea spray and the ticks began to drop off. George, being a magpie, ate some of them from the heap on the floor of his cage and crowed with joy at being home.

I woke feeling dreadful. Lost. Exhaustion exacerbates emotional reactions, and now I was tired all the time, but George's absence, while being the best thing that could have happened for both of us, had hit me terribly. At least I'd stopped opening the kitchen window, and I no longer expected him to join me when I took the dogs around the garden in the afternoons.

Friday 16 November

The month dragged dismally into a grim winter, and I am ashamed at the visceral pain I still felt at missing that little bird. And he was little; yet when he was with me, he seemed huge because his personality was so engaging. But in photographs—which were all I had left—he was just a scrappy little magpie with a droopy wing. I had another dream about him: I dreamed that George was flying across the sky looking glossy and brilliant. I called up to him—not certain if it *was* him—and held up a doggy snack. He fell out of the sky—like he did that afternoon when I first saw him dive straight down—right at me. He barrelled through the air and landed on my chest. His wings embraced my neck like a hug, and I caught him; he was a crash of feathers. I woke up feeling as if I'd been given a tonic, a boost of additional energy. Extraordinary.

A robin was flying around me all day as I worked outside in the garden, hacking foliage, digging, planting, moving stones. When I was dumping cuttings on the compost heap, I called to a passing magpie that was being hassled by two pigeons, hoping it might be George. But it wasn't.

The bird-shaped hole in my life was echoing with emptiness, so I thought I'd do a little investigating and find out a bit about adopting a bird that would benefit from the aviary. I looked up adverts for birds in a copy of the *Cage and Aviary* magazine that someone had just given me. There was an ad for "Little Owls," so I called the number and spoke to a cagey man who, when I asked who I was talking to, wouldn't tell me because I had a withheld number. I introduced myself and explained that I was just feeling my way to ownership of a new bird, and would be grateful for any advice he could give me. He appeared to relent, but told me little owls weren't a good beginner's bird and that my aviary was much too big. A second call to a man called Mike at a rescue centre was more successful, but before considering adoption of one or both of his male Harris hawks, I felt I'd have to learn a lot more about keeping birds of prey that also required exercise. He asked if I was interested in taking on a goat as he had several at the moment, one of which had apparently been sexually abused. He, too, said little owls weren't a good beginner's bird.

My search prompted a reaction from The Ex—having got rid of George at last, he was dismayed to find me trying to adopt another bird that would tie me (us) down. I, in turn, was dismayed at his admission. He didn't want to be tied down—but I did. This was my home now, and I was growing those roots that I'd hankered after all my life. The gap in the ground between us widened.

I spent an evening typing letters on the computer in the office, then found myself completely distracted looking through the old file of George photos that I have on there. I enlarged one that was taken of George preening himself on the arm of the kitchen sofa. I cried. That's enough, now, I thought.

December

Wednesday 5 December

The completion of the aviary was now painfully slow because John could only work when he was free from the other jobs he'd taken on, and I wasn't pushing him, because George had flown, and it was coming up to Christmas. The aviary seemed a ridiculous thing to have done now, yet it was quite beautiful. I still intended to grow ivy and clematis up the wire until it looked like a green room.

Thinking of my enormous, empty aviary, I phoned the local vet and left my number in case anyone ever brought in a magpie, or any kind of corvid—or raptor.

"Just corvids and raptors?" asked the receptionist, bemused.

"I don't 'do' small birds or ducks and geese," I explained, not even sure what I was saying, except that I was attempting to fill a hole in my life with what I hoped would be another magpie.

What I wanted was a bird that *needed* the aviary; not a bought, captive bird, but a rescue bird. I felt very strongly that it had to be a bird no one else wanted—a recycled bird. And I'd like it to be a bird that didn't have to leave . . .

Thursday 13 December

The first woman who phoned when the vet gave out my number had an injured pheasant that had been hit by a car. The vet hadn't taken my choice of bird seriously. I apologised profusely and told her that I was currently "full up" and couldn't take a pheasant. I resisted the urge to give her my own recipe for pheasant in pineapple sauce. If I'd taken it in, it would have either died or been released to get hit by another car. This was not the relationship I hoped for.

But Geoff, the manager of a large local pet shop where I got all my pet supplies, had telephoned: he had a crow in need of a home, was I interested? It had been brought to him in a cardboard box by someone who had rescued it from being attacked by magpies. It was either old or infirm and had become a victim. It couldn't— or wouldn't—fly.

Today was the day that I collected it. Full of excitement at the glossy black bunch of feathers that staggered around the bottom of a small cardboard box, I brought it home and called it Oscar. I dragged out the very big dog cage that I'd bought when I had George, and fixed a perch in it. Oscar appeared to like his cage; he never tried to leave it. He adopted his perch instantly. I now had a large, black crow living in a very big dog cage in the kitchen.

Every day I donned a pair of old black leather gloves and took him out to perch on my hand, and there he would sit, gripping lightly, just doing nothing; not trying to escape, not trying to fly—he never flew, he just sat. I'd stroke him and talk to him and feed him meaty titbits, but he was, I thought, just old. I couldn't see any other thing wrong with him, except what appeared to be a crow-weariness with life. Sometimes, as I sat reading the newspaper, Oscar would tip towards my chest, lean against me, and snore gently, his little crusty bird-snore.

January

Tuesday 1 January 2008

O scar had arrived halfway through December, but by New Year's Day I was worried because he had stopped eating. This coincided with a day in which I was too busy to take him out and sit with him and feed him by hand, as I so often did. He was even more subdued than usual.

When I put him back in his cage he jumped for his perch and fell, one foot gripping it as the rest of him crumpled to the floor. But the foot hung on. After a couple of seconds, he picked himself up and staggered to a spot beneath it. I reached in, moved him forwards and turned him to face the perch. He gazed at it for a couple of seconds, then jumped up on to it.

Wednesday 2 January

This morning I noticed that Oscar's poo was almost non-existent and transparent. I made a point of taking him out of his cage on at least four occasions, stroking him, talking to him, paying him attention. Then he managed to eat some mashed potato that I offered him. It seemed that attention equalled an appetite. So, after each of the other occasions when I took him out, he ate dog food from his own bowl in his cage, and ate heartily. In the evening, he ate fruit yoghurt from my spoon and seemed to like it.

In the beginning, Oscar pecked. That was how I discovered that his beak had a hidden attribute: the long outer edges were razor sharp. I was lowering him awkwardly back on to his perch in the cage one day, when he snapped, catching my lower lip (I should've shut my mouth) and skinning it in a perfect "V" beak shape which, when it started to heal, looked weirdly and embarrassingly like a triangular cold sore.

Thursday 3 January

It was now evident Oscar was definitely on the decline: he hadn't pecked me for days, but did just occasionally grab my pullover for stability when I moved, carrying him on my hand. I knew that the likelihood of ever again holding a big, hefty crow in my arms, hour after contemplative hour, was probably nil.

Here I was again, on the clock; I knew that Oscar wouldn't be around long, so I wanted to enjoy him whenever I could, and that meant most mealtimes. The dogs adapted to Oscar almost right away. George had trained them into acceptance of feathered things—but no matter how they tried, Oscar couldn't play with them—he was too world-weary; an exhausted, aged crow.

At mealtimes I'd sometimes hold Oscar in my left hand and feed him doggy snacks off the kitchen table while I ate my breakfast or lunch. He also gobbled a tiny bit of my toast and honey. When he got fidgety it usually meant that he was lining up for a poo, so I'd put him back in his cage and he'd crap straight away.

I have no idea why I was so drawn to birds, but Oscar's presence focused my day in a way the dogs didn't—they were more self-sufficient. Keeping the crow alive also gave me a purpose outside that of earning a living, wading through emails, and sweeping up piles of rubble that fell from walls where the electrician had run wires to light switches, or where radiators had been put in, as work on the house proceeded sporadically.

Saturday 5 January

I was sitting with the crow as I ate on almost every occasion. Oscar was quite relaxed, it seemed, in the crook of my left arm. On this particular day he worked his way in halting sidesteps, from my elbow to my gloved fingers, gripping them and standing up, rather than leaning on my chest. I was talking on the phone to a friend, who had called to see how I was feeling; she knew I had a streaming cold. (Feeling terrible, thank you.)

Oscar hopped on to the table and stood on the newspaper where he crapped conveniently. I cleaned up immediately but left him where he was, since he didn't seem inclined to be bothersome. I left the room to check the diary for my friend's invitation to lunch, and when I came back Oscar was standing by my empty water glass, peering down into it as if he'd known what it contained. I refilled it and put it back in front of him. He drank, throwing the water down the back of his throat each time.

Later in the evening, I left him standing on newspapers on top of his cage, where he stood until I put him away twenty minutes later. He just watched me and the dogs do whatever we were doing. He croaked his slow croak from time to time, like an old man throwing out random words into the air, to float off to other ears for interpretation—or not, as the case might be.

MY CROW

He sits in my kitchen, a dud of a crow
With a creak of a beak
And a sullen eye that disguises
His fear of movement. Tattered by magpies
Smart enough to have two
Stake him to the ground
While three others shredded his balance
And his crow-abilities, he was found
Half-dead and bloodied by some woman
Who kept him in a bath for a week,
Where all he did was fall over
Between walls of slippery pink.
My crow eats and craps like a crow;
He does these small things carefully,
His dignity compromised by tottering
In between his perch and food bowl,
And the palm of my hand, in which he rests.

In the meantime, in the world outside the kitchen, local war was declared on starlings.

Sunday 6 January

Two weeks ago, a flock of starlings had gathered in the large fir tree on the fence line outside my kitchen window, bordering Jean's next door. Jean's kitchen window also overlooked the fir tree. She (despite her fear of birds) and I had marvelled at the way a thin stream of the birds appeared to pour out of the sky, like a fuzzy smoke cloud funnelling into a ribbon that fed into the branches of the tree only to vanish behind the greenery. I felt it was such a privilege to see them, and to be so close to them—only feet away—and hear them rustling and chittering as they settled down for the night.

And it was a miraculous sight to watch them set off the following morning: they filed out of the tree the same way they had fed into it; like a ribbon, only this time, a ribbon of silky black heartbeats that expanded as it trailed up into the sky, twisting and turning, all the birds in formation. They ignored me completely, as I stood next to the tree that had been their night-time stopover.

I gave a sigh of regret, thinking that I would probably never see the like of this so close up again. But that night they returned, only there were more of them. Fascinated, I waited until after dark, then crept up to the tree and shone a torch up into the branches.

Inside, the tree was empty of foliage; the branches were bare because no light could reach them. But tonight, they were heavily laden with starlings; row upon row, chattering and whistling to each other in the torchlight, fidgeting or dozing. The tree was like a gigantic green pyramid over the speckled feathered masses. I wanted to stand and stare until the extraordinary sight was so deeply burned on my brain that I would never forget it; all those many hundreds of little feet, of black, beady eyes, the cacophony of hundreds of snapping, clattering little beaks, the riffling of many thousands of little wing feathers.

Night after night, the starlings returned, increasing in numbers each time so that they had to spread out to occupy other nearby fir trees. And by the time two weeks had gone by, their numbers were in the thousands and the disadvantage of the incomers became obvious; it was the smell.

Outside the house the smell of sulphur felt to take the skin off the inside of my nostrils and stung my eyeballs. At the base of the tree on the fence line the bird shit was piling up, increasing daily.

I'd sought out my various neighbours and found that the starling population had also spread to their gardens, and the only thing that got rid of them was noise. So, we all agreed on taking action and spread the word throughout the village, the time being at dusk when the birds flew in to roost. We would all stand in our gardens and make as much noise as possible, to prevent the starlings from landing.

And tonight was the night that, as soon as the now gigantic cloud of starlings was seen in the distance, The Ex and I stood in the front yard banging with hammers on old bits of heavy metal offcuts left from building work on the house. The noise was ear-splitting.

Some neighbours clattered tin dustbin lids together, some beat saucepans with kitchen utensils; one of the local farmers had a gun and kept shooting into the sky (at least, I hoped that was all he was doing). All through the village, in every little cul-de-sac, the racket continued and the starlings circled and circled, attempting to come down on us like a black wave out of the sky, then receding, as if the tide had pulled them back up to the heavens. Over and over again the ribbon of starlings tried to feed into one tree or another, but the noise we were making kept pushing them back into the air, the silky black cloud of their bodies undulating with alarm over our heads.

My arms felt to be dropping off as I banged away with a hammer at the bit of old sheet metal I was holding, but I didn't dare stop; neither did any of the neighbours: any lull in the noise and the black swarm slid closer to the trees where the birds would rest, until an increase in our efforts pushed them back into the air again.

The sky dulled and took on a grey-purple hue as dusk pulled in and as the starlings continued to circle, their mass increased by the minute as more and more starlings threaded in from the distant horizon to join them. We kept banging away and then slowly, as if realising there was nowhere to go now, the starlings began to peel away from their central mass and moved to trees on the outskirts of the village.

Jean next door watched from her bedroom window and told me that she wished she had a camera, to capture the swirling black clouds of speckled silk that were deterred by the noise at last.

Tonight, we'd successfully kept the birds out of the immediate trees. If we did this every night for the next two or three nights, they might get the message. The smell coming from Jean's garden, where most of the fir trees were, was stomach-churning and made it almost impossible to breathe.

Several of us repeated the exercise at dusk for a week; and it worked: eventually the starlings moved on. I was sorry to see them go, but even through a streaming, stinking cold, the smell from the front of the house made me want to retch.

Tuesday 15 January

Kitchen life around Oscar didn't change much; as with George, the minutiae of his movements and moods were my focus. I embraced the distraction of him. I found a strange kind of joy in caring for this stuttering, incapable bird, although he didn't have much of a life because he had no balance to speak of. He could turn on his perch two or three times before falling off it. I realised I was seeing something that would never happen in the wild: crow old age. I'd watch him working up to a turn, studying his landing spot, weighing up his balance.

If I had to attempt to describe how he might have felt, I'd say that it could have been akin to a human being with a middle-ear defect, who felt dizzy enough to fall over every time they moved. Every movement Oscar made had to be prejudged, and he visibly strained to do so, peering, checking, testing and sometimes falling flat on his poor little black-beaked face. I wondered what his eyesight was like.

Be careful what you wish for, the saying goes. Well, I'd wanted a corvid I could keep as a pet, and Oscar couldn't be anything else. Outside, he'd simply die. I could see he was never going to fly free and was going to need care until his end. Poor crow, poor little dud crow. He was never even going to make it to the aviary.

OSCAR FLIES

He has been unbalanced by other birds
Trying to break into his cranium
As if it were an egg.

He tilts his head forwards
And sharpens the weapon of his face

On the branch that is his perch,
Whittling a waist to it.

His intentions lie in his efforts
As he grips it like a life-belt.

Today he flapped three feet
From the top of his cage to the kitchen table
And back. This was his first adventure
In four weeks. He measures his progress
In fairy-steps and crow-staggers.

Monday 28 January

The end of the month arrived; Oscar seemed to be getting more tired. He'd lean on me when I held him, and only eat when I stroked him and tempted him. I was determined to give this crow a good ending.

In the meantime, The Ex had gone on holiday to Australia and, stuck at home in order to save some money for the ever-ongoing renovations, I was spending as much time with Oscar as I could. It was one of the perks of working from home. While part of me missed him, the rest of me was relieved to be free from The Ex's negativity and criticism.

I took some photos of Oscar, feeling that if I didn't do it then, I'd be too late, and I was right. Throughout the evening, he got weaker and sleepier. He'd been standing side-saddle on the perch in his cage for the past four or five days, which made him look very unsteady.

When he turned to scratch his back with his beak, he fell off his perch and couldn't get up; I knew the end was on its way. I put him on the newspapers on top of his cage with a bowl of food and water that he didn't touch. I stroked him. He blinked at me sleepily. I lifted him up and gave him a sip from a cup, and he drank just once. It was his last drink. Already his feet were unable to grip. Finally, I couldn't watch him any longer and I went to bed, leaving him sitting on top of his cage in relative comfort. I didn't want him to die in his cage. I cried myself to sleep.

OSCAR SLEEPS

He clutches his cut branch side-saddle,
His eyes tightly closed against the dull kitchen lights.
Usually at the flick of a switch
He'd be sharpening his beak
For a snip or a bite, watching what approaches
With his critical eye.
But tonight he is not the sleek
Occasionally staggering feathered weapon I recognise.
Tonight he crouches on his perch as if beaten.
His black feathered shawl and chest coat
Shuffle their layers so he looks
As if the wind has tossed him.
Occasionally, he sways and must remember his grip.
He snores gently, a little crow-snore.
He swallows and gurgles like a water-pipe crow-child
And something in his dreams disturbs him.
His sleeptalking sounds multiply
Until his own sudden crow-shout wakes him.
Startled, he peers out of the semi-dark
Of his cage as if to remind himself
That nothing can get him;

He is safe from attack from the outside.
But as he dreams
His innards bleed and betray him.
The damage of age chips away at his bones
Beneath his papery crow-hide.

Tuesday 29 January

I got up knowing Oscar would be dead, and he was. He lay stretched out on the top of his cage, peacefully. Neatly, even. It's rather difficult to explain how I'd become so attached to a crow I'd only had for forty-six days.

I took Widget and Snickers to the vet (bespectacled and looking barely older than twelve) for their annual booster shots. With my face still red from weeping all morning, I asked her if she ever got calls from people wanting to find homes for young or wounded crows or magpies. Sometimes, she said. And pheasants and pigeons, she added. Not interested in them so much, I replied, I like the carrion birds. I suspect she thought I was nuts.

When I got back in the car I burst into tears again. I felt as if I'd never stop. I felt that Oscar's death linked me to all the other deaths: my mother's death, my father's death, George's departure, my collapsing marriage, and all the other deaths in my life. The sense of emptiness and loss was so profound, so deep, it seeped through my veins like a sticky ink. I reasoned with myself that one cannot—should not—live without love, and those we love may die—or leave—and it is OK to grieve.

But I thought of Oscar's slow, quiet passing and was consoled by the fact he died so peacefully. He died in warmth and comfort and without being finished off by magpies. He simply went to sleep in the company of someone who cared. Who could ask for more?

*

At home, I sat in the living room, which is on the middle floor at the back of the house, and I could see various neighbours' houses out of the window. The curtains of one house were drawn; the neighbour had cancer and death was close. I'd visited him and his wife the day before; I felt ashamed at my own little sorrow for a bird when a whole human being was dying. It put things into sharp and painful perspective.

I threw myself into working up a second draft to the following week's *Times* poetry column using two poems by Tomas Tranströmer, whose work I like immensely, from his book, *The Deleted World*, because there was room, and I hated to waste poetry space. One, "Face to Face," was a poem about a miserable winter in which he and the earth spring at each other. The other poem, "To Friends Behind a Border," was about writing to friends in a country with censors watching the mail.

As I was in the mood for poetry, I worked on some of my own poems until four o'clock the following morning, because experience has taught me that the mood will change overnight—so, again, I was working with my energy even if it wasn't good for my sleep pattern.

Oscar's death, linked to other deaths in my life, produced this next poem, published first in *The Book of Mirrors*, and latterly in *Out of the Ashes*:

> The Trouble With Death . . .
> . . . is that it's never one death.
> The death of my forty-six-day crow,
> Who was already bird-battered and aged
> When handed to me in a cardboard box,
> Was attached to the happy departure
> Of a hand-reared five-months magpie,
> Which was still a bereavement of sorts.

That in turn brought home the absence
Of the husband who'd just left for eight weeks in Australia,
Which suggested the idea of his death:
In moments of weakness, a real fear.
The dead crow is also connected
To the death of my father
And the desertion of my mother
Who took her own life.
As I bury my crow in the dirt
Beneath the monkey-puzzle tree
And stroke his glossy corpse
One last time, I am unable to let him go
But unable to bring him back.
I almost have to rip him
Out of my own hands.

February

Saturday 16 February

Today, while The Ex was still on holiday in Australia, I arranged to buy a motorbike, a Suzuki 125cc Van Van. I'd just received a tax rebate of almost exactly the amount of money it would cost to buy one new; David Jones Motorcycles, my nearest dealer in Newtown, didn't have any second-hand ones, and I didn't know enough about motorbikes to buy one from a private seller. This was a step towards owning the kind of machine I have longed for since the age of fifteen, when I noticed them parked around the clock tower in North Tawton, Devon, where I spent most of my childhood. All these years I had craved a motorbike of my own; I felt that I related to motorbikes on a primal level. Whenever I heard a motorbike going by it was like hearing a call from home. The way they were put together fascinated me; I tried to find a motorcycle maintenance course somewhere near me when I got to Wales, but had no luck. I wanted to look at them, be around them, and most of all, own one. Maybe more than one.

But, for many years, because I never had the time to learn to ride one or the money to buy one in the same place at the same time, I couldn't have one. I found I couldn't bear to read motorbike magazines or watch programmes about them, because it only served to remind me of what I longed for and was out of reach.

When people ask if it's the speed or the freedom that attracts me to motorbikes (and not all motorbikes), I don't know what to tell them. Yes, a bit, but it's more complicated than that; when I'm on a motorbike I don't need anyone else. Many bikers find my love of riding alone rather puzzling, but it is all about the relationship between me and the motorbike—a thing that is both a combination of raw-looking metal components that could kill me if mishandled (or even if I was simply unlucky), that requires skill and practice to ride well, and that feels like home. On a motorbike, I never feel alone. A motorbike ride is where my thoughts settle; the simple act of riding, being focused, concentrating on the road and the other traffic and making the vehicle work for me, is like a meditation.

Obligations fall away, the air clears, and I have a sense that I have somehow escaped. I would never go for a car drive for the sake of it, but a motorbike ride is a purpose in itself. And I always take my poetry folder and a sketchbook, because it is such a joy to scribble or sketch when not surrounded by all the duties—however desirable—that the house and garden impose.

Motorbikes can have a menacing—mechanically aggressive—appearance, and that appeals too. I didn't want a friendly-looking motorbike. There has always been the added attraction that it is not normally a mode of transport associated with women, in the same way that studies have shown that the word "doctor" conjures up the image of a man, because ingrained stereotypes are hard to break away from. It appeals to me to challenge a stereotype or a prejudgement, although not simply for the sake of doing so: as a teenager I was always drawn to pastimes and occupations usually associated with men, like playing the drums, knife-throwing, wanting to be a mechanic or an engineer. But although I wore jeans, a leather jacket beneath a denim cut-off jacket with studs and chains when I went out with my biker boyfriend, I loved to dress up too.

*

I was thirty-six years old when I finally booked myself on to a direct-access course (learning on a 600cc motorbike) in London, when I was going to be spending more time visiting the UK from where I lived in Western Australia. But that was the year I met The Ex at a party near Perth and, being so in love, we had moved in together almost immediately. So, regretfully, I cancelled my motorbike lessons and life changed too much to rebook them. But it was a constant itch, as if I'd forgotten to do something very important.

Finally, at the age of forty-eight, I was going to do something about it: that little motorbike came to represent my escape from the responsibilities and difficulties of home, although it wasn't in the same league as, say, a Ducati Diavel or a Hayabusa. Until now, the garden had been my joy, but, with the impending completion of the aviary, and my construction of the aviary garden, my work would be finished (although of course the maintenance would just be beginning). I knew one passion was going to make way for another—on two wheels.

When The Ex returned from his trip to Australia in March, I collected him from the nearby station and we had a happy reunion that made me hope he'd realised how good it was to be here, with me, not there. Then I drove him into the front yard and he saw the motorbike. He immediately thought it was for him.

April

Thursday 24 April

The truth was that our life in Wales hadn't compared favourably with Australia at all. The Ex was impatient to stop work on the house and get on with the next stage of our lives; he wanted to become "someone" right now—a painter of note (or notoriety?). He wanted to leave the house in its currently dismembered state, with unfinished rooms, incomplete wiring and plumbing, crumbling ceilings, boxes of four-year-old kitchen units cluttering the hallway on the ground floor. As for me, it was my state of despondency that sent me out to work in the garden again, so I could feel as if I was achieving something towards the progress of finishing the property. (Only now, I was without the company of George.)

The Ex was too often angry and talked about going home to Australia permanently almost every day. I wondered if he'd met someone over there and was angling to get back to her. He detested the UK where it "always rained." He reminded me that he'd always wanted to return "when he got older," and of course, he now *was* older. Our fourteen years' age gap had become an insurmountable problem. Just as I wanted to work on finishing the house, he wanted to leave.

I could understand his feelings, but I wasn't prepared to sell the house of my dreams, and nor could I paint and write for the next twenty years in a house that resembled a builder's skip. The golden chalice for me was the completion of our home, which would provide the springboard (mentally and socially) from which we would launch ourselves.

He had a point. We just didn't agree on it.

However, as sole wage-earner, the real catastrophe was losing my job with *The Times*, coinciding with the departure of my much-loved editor. My last poetry column in the *Times 2* section was published today. My column initially began with a whole page opposite Caitlan Moran's brilliant column, but had been reduced to half a page after the first year. Now the new editor was going to replace me with a weekly cartoon story for grown-ups (short-lived, as it turned out).

The loss of income was devastating. But on top of that, it had more of an effect on me, as a self-employed worker, than I could ever have anticipated. Since September 2006 I had ceased to be "Frieda, daughter of Ted Hughes and Sylvia Plath" and had become "Frieda Hughes, *Times* poetry columnist." The job, the title, the association, had all been mine, with only my name attached. It had become my identity—my very own identity.

When introduced, my name is all-too-often FRIEDAHUGHES-DAUGHTER-OF-TEDHUGHES-AND-SYLVIAPLATH.

It's a mouthful, but somehow people manage to get it all out in one breath. The moment this information is given by way of introduction, it kills conversation. My parents have been dead for so long (twenty-four and fifty-nine years ago respectively, as I write this) that it seems ridiculous to be dragged back to the fact they are dead by the attachment of their names to mine, in the face of their notable absence.

It seems too much of a leap for anyone, then, to ask about anything that isn't related to my parents, but one can hardly ask me,

"How are your dead parents?" as one might ask after the health of a person's living parents. Nor is it a good idea to ask, "What is it like having two dead famous parents?" so conversation withers as these inadvisable possibilities are digested in the minds of those present, and discarded.

On one occasion I was invited to dinner in London and was to meet my hostess at the venue. She was late, so her husband, who I had never met before, introduced himself and he and I waited for her by the cloakrooms. As we waited, a couple he knew walked past and greeted him; they struck up a conversation and he, realising that I was standing there like a spare part, introduced me as: "This is FriedaHughes-daughter-of-TedHughes-and-SylviaPlath." I wondered why he couldn't just say, "This is Frieda Hughes." What was wrong with that? Or, "This is Frieda Hughes, she's a painter and poet."

His friends looked bemused, peering at me as if they half-expected to see my parents leaping out from behind me and greeting them. Nothing I could say or do now would be seen or heard except through the prism of my parents.

Now I was "the daughter of" again, also thrown back on to my own resources and initiative. I didn't belong anywhere—funny how a job, even one at a distance and not-in-an-office-with-others can lend a sense of belonging. I was rootless all over again, without either a job or a marriage that made me feel safe and supported.

The Ex, however, was delighted, as I would now have to concentrate on arranging exhibitions for my artwork, which would of course include his paintings too.

May

Friday 2 May

However much I enjoyed the motorbike, the bird-shaped hole in my life was whistling like an empty cavern, and the aviary stood monument to it. It occurred to me that a friend—a nearby landowner who had a gamekeeper—might be able to get me a crow, since they were in a perpetual war against corvids. But today one of the local vets telephoned, saying she'd heard that I liked to look after birds. She had been contacted by a woman whose cat had brought in a wild duckling the night before. I could feel my heart sink; it wasn't a crow or a magpie, but it still needed saving.

When I collected the duckling, no bigger than the size of the egg that it had hatched from, I found it in the possession of a mother and daughter in a grey concrete block of flats in a built-up area of a nearby town. It seemed incongruous that they had a duckling at all. They hadn't given it any water—just wet bread and chopped worms. (I had to give them credit for finding worms.)

Back at home I gave it a bowl of water that it immediately sat and paddled in, and I fed it ground corn grain. It was such a happy little duck—I fetched an old fibreglass fishpond from the shed, put it in my studio full of water, weed and stones to stand on, and let the duck play in her mini-waterworld. She became an ecstatic little duck.

Wednesday 14 May

Today, three and a half months after Oscar died, my landowner friend called. In his no-nonsense way, without preamble, he told me that he had a crow for me, did I want it? Was it a baby, I asked; what was its story? But he didn't know or care; it was just a crow they were going to use in a tiny cage as bait for other crows so they could entice them and shoot them. Would I like to own the crow? Absolutely, I couldn't get there quickly enough.

Following my friend's car, I drove to a part of his estate where the gamekeepers kept chickens and chicks, and the gardeners tended the kitchen garden. There was the crow, in a pen full of dried-out bits of dead pheasant. I pulled on my little leather gloves and went in to get it. It tired quite easily so I could get hold of it, all sharp edges; a wriggling, black bunch of beak and claws, protesting at captivity.

The new crow, "Oscar Mk 2," went into George's old cage in the kitchen, because Oscar's old cage was so big that I'd never catch this new, lively, angry crow if I wanted to handle it. I could see how young he was, which only emphasised how old the first Oscar was. The idea of keeping a perfectly healthy young crow was painful to me: I didn't want to keep him prisoner; he was a bird that had not been bred a captive and didn't require care for a medical condition.

I was also aware that the Royal Society for the Protection of Birds' website explains that it's OK to bring up wild birds *that need looking after* (and are not on the must-register-with-DEFRA list), with the intention of letting them go back into the wild if they can.

When I took the crow out of the cage that evening, he fastened his beak on to the glove on my right hand, and I couldn't shift him for a good twenty minutes. After several more minutes he allowed me to stroke the top of his head. As I held him, sitting at the kitchen table wanting him to get used to being handled, I felt an itching on my left arm, and when I looked down I saw the most minute specks—moving. Mites. Still holding the new Oscar, I hurried to the cupboard beneath the stairs where I keep the vacuum cleaner, brooms and animal flea powders. I had a mite spray for birds which I coated Oscar 2 with. He was most disgusted with me. Then I gave myself a quick spray for good measure.

Friday 16 May

Two days with Oscar 2 was enough; I couldn't bear it any longer. I carried him, hopping from perch to floor to perch in his cage, into the front yard outside the house, placed the cage on the tarmac drive and opened the door in the top.

Oscar 2 took one look at the sky and propelled himself out of the cage and up, up, up, into the brilliant blue and was free. He stretched into the sky, becoming smaller and smaller, and was gone. I was aware that my friend would think that I was ungrateful and never give me another crow, but I couldn't keep a healthy bird shut up like that, nor did I want to return him to his previous jail, to tempt his friends closer to their individual little deaths. All I was left with was the very, very small duckling, who I called Demelza.

Demelza couldn't be left alone; or maybe I didn't want to leave her alone—she needed feeding regularly. I filled her fibreglass fishpond with more weed from the big outdoor pond for her to play with; there were half a dozen tadpoles in the weed, and Demelza made short work of them. She lived in my studio to begin with, and kept me company as I painted, because now I had to paint for an exhibition. Curiously, the dogs had zero interest in her and she didn't appear to register them either.

Going to stay with friends, as I did on one occasion, Demelza had to come with me: I couldn't entrust her constant care to the people who looked after the dogs while I was gone; it was too much trouble. She travelled, beak tucked into her downy chest, in the palm of my hand while The Ex drove. He wasn't threatened by the duckling because it was brainless and required almost no attention at all. If anything, he seemed amused by this lump of feathered-covered flesh that appeared to have no reaction to anything except water.

Every day or so, I took a photo of Demelza sitting in the palm of my hand as a measure of her size, until her breast and her tail were falling over the edges of my fingers. She didn't ask a lot of the world: food, water—lots of water—and warmth, while she grew bigger and plumper, but never gaining in intelligence. She had no sense of humour like George, nor did she have gravitas like Oscar, nor did she have a zest for life, like Oscar 2. She just waddled about, sat, and swam in her little fibreglass pond in my studio.

Wednesday 28 May

Today at the Hay Festival in South Wales, I gave the keynote lecture for the Housman Society, which was founded in 1973 to promote the appreciation of Alfred Edward Housman, poet and classicist, and his family. His most famous book, *A Shropshire Lad*, was published in 1896 while he was Professor of Latin at University College London, containing sixty-three nostalgic poems that recounted his life.

The society also promotes literature and poetry in general, and it was in this capacity that I had agreed to deliver the lecture.

I'd been working on it for days—even The Ex said he liked it. When I'd bathed, blow-dried and made myself up, I hurried downstairs to feed the goldfish in my studio before we left, only to find that over an hour earlier The Ex had put Demelza, who was not yet waterproof, in the little fibreglass fishpond in there, with no escape, and had then forgotten about her. She had become waterlogged, but had managed to scramble on to the stone that I'd thankfully put in the middle, cold and wet and motionless, a petrified look in her eyes and an expression of panic on her tiny face, which now supported her huge and out-of-proportion beak. She was stuck, surrounded by water, in a plastic fibreglass prison with high sides and no heating. Her delicate baby fluff was sodden and plastered to her thin skin. This could kill her.

Quickly, I dried her off, but she still didn't move; I put her on a tea towel on top of the hot side of the Rayburn until she fluffed up bit by bit. Eventually, she began to shiver, and within twenty minutes she started to preen herself. I breathed a sigh of relief. I was furious with The Ex; I'd already explained that she was too young to generate her own heat. "But I've said sorry," he protested, as if that fixed things. Except that he hadn't said sorry at all. "To the duck," he explained.

When we reached Hay—where it was absolutely pelting down with rain—I read to a packed house. Afterwards, in the restaurant, The Ex told me to "shut my face" in front of our friends and members of the Housman Society. We had all finished our puddings and were waiting for him to finish also. But he hadn't begun as he was the one talking. I made the mistake of suggesting that he eat his pudding, and that was all it took.

There was silence from the rest of the diners in the restaurant. And I could say nothing more or I'd only make it worse. The public humiliation in that moment didn't need exacerbating. But it wasn't the first time he'd turned on me in public, even without provocation, and it wouldn't be the last. Several strings that had tied me to him in love, and through hardship, simply snapped.

For him too, it seemed, as when we got back to our bed and breakfast he dissolved into seething resentment; he didn't want to be with me, he wanted to be on his own, he told me. He accused me of sidelining him when I'd been paying attention to our hosts and the Housman people; in turn I felt he was jealous of any of my achievements, and that the only way to keep him happy would be to do nothing. His temper was such that I didn't want to stay—and neither did he—so we made our excuses and drove home.

The good news was that Demelza was still alive when we got back. I cuddled her in the palm of my hand and she snuggled into my fingers making little peeping noises. The Ex went to bed without me.

June

Wednesday 18 June

Demelza kept pacing the big plastic box I kept her in, in between outings and swimming sessions. I decided she was lonely and bored but didn't quite know where to find friends for her.

Then, as luck would have it, I remembered a sign saying DUCKLINGS FOR SALE on one of the country roads. Puzzlingly, The Ex wanted to come with me to choose Demelza's little companions, so I tracked them down and found myself faced with a choice of Aylesburys or Indian Runners. The Indian Runners looked a little more like my duckling than the alien-looking Aylesburys, although they stood somewhat upright, so I bought a pair, thinking that when Demelza grew up and left home, they would need each other for company.

When we got them home I put their soft, warm, yellow wriggling bodies into Demelza's box, and she went into a duckling frenzy of fear; they were so much bigger than she was, she squealed and squeaked and tried to get through the plastic wall of what, until now, had been her safe place.

Not having Demezla with me when I bought them, I hadn't realised the difference in size when I picked the ducklings out. Quickly, I grabbed them and took them back to the duck-seller's, where (to his amusement, I suspect) I changed the small Indian Runners for two extremely tiny ones.

The tiny ducks—Samson and Delilah—were much more acceptable; a week younger than Demelza, they were a little smaller. She bullied them, pecking at their beaks and feet, but it wasn't long before they all snuggled up together in a corner of the box. Later, I had them all waddling around on the kitchen table, but the two Runner ducks fell off the edge right away. Fortunately, they appeared to be made of rubber and didn't break anything.

Now that Demelza had friends, she'd stopped pacing in her box and being agitated. Making plans for their future, I bought stakes and welded mesh; I was going to make the ducks a run that would encompass the entire little back lawn adjacent to the aviary. And when the run was built, I would buy a large chicken hut, so I could shut them in for the night to keep them safe from foxes.

Thursday 19 June

Despite our unfortunate scene at Hay, the Ex was working on the blockwork wall that was going to be the inside skin for the stone exterior of a small koi pond I was building in the aviary. I love to sculpt river stones together, wiping the mortar so the joins are seamless and undulate with the surface of the stones, but ordinary blockwork bores me because preparation for levels is needed, and truthfully, I haven't the patience.

Encouraged by his helpfulness, I initiated a conversation about our future. Our conversation began well; he talked about needing a business plan for his artistic career and I agreed that it was an excellent idea. But when we each listed our intentions and expectations of the other and discussed the results, it seemed he expected me to do everything, and the amount of work it would entail left me breathless.

We had once been so unbelievably happy, so blissfully part-nered, so perfectly compatible and so much in love, that I couldn't believe it was not possible to talk to him about it and resolve what was eating him. But I somehow seemed to have become the enemy, the competition, the withholder of the realisation of his dreams, and there was nothing I could do about it.

In order to have peace tonight, I had to persuade The Ex that I had only thought about contacting galleries, and hadn't done any-thing about it, and probably wouldn't.

I was now seeing a specialist who was trying to determine why I was nauseous all the time, coughing blood, and why I'd lost my appetite; it was almost impossible to eat. Acid reflux? I was living on soup and Omeprazole.

July

Wednesday 23 July

Demelza wasn't there when I went to put the ducks away; there was no sign of her; she'd flown over the fence. After chasing around the rest of the garden searching for her, then widening my search to the street, I finally found her on a neighbour's front lawn, padding through the clipped grass looking thick and stupid. I had to herd her back to the run in my own garden, since she wouldn't let me pick her up any more. I knew she had to leave, and I was fine about that; Demelza and I never formed an actual relationship: she was very different to George or Oscar, and brainless by comparison.

Thursday 24 July

I let the ducks out of their duck hut in their run and picked up Demelza. Her body was compact and sleek in my arms and her little head swung from side to side in a panic of wonder. I walked her down to the big pond in the garden and released her into the water. While my feelings for Demelza lacked the passion I'd felt for George, I'd developed a real affection for her, and I'd be lying if I said I didn't shed a tear.

I wanted her to know where the pond was and to be comfortable on it, while she had a whole day to accustom herself to it. The following day, of course, she might be dead, having not survived the foxes during the night. I worried about her, but I couldn't catch her by this time, even with a big net; she was too quick. Which gave me hope for her.

She dived in and out of the water, threading it like a needle; she stretched up to her full height and flapped her wings; she rapid-nibbled the weed and fished. She bathed, the water running off her back without affecting her feathers at all; she was in her element.

The following day I found Demelza was still on the pond, eating and diving. She ignored me completely; I was nothing to her now. But the day after that, I was out in the duck run washing out the duck bath, and she arrived at the gate of the pen, waited for me to let her in, then joined the Indian Runners. There was a great ducky reunion, they were all excited to see each other, and she stayed the night in the duck hut. I was impressed that she'd waddled all the way up from the pond and had found us.

When I let them out of the hut in the morning, Demelza looked up at the sky, heaved her duck-bulk into the air and flew up and over my shoulder, skimming my head as she did so. She did a single perfect circuit over the roof of the house, then headed off for the River Severn. I knew that I wouldn't see her again; my job with her was done, just as it had been with George—and even Oscar 1 and 2.

However, I still had Samson and Delilah . . . they now lived on the pond in the big aviary that I'd built for George. It was finished at last; a gigantic cage that hadn't yet been softened by greenery.

September

Wednesday 24 September

My first motorbike test in August had not been the success that I'd hoped. To begin with, The Ex was ill with labyrinthitis, so every time he tried to get up, he felt as if he was going to throw up. Not wanting to be left home alone, he managed to reduce me to tears as I left for the test I'd waited so long for and practised so hard for. And it was raining.

During the test I'd put my foot down on the final U-turn, which was an instant failure (although I didn't know this until the test ended). I had gone off to practise afterwards and done everything beautifully. My wish to pass my motorbike test—and buy a bigger bike—was all-consuming. And as I knew I would go on taking my test until I passed, I'd chosen a motorbike and bought it already, unsure of whether I was being impulsive or determined. It was a black GSX650 Suzuki and looked the business.

Now that the fulfilment of my most deeply felt desire hung on passing my test, the fear of failure escalated, eroding my confidence and eradicating my hours of practice on the Suzuki 125 (4,000 miles). But I'd put the experience to good use, nonetheless, and wrote an article about failing my test for *The Times*. But when I failed my second test—also on the U-turn—I realised that the

U-turn was a challenge because it meant riding in a semicircle to come to a halt at the feet of the examiner. It wasn't the action, it was the man I found daunting.

By now the summer days were growing shorter, and I was preparing for the following day when I was to take my third (third—the shame of it!) motorbike test. I'd flown through the theory part of it, and the hazard awareness—apparently the fastest applicant with the highest score that fortnight, said the old gentleman overseeing entries and exits to the test venue.

As my two previous motorbike tests had both taken place in the pouring rain, my glasses misting up inside my helmet, I'd made sure that this time I was prepared—I'd invested in contact lenses. I also knew that I wasn't a natural and had to work much harder than someone half my age in order to be good enough. So, in an effort to conquer my fear of U-turns, I persuaded the manager at David Jones Motorcycles, in Newtown, to allow me to practise U-turns and figures of eight on their forecourt on their old 600cc test bike. On the forecourt I didn't need an instructor as I would if I was on the road. Somehow, David Jones maintained his sense of humour even after I burnt out two clutches, and only charged me for the second one.

Thursday 25 September

After avoiding several emotional trip hazards laid down by The Ex on my way out of the front door to attend my "motorbike lesson," as if to delay me intentionally, I found that preparation for my test was with an instructor I'd not had before. He had different tactics. "When you do the U-turn," he told me in a military tone, "I WANT YOU TO RIDE OVER MY FOOT!" Now, he was shouting. I did as I was told, and he withdrew his foot in the nick of time.

Then he noticed that there was a man in a pale blue car watching us from the other side of the road and commented on it. Being an otherwise deserted back road on the far side of town, it was odd to find anyone else there. Instantly, I recognised The Ex and rode over to him. How had he found us?

He'd been driving past on his way to the supermarket, he told me, and had seen us from the main road. This seemed unlikely—the supermarket was on the way into town, and he'd driven past it to reach us, and the road we were on was hidden by trees and couldn't be seen. I didn't like to think what this signified. Fortunately, he had no idea that I was about to take another test.

When, an hour later, I took the test with the same examiner as my first and second attempts, and he asked me to complete the U-turn, I mentally superimposed my instructor over him, bellowing at me, "RIDE OVER MY FOOT!" That, and dragging the back brake for additional slow control, which no one had ever suggested until this morning, got me over the finish line.

The examiner told me I'd passed; I asked if I could hug him and he had no objection. Then I ran to David Jones's yelling, "Wrap it up! I'm taking it with me!"

My new motorbike immediately became my primary means of transport, and four months later, after another 4,000 miles, I traded it in for a black Suzuki GSX1250 that gets me to London and back in a day, easily.

In the meantime, Geoff, who'd found me Oscar 1, had news for me—someone had called him wanting to find a home for a pair of Bengal eagle owls. He intended to have the female—the bigger owl, because he'd already got a male—and I could have the male. It needed training, apparently, which I took to mean it was feral.

Thinking quickly, I worked out that I could keep the owl in the unfinished bathroom on the middle floor until it could go out into the aviary. At which point the two Indian Runner ducks, who'd been enjoying their easy access to water, would have to go back to their pen on the back lawn. I could return them at times when the owl was tethered, just in case they didn't get along.

October

Thursday 9 October

Today was Owl Pick-up Day, and I could hardly contain my excitement: I was going to get a real, live Bengal eagle owl. It was never a bird I'd thought of choosing, as I was still focused on crows and magpies, but it ate meat, it was stunningly beautiful, and it NEEDED A HOME because the current owner didn't want it any more. That last bit was the fish hook in my heart.

Geoff and I met in a car park and I followed his car to a suburban house on a well-to-do modern housing estate, which seemed an unlikely place for a pair of large owls. A woman showed us to my new lodger: he was in a small, muddy aviary with a bird bath of filthy water. She told us that she threw day-old chicks (dead, frozen, defrosted) to him every day, but no one handled him.

Then there was the kicker: the owl had a broken wing, which stuck out at an odd angle; he would never fly. So, that was why no one else wanted him, which meant that I wanted him all the more, although my heart sank; if his broken wing stuck out it meant that he could never be held bodily, or wrapped in a towel for beak and claw treatment, or the wing would break again. (If a bird won't keep still for that kind of attention, a towel-wrap is the safest way to restrain them.)

Once we'd caught him, I carried him home in a box with a

bow perch (shaped literally like a bow—as in "arrow") borrowed from Geoff, and a falconer's glove that the woman had given me, since her husband didn't need it any more. I observed that it only appeared to have been used once.

Geoff, who had a couple of owls and an assortment of falcons of his own, parked the perch on my front lawn and showed me how to hold the owl—Arthur—so that he dangled by his legs. Then I had to scoop him up from behind and sit him on my gloved hand. It worked! Arthur gazed at me malevolently through a pair of the most beautiful orange orbs with little black centres, shrunken in the sunlight. Those black pupils enlarged to obliterate his orange irises in the dark. They appeared to be bottomless wells—I could look into the black but see nothing beyond.

The outer edges of his eyes were rimmed with a thick, black, khol-like line, and a smudge of black feathers streaked from the top of his eyes upwards to meet with the base of his owl-ears.

These are not actual ears, but feathers that rise and fall with the owl's mood. They can be very upright, like rabbit ears, or flatten down completely and become invisible. Arthur's feathers indicated everything about his mood: upright could mean he was challenging and alert, flattened could mean he was cowed and scared. Sometimes they seemed to just flop sideways when he looked puzzled.

The broken wing gave Arthur a slightly lopsided stance and he'd gaze at me with his head slightly tilted as if waiting for the answer to a question.

When Geoff had gone, I left Arthur on his perch on the lawn for an hour or so to let him settle, before bringing him indoors on the glove, still tied to his perch. My heart was thudding inside my chest—would I be able to handle this big, ungainly bird?

I placed the incredibly heavy perch on the sheet of plastic in the middle-floor bathroom, spread a bag of pea shingle around the base of the perch to weigh the plastic down, and let the owl flop on to the shingle. He spread his wings and puffed himself up to make himself look larger, hissed at me like a cat, and made snapping noises with his beak. He was definitely a pissed-off scared owl.

I looked in on him later to toss him three half-chicks that Geoff said would be enough for him. The defrosted chicks vanished in seconds. I walked away, then walked back and they'd disappeared. That was a relief; he had an appetite.

Fascinated, I ate supper with the owl sitting on my left arm as I rested it on the table. As long as he was on my arm, he didn't hiss and spit or try to bite me. I loved it, just as I'd loved sitting with Oscar, the ageing crow, when I was eating too; it's sort of multi-tasking. I got to feed myself and spend time with the birds—and feed them into the bargain. Arthur sat on my gloved left hand all the time and allowed me to cautiously stroke the top of his head with one finger as he hissed slightly, but then he settled. I was riv-eted by him. Smitten. Fascinated.

As the days passed, I explored Arthur's idiosyncrasies and dis-covered that if he was on a leash and I put my hand down on the floor beside him, he would automatically climb on to my gloved hand and then up on to my left shoulder. Then he'd snuggle up against my left ear—possibly because my shoulder wasn't very broad. I told Geoff this in a phone call.

"He's not making friends with you," he pointed out, "he just thinks you're a tree."

Thursday 16 October

If he tried to fly, Arthur would spin around in three flaps and end up facing backwards. His broken wing acted like a helicopter blade, which meant that he rotated in the confusion between his good wing and his broken wing.

So, I took him to the vet. At the surgery, where they saw mostly run-of-the-mill dogs, cats, sheep and cattle, and perhaps an occasional rabbit, they all wanted to have a look at him.

He was sedated so his damaged wing could be X-rayed, and that's when I discovered that it already had the telltale signs of being pinned in a previous operation. The hollow bones had been irretrievably damaged, and nothing further could be done. A wash of disappointment swept over me. They gave Arthur back to me while he was semi-conscious. Awake, he would have been wild. But now he lay heavy in the cradle of my arms, his head resting in the crook of my elbow, totally defenceless. I felt so desperately sorry for him.

It wasn't long before I moved Samson and Delilah out of the aviary and back into their duck pen, to be shut in the duck hut at night, so Arthur could have the aviary to himself.

The aviary pond was now green with duck poo—like pea soup. I checked the UV light on the filter, but it seemed to be working. I rinsed out the filter sponges in pond water as you should, which was a bit ridiculous, since the water was, as I mentioned, like pea soup. Tap water kills the good bacteria—and that, in turn, kills off the fragile ecosystem in the pond and, eventually, the fish.

The koi that I'd put in several weeks earlier, however, hadn't been seen in a while. I imagined that they'd died, although I hadn't noticed any little corpses. Eventually, I just left the water as it was, cleaned out the filter weekly, and resigned myself to my belief that the koi were no longer alive. Weeks later, when the pond had cleared somewhat, I saw that I had two koi left; they were now over a foot long and looked like mini-fish hulks. Duck shit, it seemed, hadn't done them any harm at all.

November

Tuesday 25 November

Today, to my horror and amusement, three large boxes of poems arrived; I'd agreed to be a judge for the National Poetry Competition. The sheer weight of them was extraordinary. Stacked vertically they were over 3 feet high: I read poems for breakfast, lunch and supper; tea breaks, coffee breaks, or "it's raining outside" breaks. I was up to my ears in other people's poems—no one had mentioned that they wouldn't be sifted first . . . As a result, I was spending a lot of time in the big, chaotic kitchen with Arthur, because that's where I read the poems and sat still enough for him to sit on my shoulder.

Arthur would remain motionless, seemingly content, crapping quietly down my back, over the big lumberjack shirt I used to cover my ordinary clothes and protect them. Any spatter was caught by the dust sheet I'd put on the floor beneath my chair. (If there is one lesson I had learned, it is that one cannot spend time in the proximity of birds without bird shit being a feature of the landscape.) His quiet presence, and the muted grip of his talons on my shoulder, were peculiarly comforting, and it made me smile to think that I wasn't being kept from spending time with my owl by my agreement to read several thousand poems.

But whenever I put Arthur back on his perch or, later, back into the huge aviary all on his own, I thought about all that space I had left available and realised that one owl might not be enough; there was room for more. And then there was the duck run that could easily be turned into another, smaller aviary.

The idea of acquiring more owls felt a little like dangling my foot over the edge of a precipice and wondering if the ground was a small step below, or so far that the fall would break bones. I knew very little about owls, and what I could find on the internet didn't tell me how to look after them. I wished there was some way I could meet a remarkable owl-woman in North Wales who'd been mentioned to me; she'd be able to tell me everything I needed to know. I could find her through the North Wales Owls' Trust, someone said. But there was no such thing (I didn't realise they meant the Owls' Trust, which is in Llandudno).

Neither of us knew it yet, but eight years later, by which time I had been given other owls, we were going to meet by accident at a veterinary clinic in North Wales, each carrying an owl. Pam would subsequently give me two of my most precious birds. The first of these was Wyddfa, the desperately confused two-month-old male snowy owl chick with a damaged wing that she had taken to the vet. Wyddfa would help to assuage my grief for the unexpected loss of a bird I had desperately longed for—a gigantic Eurasian female called Samantha. She had developed a hole in her gizzard that could only kill her.

As I write this, Wyddfa sits on his favourite perch on the floor in the kitchen near the kettle, where he has been living for the past six years. He is no longer confused; he knows he can't fly and appears to have accepted the fact. Sometimes he trots over to his perch by the oil-fired Rayburn for a change of scenery. Once, I put him outside in the snow where he ought to belong—he looked at the big, red front door and saw it was still open. Then he ran, as fast as his little owl-legs could carry him, back to the warm kitchen, back to the Rayburn, back to all the other owls. Back home.

Epilogue

The months that followed Arthur's arrival were a series of highs and lows. The good news was that during the summer X-rays and an MRI scan had identified a collapsed disc in my lumbar region, worn facet joints and arthritis in my lower spine, for all of which I received a round of nerve-block spinal injections. Agonising, but not as bad as the back pain. While they didn't get rid of the pain completely, they took a couple of points off its escalation, so that I could function without the disruption of misery on top of everything else.

When I finished the garden in October 2008, I joined a local gym to improve my core strength and manage my pain better. I have weight-trained since my early twenties, with the exception of the four years I spent working on the garden, and it has made it possible to continue to function.

But while my back pain was improving, I'd been seeing three specialists in hospital, for various puzzling medical problems that appeared to be worsening, one of which was the persistent cough that brought up blood. Sometimes it was so bad I couldn't breathe and struggling for breath made my spine hurt. I'd also lost about 20 pounds in a period of six weeks and the nurses at the doctor's surgery thought that I was diabetic (although I wasn't). I looked like death's older sister.

Nothing the specialists could come up with seemed to help. At one point during the year, in April, I'd bought two red-breasted turquoisines and five Rosa Bourke's, beautiful species of parakeet—two were pale pink and cream and three had darker, much prettier feathers. I loved those little birds, and kept them in two gigantic cages at the back of the enormous kitchen where I could see them often and listen to their exquisite voices. Their birdsong lit up the air and populated the ground floor of the house.

But the chest specialist said I had to get rid of them, which I found truly depressing. He said that the dust from the feathers might be irritating my lungs. The pet shop was good enough to take them back and return my money. But my health only worsened.

I hadn't mentioned Arthur to the chest specialist as Arthur spent most of his time outside now . . . and no one else would want him anyway. At any rate, I wasn't parting with him.

By December I was certain that the root of the problem was my deteriorating relationship with The Ex. For years I felt we had been a good team, but now he appeared to be directing all his bottled-up anger at life towards me. It was almost as if we had fallen from the Tower of Babel and no longer understood a word the other said. Or maybe he just didn't want to hear me. Almost every day of the last six months of our marriage, I'd take my breakfast to the kitchen table where he would already be eating his toast and greet him with a cheery "good morning!" and he would raise his hand, palm against me, and say, "If you want to speak, talk to the hand, the head isn't listening." Then I wouldn't see him for the rest of the day unless he came to my study or office to tell me that he wanted a divorce. I always said "yes." Then he'd change his mind. It was a form of torture. I couldn't believe this was the man who had professed undying love and with whom I'd worked for a future together.

He insisted that he wanted a divorce weekly now—sometimes daily—so I did my utmost to grant his wish, only to discover that he didn't really mean it. Then he did. Then he didn't. Then did, then didn't. So, then I did and that was the end of us.

It was Christmas Day when it all came to a head; I couldn't take any more, and on 31 December he left for London. Two days later he was on a plane back to Australia. It was what he'd really always wanted and the root of at least some of what had gone rotten between us. England had not thrown its doors open to him the way he'd hoped it would, and Wales was just too wet for him.

On New Year's Eve I sat in my kitchen at home with Arthur the Bengal eagle owl and of course Snickers, Widget and Mouse, with the Indian Runner duck duo outside in their pen. Loneliness did not engulf me; I opened a bottle of Veuve Clicquot and celebrated my new freedom. I did not feel sad to be on my own on New Year's Eve, but full of joy at the peace and tranquillity in the house.

The whole world seemed to spread out before me and shine; my life was my own again, full of possibilities, and I was going to be able to pursue them. A deep, inner happiness crept over me.

Arthur, on the end of his leash, climbed up my gauntlet on to the sleeve of my thick, padded work shirt, then up, up, and on to my left shoulder. The sensation of his weight, his steady grip, and the pressure of feathers against my ear, reminded me how incredibly special he was—a proper Bengal eagle owl, not a budgie. No one had wanted Arthur, but to me he was a daily delight. The absence of my husband and lack of any family made me conscious of the fact that my pets filled gaps: my lifelong love of animals and birds had not abated.

By 5 January almost all my medical symptoms had disappeared, and I was beginning to put a bit of weight back on. I no longer coughed up blood. I didn't even look like the same person, and the solicitor dealing with the beginnings of my divorce didn't recognise me within a week—I looked ten years younger and felt marvellous. My suspicions were correct; all this time my "illnesses" had been stress-related, and I'd been ill for more months than I cared to count, deteriorating as The Ex became more and more a stranger to me despite all my efforts to gather up the unravelling threads of "us."

I counted my blessings, blissfully unaware of what lay ahead, how difficult the divorce would be, and the sorrow to come. Nor could I guess how many more owls would arrive to populate my kitchen and my aviary and take over my life, becoming a source of joy and equilibrium when the going got tough—all because of a little magpie called George.

Acknowledgments

My heartfelt thanks to the following:

Lauren Wein, Yvette Grant, Amy Guay, and the team at Avid Reader Press and Simon & Schuster US, who have been involved with getting *George* on the bookshelves. Cecily Gayford, Georgina Difford, Sarah-Jane Forder, and all at Profile Books, who are doing the same for *George* in the UK.

My literary agent, Antony Harwood, who has waited patiently for something to hatch.

My long-suffering neighbours who put up with George's attentions at the time when George was at his most interested in everyone and before he discovered that the sky was not a limitation but an open invitation; to my plumber, my electrician, my cleaner, my roofer, and various builders and The Ex, because even as we grew to misunderstand each other, he was part of my story—and George's. To all those people who may have wanted to shoot George but didn't. To all those people who fed, indulged, and entertained George during his wilful adolescence.

To marvellous Bel Mooney, writer, journalist, and agony aunt, who introduced me to Sandra Parsons at a boozy literary party, when Sandra was editor of T2, part of the *Times* (London). To Sandra, who offered me the job as poetry columnist for T2 that same night, and to the glass of wine that rendered me too bold to refuse. To the very trimmed box bush in the fancy planter that broke my fall when I sat in it, having inadvertently caught one of my six-inch platform heels in the Yorkstone pavers on the way out of the party.

To Kath and Andy Joseph, Neville Davies, and all at the Derwen Garden Centre, Guilsfield, who helped me indulge my love of over-planting during the four years it took to build my original garden—into which George was propelled—and their similar help to do the same when I bought the house next door for my gallery and studios in the middle of the Covid pandemic, and went completely over-the-top in stuffing every new flowerbed with plants, in the company of a pair of magpies who may, or may not, be related to George.

About the Author

Born in London in 1960, Frieda Hughes, the daughter of Ted Hughes and Sylvia Plath, is an established painter and poet. She has written several children's books, eight collections of poetry, articles for magazines and newspapers, and was the *Times* (London) poetry columnist. As a painter, Frieda regularly exhibits in London and has a permanent exhibition at her private gallery in Wales, where she resides with fourteen owls, two rescue huskies, an ancient Maltese terrier, five chinchillas, a ferret called Socks, a royal python, and her motorbikes.